D1572010

BUREAU OF MISSING PERSONS

BUREAU OF MISSING PERSONS

WRITING THE SECRET LIVES OF FATHERS

Roger J. Porter (signature)

ROGER J. PORTER

CORNELL UNIVERSITY PRESS
Ithaca and London

First published 2011 by Cornell University Press

Printed in the United States of America

Library of Congress Cataloging-in-Publication Data

Porter, Roger J., 1936–
    Bureau of missing persons : writing the secret lives of fathers / Roger J. Porter.
        p. cm.
    Includes bibliographical references and index.
    ISBN 978-0-8014-4987-1 (cloth : alk. paper)
    1. Autobiography—Authorship.   2. Fathers in literature.   3. Secrecy in literature.   4. Deception in literature.   I. Title.
    CT25.P664   2011
    808'.06692—dc22   2010052648

Cornell University Press strives to use environmentally responsible suppliers and materials to the fullest extent possible in the publishing of its books. Such materials include vegetable-based, low-VOC inks and acid-free papers that are recycled, totally chlorine-free, or partly composed of nonwood fibers. For further information, visit our website at www.cornellpress.cornell.edu.

Cloth printing   10 9 8 7 6 5 4 3 2 1

To Jennifer, with Love

"Why do you want to go so far into it?" asked Alka. "Why do you want to know so much about your father? He borned you, that is the great thing."

—Germaine Greer

"Thou shalt not uncover the nakedness of thy father," says the commandment.

—Germaine Greer

Children whose parents do not make them blush are irrevocably condemned to mediocrity.

—Emil Cioran

In writing about a father one clambers up a slippery mountain, carrying the balls of another in a bloody sack, and whether to eat them or worship them or bury them decently is never cleanly decided.

—Geoffrey Wolff

Contents

ACKNOWLEDGMENTS

John Eakin has been a constant champion of my work, and his insightful critique of the manuscript proved to be invaluable. His friendship has helped me throughout, and I, like so many other writers on Autobiography, always benefit from his sage counsel. Richard Freadman has been a loyal and sympathetic reader, and chimed in with beneficial, astute criticism and suggestions; he ran a wonderful conference at Latrobe University in Melbourne where I first presented the ideas that led to this book, and I am grateful for his profound understanding of the issues. At another conference Peter Brooks lent a careful ear to some early words that found their way into the book, and was reassuring that the project had merit. Other organizers and chairs of conferences on Life Writing where I presented portions of the book include Rocio Davis, Alfred Hornung, Craig Howes, and Alexandra Wettlaufer, and I am grateful to them. As always Howard Wolf constantly prodded me in directions I had not initially considered, giving discerning advice and continual support, and encouraging me when I wasn't sure my approach was on the mark. Ellie Langer, one of the most trusted writers I know, was a careful reader of portions of the text; her clarity and integrity were models to aim for. Other students of life writing who have been helpful in a multitude of ways include John Barbour, Tom Couser, Rebecca Hogan, Joe Hogan, David Parker, Gene Stelzig, and Julia Watson.

I am grateful to Reed College for a summer grant and a paid leave award which allowed me to do much of the work on the book; my colleague Peter Steinberg, former dean of the faculty at Reed, has been unstintingly supportive of my work.

Peter Potter, editor in chief at Cornell University Press, was enthusiastic about this project from the start, and I deeply appreciate his wisdom along the way to publication. I am also pleased to acknowledge his assistant, Rachel Post, and my editor, Susan Specter, for their valuable assistance in getting the book into print.

Portions of this book, in slightly different form, were published elsewhere and are used here with permission. These publications include "'Love is No Detective': Germaine Greer and the Enigma Code," *Life Writing* 3 (2006): 3–16; "Finding the Father: Autobiography as Bureau of Missing Persons," *a/b: Auto/Biography Studies* 19 (2004): 100–117; and "Inquiry and Denial: Helen Fremont's Anguish of Silence," *a/b: Auto/Biography Studies* 23 (2008): 65–79.

Introduction
The Child's Book of Parental Deception

When Mary Gordon sets out to learn about her long-dead father, whom she worshipped as a child and who imbued her with his devout Catholic faith, she makes a number of startling discoveries: he had a previous family of which she knew nothing, he was not Catholic at all but a Jew who had written encomiums to Hitler, and he edited and wrote for a pornographic magazine. When Mark Kurzem perceives his rueful father is plagued by a past untold for over a half-century, he gradually unearths a dark truth about him: as a Jewish child his father barely escaped being killed with his family in the Holocaust and was rescued by pro-Nazi Latvian soldiers, spending the war years dressed in a miniature SS uniform and gaining celebrity as a "Nazi child warrior." When Bliss Broyard's father lies dying, she finds out that he is a black man who has successfully concealed his race from his children and passed all his adult life as white. And when Germaine Greer decides to investigate the reasons for her father's long depression, she uncovers the facts beneath his life-long secret identity and his lies about every important event in his life, including his origins. In powerful autobiographical narratives these adult children have dramatized the poignant and secret lives of their furtive fathers and their search to unearth those concealments.

My book explores these and numerous other intensely human dramas of secrecy and deception in memoirs by children each of whose fathers maintained and perpetuated a clandestine existence. How the child learned about the father's covert life, the effect it had on the inquirer's own sense of self, and the way the autobiographical writing investigates and reveals the entwined identities of parent and child are my subjects.

In recent years autobiographies and memoirs have been preoccupied with secret lives. The life writing that has captured my interest recounts the uncovering of family secrets, especially in works in which a biography or reminiscence of the writer's father is contained within the son's or daughter's autobiographical text. Such writing tends to focus not only on the *facts* of the father's secret life but also on the writer's *active search,* usually in middle age, to learn what was not known and could not have been remembered about him, given how he withheld information, absented himself from the family, deceived it, or generally maintained a false or covert identity.

These autobiographical children are compelled if not consumed by a desire to know, frustrated when parental evidence is erased, reluctant to be condemned to uncertainty, tentativeness, doubt, or to a father whose identity is baffling, problematic, or inauthentic. What Paul John Eakin has called "the story of the story"—here not merely the *exposure* of the parent's secret but an account of how the autobiographer brought that identity to light—is neither a supplement, an epiphenomenal narrative, nor an aide-mémoire, but an account of equal importance to what is discovered. Often the process of the unraveling is the main story, the tracking of secrets as central to these narratives as the nature of the secrets themselves, secrets that, when probed, shed light on both the parent's identity and the child's own. The writer's frustration at having been subjected to uncertainty is palpable, particularly when the parent is dead and the child unable to ask directly the urgent questions that tend to motivate the search. The findings are often darker than initially expected, and as the child gathers unwelcome, even ominous material, we perceive how family memory has been directed, manipulated, and distorted to protect the secrets. Because the fathers are disconcertingly obscure or fraudulent, the autobiographers are often desperate to unearth what they suspect but cannot prove, or what has long baffled them, or what has come as a sudden shock of unfamiliarity that begs for investigation.

There is enough in common in the texts I deal with to justify a designation of this subgenre of life writing. Let us call it "The Child's Book of Parental Deception," since these texts regard the fathers from the perspective of adult children who suffered parental mystery and equivocation. This rubric provides an initial logic for the study. Though I give the title "Deciphering Enigma Codes" to one of the chapters, this concept may stand for all the kinds of secrecy I explore, including religious, sexual, criminal, racial, or that which pertains to one's origin and various forms of identity. It is plausible to regard the detective work or the cracking of parental codes as an autobiographical trope, whether we are investigating behavior, memory, documents, or archives, any of which might yield up the nature and significance of buried family secrets.

Indeed I regard the narratives by these adult children as crime stories, variants of detective fiction functioning as a corrective to the parents' nonfiction. The Australian feminist Germaine Greer, in the throes of guilt about her investigation, declares almost in protest against her project "love is no detective." While some of the authors are indeed "detectives" whose declared love for their parents appears compromised or undermined by the investigation, this is not true of all of them. Many are detectives who *do* love, others come to love what they discover or *despite* what they discover, still others discover that love was there all along. The writers' fathers have frequently scattered clues, like diabolical criminals enjoying the game of deception but also daring to be found out by their sleuthing offspring.

While daughters have written nearly half the texts I examine, with only two exceptions all of the works focus on secrets maintained by fathers; the exceptions give no special prominence to mothers, the secrecy in those cases perpetrated by both the parents. Why are fathers the overwhelming majority of the narrative subjects in this study? Coincidence? Hardly. Unconscious choice by me, a male writer interested in how men have lived furtively and surreptitiously? Quite possibly. Stories of missing and secret mothers exist, to be sure, but there are not so many. One reason for the infrequency of children's narratives about mothers' secrets may be that children tend to be protective of their mothers, believing it would be unseemly to expose any secret lives they had led. Fathers are fair—or fairer—game, this argument would go, on the grounds that they appear less vulnerable to narrative harm because many of them have sought the very secrecy their children find so disturbing. There are memoirs by children about difficult mothers, but relatively few about maternal secrecy. There seems to be a clear gender difference in both the prevalence of secret lives and the impulse of their children to write about them. Since women traditionally rooted much of their identity in motherhood, they may have had fewer occasions to live the kind of concealed existence that men not only managed but often sought and eagerly embraced. Men of course have frequently gone off to war—in a number of texts I discuss battlegrounds are the sites where secret lives were established—and men go on the road, away from home and family and where several of these subjects sought an alternative world in which to live out their hidden stories. In one work I treat the father deserted his own family, creating second and third families that, for a while, knew nothing about the others; in another case the father's passion for his work trumped any commitment to family. Families had only a tenuous hold on these fathers, and their furtive lives were cause for not a little pride.

Focusing on fathers has allowed me to think about the particular relation the children have with these figures of authority, and how such emotions as shame, blighted love, and the fury of disappointment figure in the competitive and collaborative dynamics of these paternal relations. To their dismayed children the secret fathers become objects of intrigue, figures of fascinated speculation; but because they have let their children down they frequently become targets of rage as well. The story lines I trace throughout the book suggest that the sons who expose their fathers are often competing with them for mastery—either for control of their life narrative, for the definitive interpretation of their story, or for power within the family—even when telling the story purports to be a gesture of affiliation. The daughters who do the same usually act to free the father from his secret, rescuing him as it were from the need to remain hidden from the world or even from himself; daughters wrestle with their conscience, often apologetic for their loving betrayal.

The need to unmask concealments and to disclose truths may be greater in urgency but not so different in kind from the driving force of much of life writing. These texts bring to the fore and make explicit—in both content and approach—the way autobiography depends on an inquisitional practice regarding the origins and performance of selfhood. While the stakes seem higher in this subgenre for reasons I've enumerated, probing for truth is of course a common trope in auto/biographical texts. Even in these somewhat specialized instances, the drive and commitment to investigate culminates in a satisfaction common to autobiography. Family sleuthing is an aspect of a broader autobiographical quest for identity.

The works I treat are problems in knowledge and interpretation by the children about their familial pasts, exposés of secrets the father was assiduously bent on maintaining. I approach the study of these texts by postulating that in the course of their investigations and their writing the adult children frequently engage in a struggle for power with their fathers. We will see how those children desire a story that was denied them earlier, one that connects them to the family in the face of silencing and mystification. My argument is that in the context of these deceptive and sometimes contentious relations, the children have no clear standing in the family story, indeed no assured sense of self, until they engage in the act of uncovering and narrating. I am interested in what we might call counternarratives that occupy contested spaces in the family history. This is especially true when the fathers have, for reasons rational or dissociative or psychopathic, taken on multiple identities or seem to have no identity at all, effectively nullifying the child. I examine the way these projects of self-fashioning effectively become modes of resistance in the face of the paternal domination. This is generally no less true when there is a strong residue of love in the accounts, even if there is collaboration from a living father.

The book has a five-part design, each of the chapters focusing on a different aspect of familial concealment. In the examination of the specific texts, I attempt to analyze what we might call "life writing in action" to show what is involved in that act and to suggest the psychological, identity, and therapeutic stakes for the father who maintains the secrets and for the writer who uncovers them.

I begin with three dramatic works describing how a parent's need to hide his or her religious identity led to a lifetime of secrecy. "Faith-Changing for Life" discusses accounts of Jews caught in the Holocaust and forced to conceal their Judaism, as well as the necessarily complex impact on their children when they learned of the parental deceptions. In these works, secrecy enabled the parent literally to survive, but it also entailed shame, self-abnegation, and in several cases a desire to maintain the subterfuge long after the situation requiring it had passed. Because the secrets harbored by their parents are so alarming, the children struggle to tell the stories with accuracy and compassion, fervently concerned to do justice to their parent's horrific experience. In this chapter I am especially interested in the relation of the inner narrative (the parent's story) to the outer one (the child's account of the story he or she has been told or has ferreted out).

In the second chapter, "Deciphering Enigma Codes," I group five works involving searches for fathers who, during the childhood of their sons or daughters, undertook to obscure if not erase their own identities. In each case their secretive lives produced unintelligible gaps in their stories, blind alleys, and deliberately misleading clues, making the writers' later attempts at reconstruction extremely difficult. In one case the father had helped solve the famous German "Enigma" code in World War II, and in his daughter's eyes is himself no less baffling a code, she a parallel code-breaker. Several of the writers frequently regard themselves as hunters stalking concealed quarry who attempt to throw any pursuer off the trail. The writers desire to get to the central truth of the lies and distortions and display considerable resentment for the fathers' attempts to remain inaccessible. At the same time they reveal guilt for unraveling and conveying the deception, as if their projects were ineluctably transgressive.

The third chapter, "The Men Who Were Not There," centers on four fathers who were absent—literally and figuratively—from their children's' lives. While all the writers in this study seek to understand their fathers in the face of their opacity, the memoirists of this chapter especially concern themselves with the nature of the detection. Paramount here are the details of the quest for knowledge, including the modes and procedures of the investigation. One child, unable to fathom his father's secret existence, sits solitarily in a room and thinks about him in relation to other fathers, fictional and historical; others conduct interviews, assemble stories, visit memorable and symbolically significant sites, or scrutinize physical evidence including letters, diaries, and photographs.

The fourth chapter, "Becoming One's Parent," focuses on several autobiographies where the inquisitional children, despite initial assumptions to the contrary and the desire not to be who their parents were, discover a surprising resemblance to them. The children experience a profoundly ambivalent reaction to this discovery, both dismayed by the unexpected connection and curiously pleased by it. Since the writers often presume a superiority to their subjects, this finding, frequently made in the course of the autobiographical writing, forges links that may or may not be welcome. Alongside the writers' fascination with an uncanny resemblance to their parent we find an anxiety regarding a potential loss of individuality; too much likeness undermines claims of uniqueness and threatens identity. On the other hand, in the process of acknowledging the unexpected connection the autobiographical children may reaffiliate with their fathers.

The fifth and final chapter, "Breaking the Silence," discusses two parallel texts: in one a black woman learns her father was a distinguished white man; in the other a woman who thought she was white learns on her father's death that he was black. I couple these works not only for the obvious reason that in contrary ways they reverse the racial identities of father and daughter but because as each writer exposes the secretive father she celebrates a new and self-confident identity with all its racial complexities.

Why have these kinds of autobiographies and memoirs become popular at this time? I suspect because such works reveal the struggle of previously bewildered children not only to search out obscured truth but to recreate themselves and assert a resistance to their situations of being unaware and deceived. These texts represent the multiplying of opportunities for self-fashioning in our day, and we could regard them akin to the discourse of formerly colonized figures in the empire who "write back" against power and the threat of nullification, insisting on the right of self-representation and regained authority. These are compensatory texts, and the adult children seize the opportunity to write against implicit if not overt silencing, countering long-standing violations of trust, intimacy, and affection with narratives expressing their commitment to truth, if not always to reconciliation. We take a certain pleasure, I believe, in seeing how the writers compose their own version of, and gain control over, the family story, even as they concede the limits of their knowledge.

What distinguishes these texts from other memoirs? It is important to note that they are not works of false or recovered memory, nor are they accounts or the "working through" of traumatized survivors of sexual or other abuse recalled at a later date. They do not scapegoat their fathers for any professed difficulties in the world, and their motives have little to do with accusation and retaliation against abusive subjects. The works in this study are nevertheless what I'd term "emancipatory texts": the writers attempt to free themselves from conditions of ignorance imposed on them and in the process reevaluate the nature of the child-parent relations that so perplexed them earlier. What distinguishes these texts from more simplistic autobiographical family narratives, where either vengeance or propitiation dominate, is that they do not express exclusively either resentment or love toward their fathers. Addressing what she terms the life writing of reconciliation, Patricia Dutton notes that the autobiographical "I" of such works is paradoxically "both plaintiff and arbitrator in this volatile polemic" (735). The distinctive appeal of such works inheres in their complex and often anguished stance, now seeking requital, now rapprochement. Their intensely felt grievances are seldom resolved without ambivalence, and part of the power of such texts lies in the writers' dramatization not only of their relation with the fathers but with their own consciences as they negotiate decisions about attitude, point of view, and tone.

When I first mentioned my project, to academics like myself or to friends and acquaintances, nearly all the persons with whom I spoke acknowledged the presence of troubling secrets in their own families; they affirmed that few subjects so fascinate and intrigue them as suddenly becoming aware that someone they were close to and thought they knew intimately turned out to be unfamiliar if not unimaginable. When that person is a parent, the shock could not be greater. Seeing ourselves reflected in these complex accounts is inevitable, and necessarily provokes questions about our own identity, either as autonomous beings or members of a family constellation. These gripping stories are highly generalizable even when not identical to our own. They make us wonder how *we* would confront such ambiguous figures and their complicated histories and how *we* would respond to disturbing material that throws everything we believe in and cherish into doubt. Reading how others have felt about a parental veil of secrecy *and* gone about lifting the veil, as well as composed a narrative making the furtiveness public, will likely stir in readers a curious mixture of uneasiness and fascination. I imagine that even the most circumspect are not only drawn to the mysteries of those close to them but may fancy themselves inquisitors peering into secrets and bringing them to light, even as they fear to pry and intrude on the privacy of others. Family concealments are naturally alluring, even though uncovering them may produce guilt and anxiety, and the self-conscious narrators may vacillate between a romantic if not an erotic quest to connect with a beloved object and a concern that in doing so they themselves may turn out to be a family betrayer.

Given the narratives of entangled lives and the questions they raise about motives for the secrecy, it is not difficult to imagine the reader posing many of the questions raised either directly or implicitly by the autobiographers. How might our own sense of identity be affected by the discoveries of subterfuge? If we were to speak and write about those secrets, how might it change our relations within our family—with siblings, with children, or with the other parent? Do we suspect there's an impulse of revenge in the sleuthing and the reporting? Would writing a father's secret life be compensation for our feelings of victimization? Would we get our own secret pleasure in all this? Could we be sure we were representing our father to the best of our ability and not deliberately distorting things to make our case? Since these accounts have the effect of "outing" a parent, would we have ethical qualms about doing the same, and should we? Might there be a therapeutic gain in speaking out? And finally, perhaps the most startling question of all: Do we have secrets of our own, and if so will our children expose and write about *us*?

What drives our desire to track down these fathers? The reason may be no more complex than a need to have a story that connects us in a meaningful way to family (or tribe or community). We may plausibly claim our identity is a function of the story we accumulate as a member of a family. But if we come to believe the story is constituted by secrets and lies, we will doubtless desire to set matters straight in order to pass on to the next generation a more accurate version of *our* story. The impulse to align oneself with, or conversely to distinguish oneself from, a parent may come to the same thing: a wish to understand origins, validate (if only narratively) our discovery, and establish something like an inheritance theme. I would note that almost all the texts I examine in this book were written in middle age; it seems we begin to think seriously about these matters at that stage of life because then we are prone to be more like our parents than we were willing to admit or contemplate. Family secrets necessarily fragment and disrupt continuity, deposing us from our place in a comprehensible relational narrative. Middle age appears to be the time when relations are subject to scrutiny, condemnation, or repair.

We are intrigued by such secrets because any felt uncertainties about our parents necessarily cause us to raise questions about ourselves. The works I discuss do not represent a mere casual interest in family history or a commonplace "roots" phenomenon. Rather the search for the parent implies an imperative necessary for the child to come to terms with him- or herself. The adult children inquire for their very lives, their ignorance of the parent often a cause of personal trauma as they unravel the secrets. If falsified identities, outright lies, buried lives, and omissions by a parent help determine one's own story, any attempt to recast the parent's mendacious past almost inevitably becomes an effort not only to explain what was incomprehensible but to reclaim one's life. Chronicling the family story anew and aright is a step toward understanding oneself as a participant in it. As Nancy Miller argues, "We don't choose our families but we get to revise their myths" (*Bequest* x).

The title of Greer's memoir, *Daddy, We Hardly Knew You,* could stand for all these works; whether the authors finally *do* know Daddy is not easy to apprehend, for despite the research and the excitement of the discoveries, the revelations in these accounts are always partial. These undercover narratives are rife with hiatuses and gaps, tentativeness, doubt, and irresolution, typically moving between speculation and uncertainty. Often there's a sense of incompleteness, of things that will never be fully known about a figure provisional at best, of assumptions that can never be verified. Parental deception may have caused problems in the first place, but despite the children's hope that full truth can be attained, their texts settle for less than complete understanding. The unmasking hardly guarantees that truth will be accurate or definitive.

A passage from Philip Roth's *The Human Stain,* with its radical skepticism, is relevant to the limits of these inquisitional narratives: "What we know is that . . . nobody knows anything. You *can't* know anything. The things you *know* you don't know. Intention? Motive? Consequence? Meaning? All that we don't know is astonishing. Even more astonishing is what passes for knowing" (209).

So a common trope is the writer's frustrated realization that far more remains to be known than even the most meticulous interrogation can disclose. These secret lives may be intense and powerful versions of a more general opacity in autobiographical relationships, constraining us to ignorance about others and to the desire, indeed the imperative, to learn more. Since the parents in many of these accounts have lived lives of multiple aliases and plagiarized identities, it is no surprise that writers trying to define such slippery subjects are necessarily speculative and conjectural. I think of these texts as if the writer were conducting in them a kind of séance, interviewing ghostly after-presences whose vague memory lingers in the child with painful effects.

Penelope Fitzgerald, in her novel *The Blue Flower,* suggests, "If a story begins with finding, it must end with searching" (112). Many of these texts begin just that way—with a discovered cache of documents, a locked trunk, a recently opened drawer or box, a photograph or a letter that begs to be read, explained, and interpreted. Frequently it takes such a finding to initiate the search for information and knowledge previously concealed. Amassing clues, data, and facts, these writers, sleuths of selfhood, gather and sift evidence in the documents, attempting to establish a degree of certitude. But how can the ending be a searching rather than a new finding? Since in these texts inconclusiveness is more common than certainty, the secrets have a way of proliferating so that any given "solution" inevitably raises further questions, a process that impels the quester into continued searching, perhaps into an infinite regress of surmise. Few of these works conclude in triumph, but commonly strike a note of frustration, even exhaustion in acknowledging that more work needs to be done with no guarantee of definitive knowledge.

We tend to believe that when autobiographers compose their work they sit at a desk and, as the song goes, try to remember that kind of September. A memoir, after all, implies a concerted act of recall; and however much one acknowledges there will be distortions and gaps in the representation of the life—deliberate or inadvertent—and lapses in memory that skew the account, common belief holds that the individual memoirist is the repository of the past, contains within him- or herself the memory necessary to begin the autobiographical enterprise. But in this study the autobiographical texts generally run counter to the assumption that life writing begins with an act of remembering. In autobiographies that uncover secret lives, even willed acts of recall cannot resurrect the past with much accuracy: either what is remembered is partial or false, or there was too much duplicity and evasion to base memory on anything concrete. In cases where the father was hardly present, the writer has no significant memory of him at all. Elusive parents leave memory voids. Where there are only fragments of memory or nothing solid to provoke it, the autobiographer may turn to external records from an uncertainty regarding subjectivity: forms of material and archival evidence such as documents both public and personal, parish or police records, court papers, genealogical accounts, birth or death certificates, medical and military records, newspapers, employment files, letters, photographs, iconic physical objects, and the like.

I am not claiming that "knowledge"—always provisional to be sure—gained through evidence and research is more definitive than "knowledge" gained by memory, merely that it is accessed differently, though it might be useful to ask whether there is something especially reassuring about a physical artifact used to substantiate and confirm premonitions about the past or to replace memory. Do scraps of tangible, palpable matter, *objets d'outre-tombe,* speak to a definitiveness that mere memory cannot achieve? Or are they equally fallible in postulating any "truthful" reconstruction of the past? It is not surprising that the autobiographers resort to hard evidence in the face of parental barriers thrown in their way, and one of the compelling features of these texts is the way autobiographical "researchers" assemble and interpret such information, evaluating its evidentiary reliability.

If we regard such texts as in part *biographies*—that is, autobiographies encompassing the stories of others who have played significant parts in the writer's life—then an emphasis on research is hardly surprising. What else does a biographer do but uncover documentary evidence, determine its importance, and use it to interpret the subject under study? In these texts the line between autobiography and biography becomes blurred; it is crucial that the writers cannot understand themselves until they understand the parent, so inextricably are they entwined. Eakin, in *How Our Lives Become Stories: Making Selves,* has persuasively argued that the inevitability of autobiography being "relational" complicates the issue of selfhood, for assumptions about a traditional, self-determining model of identity, in which agency and autonomy alone define the self, cannot hold up. Thus a porous boundary between autobiography and biography finds its counterpart in the equally porous boundary between seemingly discrete but nonetheless profoundly relational selves when they share intimate family lives, however isolated from one another they may at times have been. In the broadest sense these are arrestingly collaborative texts, twinned and conjoined stories, double narratives in which the writer claims the authority to reauthor the life of another.

In some of these texts the writer seeks reconciliation rather than blame. Far from castigating, defaming, or punishing their fathers, such authors take a more generous view than we might expect, with a focus on commonality, identification, and inherited traits rather than difference. In J. R. Ackerley's *My Father and Myself,* a gay English writer learns to his delight that his father may have had a secret homosexual life, a discovery that dissolves Ackerley's ancient fear of his father; and because the father also had a hidden second family he, like his son, understands (doubly) the necessity of a secret life. In a text portraying Holocaust survivors who hid their Jewish identity long after they found safe haven in America, Helen Fremont's *After Long Silence,* the daughter defiantly confronts her parents with their deception but at the same time writes understandingly and not unsympathetically about their ordeal in Europe and their plight in the new world.

However angered the adult child may be when discovering the parent's concealment, there is often a grudging admiration of the seductive power of the secret life, which can display invention, will, and improvisatory self-making. Secrets are irresistibly attractive to such writers, goading them to match authorial wits with the older person, both of them adept at a form of creative energy. The writer and the parent may be regarded as rival biographers. In Geoffrey Wolff's *The Duke of Deception* the son narrates examples of his father's duplicities and fabrications, his own artful story-telling sharing something with his father's artistry, albeit the latter was a *con* artist. Wolff's text veers between disgust for the jeopardy in which the father placed others— especially those close to him—and admiration for his father's self-confident ability to live as he wished without caring for the consequences. As Wolff recounts, a friend of his once told him that writing about one's father is always marked by ambivalence: "one clambers up a slippery mountain, carrying the balls of another in a bloody sack, and whether to eat them or worship them or bury them decently is never cleanly decided" (*Duke of Deception,* 11). Such texts ask us to reassess attitudes previously perceived as judgmental.

But at other times a less benign tone is apparent. This often occurs in texts lamenting that the child had not been at the center of the father's life, or in texts expressing a fantasy of rescuing the concealed father from oblivion— bringing the Lazarus-father back from the dead or from death-in-life—and thus gaining power over him. Some of these texts are hedged around with disillusionment and disappointment at the parental secrets; still others are full of vitriol. Narratives focused on betrayal seldom generate any desire for reconciliation. Here it might be useful to quote from Roth's *Exit Ghost:* "The man in control of the words, the man making up the stories all his life, winds up, after death, remembered, if at all, for a story made up about him, his covert brand of baseness discovered and described with uncompromising candor, clarity, self-certainty, . . . and with no small measure of delight" (275). There may indeed be a kind of retributive pleasure, and we should not underestimate how rewriting a parent's history not merely sets the record straight but asserts the child's newly felt supremacy, a note of fury sublimated into the triumph of detection. But occasionally these works express such a sense of sorrow as to overwhelm any pleasure the writer's investigative prowess might provide.

These dark stories reveal in the children a mixture of fascination, sadness, pain, and shame as they confront and represent parental duplicity. The offspring seem unremittingly haunted by the discovery of their fathers' disgraced past and they continue to mourn—as much for their own as for their parents' lives—unable to resolve their feelings in the face of the imposture they have been obliged if not forced to confront. Even when their disclosure affords some relief as well as the possibility of regaining a lost closeness, at times there is little forgiveness, for the wounds are simply too deep.

Since we may presume that in most if not all cases the parents would have greeted the publication of their story with alarm, scorn, or worse, I want to raise another issue fundamental to these works. I refer to an ethical dimension of these writers' investigations, exposés that might be described as the involuntary or implicitly compelled confessions of the fathers, extracted through the research of the autobiographical children. "Thou shalt not uncover the nakedness of thy father," Greer quotes from scripture (109), but she proceeds to do just that, hunting down her father's deliberately concealed origins and childhood.

Several of the autobiographers, probing for information about their fathers, guiltily refer to themselves as Noah's child gazing on the father's nakedness; their invocation of the taboo act suggests how dangerous they perceive their project of uncovering the father's concealed identity to be, but they proceed anyway because at stake is not only the father's genealogical identity but their own sense of self. If the fathers have cursed them *with* and *to* ignorance, they fight to gain the high ground of authenticity.

Of course we live in an age where the revelation of secrets comes easily, *too* easily. Talk shows, Facebook, and MySpace, indeed the entire culture, encourage willful public confession and self-exhibition unthinkable at an earlier time. If the autobiographers of parental secrecy feel a need to divulge their findings and expose family matters that some would argue ought to remain hidden, they do not, like the social networkers, bare those secrets casually. The tone of these texts suggests that the knowledge and the disclosure come at considerable cost. Because these writers recognize that the father's self *is* the secret, the writers tend to be highly self-conscious about performing the disclosure.

Nevertheless, Nancy Miller considers some perfidy by children who write personal narratives about their parents to be both necessary and healthy: "The betrayal of secrets is a requirement of the autobiographical act. . . . That broken bond is essential to the making . . . of autobiography" (*Bequest* 124). For Miller a "broken bond" between parent and child is also a requisite for the latter's achieving identity. And the biographer Diane Middlebrook protests against any demand of autobiographical circumspection that would blunt or evade biographical truth, indeed of any ethics of life writing that might inhibit the writer. She applauds the apothegm of her biographical subject, Anne Sexton, who asserts, "The dead belong to the living" (171–172).

On the other hand a study by G. Thomas Couser, entitled *Vulnerable Subjects: Ethics and Life Writing,* argues forcefully for resisting the right "to infringe on another's right to privacy," especially when the subject is "vulnerable" to narrative harm, as is the case of a child or a disabled person, indeed of virtually anyone in a close or family relation to the writer; even, in fact, of a subject who is dead. Death, Couser argues, is not a state of invulnerability to harm but the condition of "maximum vulnerability to posthumous misrepresentation because it precludes self-defense. Thus we trust that after we die...secrets we may have divulged will be respected, either by being kept or by being communicated only to certain parties or in certain ways" (16).

We might ask with Couser, what *are* the obligations devolving on autobiographers regarding such ethical issues? "To what extent, that is, is our freedom to narrate our own [and certainly others'] lives restricted by the rights of others to privacy?" (7). Are there circumstances in which it would be acceptable to breach the trust given and expected in return by parents, even dead ones? Does writing about a person who probably did not want to be written about constitute a violation of trust such that ethical concerns trump the desire for knowledge or for self-understanding, especially when, as in some cases here, writing about the parent is tantamount to "outing" that figure? Or does an imperative for self-understanding achieved through an understanding of the parent(s) take precedence over the implicit wishes of those secret-bearing parents, even when they are dead?

Given the fathers' presumptive desire to remain concealed (after all, concealment is a large part of who they were), when the children disclose those secret lives does such disclosure constitute family treason? And who determines that? If a trusting relation were utterly lacking in the writer's childhood, is the child granted more freedom to disclose? Couser, who urges discretion and caution in life writing, fears that "over-writing [others'] stories—imposing an alien shape on them—would constitute a violation of their autonomy, an overriding of their rights, an appropriation of their literary, moral, and economic property" (19). But this raises the thorny issue of how we can determine auto/biographical *mis*representation, and what constitutes "correct" or "justifiable" representation.

Some would argue that respect for others is essential when writers describe them, though how one defines and evaluates respect in specific instances is hardly clear. Gossip, attack (whether in the name of self-justification, vindication, or explanation), and judgment are all slippery terms. Should an ethics of life writing restrain the desire to judge another person if judgment involves a revelation not countenanced by the subject? And if so, what criteria need be invoked to enjoin auto/biographical representation of others? While it is certainly difficult to determine in just what ways the subjects of these texts are vulnerable, and whether and in what ways injury is done to them by the writing, writers should probably be extra-alert to such possible harm. But one could argue this is especially treacherous territory because while the child may have been particularly close to his or her father and may understand exactly what is most private, personal, and precious to him, that child could also have felt violated by the paternal secrets and thus might seek a form of justice in writing the untold story. Some might argue that any harm done to the subject (perhaps the "harm" to a reputation in a posthumous account) is justified by a therapeutic gain achieved through the writing, particularly if that writing purports to be fair and accurate and not to debase in a willful act of revenge. The revelation might benefit writer and readers alike, usefully illuminating the lives of both secret-keeper and discloser, especially the complex relations between them.

Richard Freadman, in a powerful essay entitled "Decent and Indecent: Writing My Father's Life" that addresses his initial qualms about revealing what he imagines his deceased father would have wished to go unspoken and unwritten, asks how far into the privacy of an intimate Other a writer ought to go, even if that person has himself broken the bonds of intimacy. Are we always obliged to honor someone's wish for circumspection? Since, Freadman wonders, we don't have contracts about such things, should we have an implicit trust about them, a trust that extends both ways? And, perhaps most significantly Freadman worries, if we believe it is important to tell our own story that necessarily involves the Other, who exactly should decide on the propriety of the telling—the writer or the Other? Freadman believes in mutual trust; thus he can say about his father, "He trusted…my trustworthiness. So he would have trusted me to act *in a certain spirit* in situations that required complex ethical decisions, even where he could not predict what precisely those situations would be" (132). Not all the subjects in this study are so fortunate nor their authors so generous as to presume a mutual trust in the other's trust.

I want to suggest, briefly and tentatively, that while the parents in these texts like anyone have rights to privacy, it is not always easy for the memoirist to know precisely when or even if he or she has abused those rights in disclosing the secrets the parent so carefully tried to conceal. If sheer and palpable vengeance is the sole motive of the writing, or the accounts bristle with meretricious and sensationalistic detail, the abuse cannot be justified. But if the motive for the uncovering is understanding, and disclosing the secrecy results in a reciprocity of shared accounts of *others*' similar experiences, then the writing and publication seem to me to be valuable. The narratives I discuss in this book, as I suggested by comparing them with the facile storytelling in social networks, are exacting in tone, complex in point of view, and deliberate in attempting to be faithful to their subjects. While some might argue that the writers infringe on their fathers' privacy, I believe these writers demonstrate respect and care for the integrity of their subjects, even as they condemn violations of truthfulness. These stories uniformly show sensitivity to the character of the other, even compassion, albeit the writers are inevitably dismayed by the behavior of their paternal secrecy-keepers.

Should these stories of lying and fabrication be written if consent is not forthcoming? Because of the fathers' conduct, especially in relation to their children, it is the *writers* who have been and may continue to be in the more vulnerable position, and who have felt betrayed. Their need to understand who they are and how they have been formed by the paternal secrecy has provoked this particular kind of life writing, through which the adult child may seek to regain a closeness that the secrecy either precluded or threatened to rupture. The father may not, or may not be in a position to, affirm that truth, but these texts often express a desire for a lost closeness that the children, by narrating their parents' and their own story, hope at last to repair.

CHAPTER 1

Faith-Changing for Life

I begin this book with a chapter on three memoirs about Holocaust survivors whose startling stories disclose their life-saving secrets. All three texts reveal that under circumstances in which one's very identity could be a death sentence, the need to conceal that identity was absolute. Though each work is quite distinct from the others, the adult children exposing their parents' concealed identities and narrating those problematic lives explore equally dramatic dissimulations.

Mark Kurzem's *The Mascot: Unraveling the Mystery of My Jewish Father's Nazi Boyhood* recounts a son's interrogation of his father who reluctantly and gradually unveils a story of his childhood rescue by pro-Nazi Latvian soldiers and his becoming their "mascot" for several years, decked out with a child's Nazi uniform, during their deadly *aktions* against Russian Jews. Because as a child Alex Kurzem had to conceal his Jewishness from his rescuers, he eventually repressed all memory of his religion, and for much of his adult life barely knew who he was, fearing to acknowledge even the glimmerings of a former identity, ashamed of his past and fearing to be vilified if the secret of his trafficking with Nazis were to emerge. Michael Skakun's *On Burning Ground: A Son's Memoir* tells the story of his Jewish father who, in imminent danger during the war, managed through astonishing ruses and subterfuges to procure false identity papers, eventually joining the Waffen SS, the front line combat wing of the Nazi Party. He became a Nazi soldier to save his life, but lived for years with guilt, fearing he had betrayed his faith and his very being. In *After Long Silence* Helen Fremont learns that her parents, whom she believed to be Catholic, were actually Jews who survived the Holocaust by hiding the truth, maintaining their adopted faith in the United States long after it was necessary while pretending they had never been Jews. In the face of massive resistance as well as outright hostility and denial from her parents, Fremont slowly and painfully extracts their secret, but in the course of eliciting the story and forcing the truth suffers their accusation of betrayal, even of replicating efforts of the Nazis to penetrate and uncover a camouflaged Jewish identity.

In these stories secrecy attains its most dramatic form because it is fundamental and essential; altering or masking truth had to be an imperative of the highest urgency. A child's Nazi uniform, an SS uniform, or the Italian soldier's uniform with which Fremont's mother disguised herself are all metonyms for identity itself, suggesting how changing one's shape became the only means to cheat death. But the fact that these parental stories have a common setting in Nazi Europe is not the only rationale for their inclusion in this study, nor for their opening the discussion. These works provide common key themes that will appear throughout this book, and they raise fundamental issues of identity, responsible storytelling, and adult child-parent relationships when the writers attempt to probe lives that are painful to disclose and, when revealed, threaten to reconfigure long-established relations. These works portray a child who encourages a more or less recalcitrant parent to speak, while they dramatize a troublesome dilemma involving a fear of intruding into another's life and making a private past uncomfortably public. We perceive what it feels like to be a sometimes unwelcome inquisitor, a teller of a tale that may produce guilt in the speaker, and humiliation in the subject. The children wonder whether they should urge or even force the story, or rather spare the other's (and perhaps even their own) suffering. These accounts raise a serious question about the traumatic past: Ought it to be forgotten or left alone?

Another theme common to these texts is the question whose story it really is. The child effectively appropriates the narrative, in the process controlling the parental image and determining how the account will be shaped and framed. These narratives constitute what we might call "blended" stories, and in the course of their investigations, the writers undertaking to pry and expose the secrets may establish a more complex attitude to their parents than was apparent before they began their projects, especially given the intimacy of the process of working together notwithstanding that the writer may encounter resistance and resentment. The relation is somewhat analogous to that of the detective's fascination if not admiration for the person he tracks down, even his identifying with the subject of inquiry in the process.

Yet another recurring theme in these texts concerns the matter of multiple identities. To survive the protagonists were forced to take on a range of roles and identities; as a result the interrogator often has a difficult time penetrating layers of masks and negotiating a labyrinth of ongoing concealments. When secrets are exposed and brought to the surface there may be even greater depths of concealment that never see the light of day. Beneath every secret lie other ones. Secrecy made public may not be the real or ultimate one; nor can secrecy be easily unveiled. We inevitably wonder if any exposure is sufficient to end a fetishization of the parental secrecy. In no small measure this problem leads to a corresponding difficulty in establishing the parent's claims for truth, so that a continual suspicion haunts these narratives.

In the course of this chapter we begin to see how urgent it is for the writers to understand themselves and their origins as they investigate their parents. Why, aside from mere curiosity, the children seek this knowledge in the familial context they explore is an issue implicit in each work I discuss and an abiding question as the children probe the possibilities and limits of their relational lives.

The Wounds of Memory: Shame and Discovery in the Kurzem Family

When writing or speaking about the Holocaust, survivors frequently vacillate between a numbing distance from the experience erected against disturbances to the individual's functioning system and intense emotion that threatens to break through the protective shield and the carefully constructed defense mechanisms. Secrecy, repressed memories, or selectively euphemistic memory can all serve as barriers against trauma that has not been worked through (principally the recollection of horror, whether experienced, witnessed, or even imagined), while the emotional breakthrough may come as a relief or conversely may intensify the initial trauma. In Mark Kurzem's discovery of his father's long-repressed story of an alliance with evil, these dynamics are dramatically disturbing.

Recorded by his son Mark, Alex Kurzem's shocking account of Holocaust survival, which oscillates between these twin responses, is no commonplace tale of endurance and survivor's guilt. At its heart is a secret life probably unlike any other experienced by a Jew in the Shoah, one that filled the father with such self-loathing that he had been unwilling to reveal it for over half a lifetime. In the course of learning the story, his son vacillates between on one hand a desire to end the father's paralyzing silence and elicit authenticating detail and on the other hand a temptation to spare the older man's self-recrimination by putting a stop to his own investigatory practice and to his father's recall.

Kurzem's account of the gradual unfolding of his father's story explores a collaboration precipitating the son into a relation with the older man that is new and troubling. But it is as important to him as it ultimately is to the father to engage in the painful uncovering of the past. If any work establishes just how difficult it is for the adult child to remain the cool, detached investigator, Kurzem's narrative (along with Mary Gordon's memoir discussed in the next chapter), is the one. At each stage of questioning and recording his father, the son asks himself if it is necessary to continue, and, as the older man's memories gradually return and "facts" are revealed, the emotional cost of the son's prodding the disclosure is balanced against the potential gains of the father's freedom and of the two men gaining a new closeness. This text is an exercise in continual balancing of competing impulses.

The Mascot: Unraveling the Mystery of My Jewish Father's Nazi Boyhood (2007) explores his father's startling past in a narrative that goads him to reveal a life shrouded in mystery and deliberately repressed memory. In the process the son joins with his father to uncover and understand that past, learning in the course of the investigation that he himself is hardly immune from the pain of a "dislocated" identity (146). Because his life is so linked to and implicated with his father's, as young Kurzem struggles to explain the brutal facts of the father's boyhood—a set of circumstances the father has denied for over fifty years—he is forced to reevaluate his own sense of self and his relation to the father. Parental secrets and attempts to discover them ripple through the family, and Mark's interrogation alternately estranges and solidifies father-son bonds, compelling him to turn inward in ways he never imagined.

I want to contrast Daniel Mendelsohn's desire to let the past belong to the departed with Kurzem's understandable need not only to inject himself constantly into the account but to make himself a significant partner in his father's story. In Mendelsohn's moving narrative describing his mission to learn how several relatives died in the Holocaust, he ultimately resists ownership of the story, ceding it to the victims rather than claiming it for himself. In *The Lost: A Search for Six of Six Million,* despite a commitment to knowledge as obsessive as Kurzem's, Mendelsohn argues that stories of a familial past, especially one of terrible lives and deaths suffered, are never the property of the researcher or the narrator of the events, only of those who lived that past. The story belongs to them, not to the storyteller, however passionately engaged the latter may be. In a self-effacing gesture Mendelsohn acknowledges "at the very moment I had found [my ancestors] most specifically, I felt that I had to give them up again, let them be themselves, whatever that had been" (502). But perhaps because the object of Kurzem's search is still alive and is someone with whom he has spent his entire life, he cannot surrender his share in the story, given its effect on him and the new ways in which he is compelled to view his father. In this memoir of a haunted and haunting past, searcher and subject join in the exploration and its troubling consequences. As one figure in the memoir declares: "The shadow never leaves you, does it? Even if you're from a later generation" (307).

It is indeed the strangest of tales. When he was five, Alex Kurzem (born Ilya Galperin) witnessed in a town square outside his home in Berlarus the execution of his mother and siblings by the Nazis. Alex's father had earlier gone off to fight as a partisan against the Nazis and, unknown to Alex, survived the war. Alex harbors vague memories of having escaped the killings by fleeing immediately before the massacre to the forests near his village and of having survived on his own until he was rescued by a battalion of pro-Nazi Latvians fighting against the Russians. One of the soldiers discovered the boy was Jewish, and for reasons not entirely clear warned him to hide his circumcision, which the boy managed to do for years. Taken in and adopted by the soldiers, eventually given small uniforms modeled first on that of the Wehrmacht and later on that of the SS, he traveled with the battalion for several years, becoming renowned throughout Germany as a child Nazi warrior. The subject of many photographs, extensive publicity, and a film shown throughout the Reich (his son concludes he was used by the Nazis "as a propaganda tool—a little mascot"), his celebrity eventually reached the attention of Hitler (375). Unbeknownst to almost all of his protectors, a Jewish child had been made to symbolize German racial purity. The boy spent several years with the soldiers and may have witnessed massacres of Russian Jews, including the torching of people in a synagogue. Eventually adopted by a Latvian businessman and Nazi Party member who gave the boy the name Uldis Kurzemnieks, he emigrated after the war with the man's family to Australia, where he eventually married and raised a family. Years later a group of anti-Semitic Australian Latvians warned him not to reveal the work of the battalion in killing Jews; some of its soldiers had been condemned and executed by Soviets after the war, and the Latvians feared further reprisals. At the same time Alex Kurzem dreaded exposure and retaliation by Jewish groups for collaboration with the Nazis were his wartime activities to be made public. And so he harbored a double secret: his Jewish origins and his "Nazi" past. Worried lest either fact be discovered and endanger his family, he maintained a long silence and showed no interest in uncovering his roots or probing and confirming the dimly remembered facts of his childhood.

The secret within the family (or rather the father's secret withheld *from* the family) reproduces something like the so-called latency period of survivor silence in the fifteen or so years following the end of the Holocaust. The elder Kurzem never spoke to his wife and children of his Jewishness; whether he forgot or repressed the fact, or simply didn't know, is hard to say. The father often entertained his family with the tale of his rescue by kindly soldiers and subsequent adoption, but not much more; over the decades he delivered "an edited version of the past" (117). Tortured by his memories as well as by his *lack* of them, Alex both withheld much of what he did recall and made no attempt to explore a past he had comfortably forgotten. When he finally begins to talk to his son about his wartime experiences, he is confused about many details: Was he present at various execution sites, even participating in the killing of Jews? Before he opens up to Mark, the only person to whom Alex confided his suspected origins and his activities was an Australian Jewish lawyer, who advised him to forget the past since no one would believe it: "'Your past is a lost cause!' That was that—I buried my past," is Alex's laconic response (142). Hiding his identity not only from others but also from himself turns him into a doubly secretive man—fearful, uncertain, emotionally numbed, a stranger to everyone: "I was dead to this world" (354).

It is not obvious what impels Alex gradually to reveal his wartime activities to his son. We can speculate that he needs to lift a burden represented by a lifetime of self-laceration. Or perhaps in late middle age he is troubled with not knowing who he is, not even his real name, and needs to repair the gap in knowledge.

> It's as if there are two men inside me, and one of them has been asleep for more than fifty years. Now he's waking up, and the two are not getting on so well. . . . The one that is waking up, well, he won't be pacified. It's as if he's whispering in my ear over and over: "Find out who you are. Now!" So I'm taking his advice. It's a simple wish—I want to know who I am. Doesn't every person have that right? . . . There must be someplace I belong. Am I Jewish? Am I Russian? Am I Latvian? Am I guilty or innocent for what happened to me? The more I talk about my past, the more confused I am. (189–190)

But the desire to know these things cannot easily or comfortably be gratified, for the two selves—an original and a "long-manufactured" one (190)—cannot easily be reconciled. Furthermore, he needs to understand the relation between those selves, as well as his motive for clinging to one in order to deny and conceal the other.

The Mascot begins with the father's visit to his son at Oxford, where Mark, then 40, is doing research on Japanese rituals, performances of concealment he will come to recognize in his father's behavior. Alex refers obliquely to fragments of his childhood past, occasionally dips into a battered and familiar briefcase to extract a photo of himself as a child in an SS uniform, and mentions two words—"Koidanov" and "Panok"—unidentified names that have haunted him for a lifetime. Mark senses his father wants to explain the photograph and to press on with stories about his role in the war, but the father backs off and retreats into embarrassed silence. The father has difficulty advancing his account; more than once he stops just short of revelation and clarification, the rhythms of his narrative characterized by what we might term a *confessio interruptus* resulting from accumulated guilt and continuing fears. The visit ends in mystery and mutual frustration. Thus begins a pattern of abortive revelations, hesitations, frustratingly incomplete narratives, and abrupt silences, often on the verge of a crucial disclosure.

As Mark takes down the story over many late nights at his parents' Melbourne kitchen table, the father is troubled as much by his own storytelling as by the contents of the story itself: "to be truthful, I don't want to remember anything of what happened to me. Who in his right mind would? But the bigger truth is that I am more terrified to forget. I am trapped" (100). Silence is part of the story, a marker of shame and an attempt to stop the narrative lest telling it will make him feel increasingly guilty about a role for which he already feels uneasy. While the father unfolds his story, awkwardly and with encouragement from his son, Mark perceives himself as a "detective...record[ing] the minutiae of my father's story" (82). But like so many narratives of filial inquiry, the text is not only a record of attempts to probe a recalcitrant older man's past but also one of ambivalent collaboration. Mark regards his father's cautious and diffident revelations, hesitant gestures of show-and-tell, as a "tentative invitation to be his companion" (31), and this reaching out gratifies him. Yet he feels increasingly anxious as the father slowly unwinds his story: "My inner life had been churned up in ways I was not yet able to fully understand" (136).

Parallel to the father's impulse to withhold information is the son's reluctance to play the inquisitor: "I immediately regretted the way I had cross-examined my father" (127). Some of this reluctance undoubtedly stems from the son's unwillingness to torment the father by opening the wounds of memory, but some of it stems from a fear of what the son might eventually witness: darker and more hideous revelations from the killing grounds and of his father's relations to the Latvian SS. Though vexed when his father retreats into himself, Mark is nevertheless concerned that further interrogation will elicit an admission that Alex was complicit with the Nazis, perhaps that, urged on by the soldiers for their amusement, he even killed Jews; or that the disclosures will bring retaliation against the family; or, perhaps most important, that the father will break down in the process of divulging his past, surrendering the armoring mechanism he has needed for survival, indeed for his very life. But Mark wants the truth to emerge because he believes in accuracy and honesty, seeks to free his father from doubt and ignorance, and hopes the elaborate process will bring them closer. His project is not merely to unblock his father but to gain a relation that years of parental repression have prevented.

No matter how difficult it is for Mark to see a new person, an "unadorned man, the raw human being" beneath the familiar, comfortable face, he believes in the importance and the cathartic effect of his father's effort to speak. Yet he understands the danger of convincing him to do so. He risks alienating himself from his father, even coming to be regarded as a Nazi prying into the very secrets that the older man has so carefully guarded. The father senses that once he has begun the process, he may encounter unsuspected demons: "My memories are here inside me like vipers inside my bones gnawing their way out" (47). But as Mark prompts his father's admissions while struggling to keep him from "drowning in the horrors of his past" (213), at every turn he risks the older man's resentment and estrangement. Still he presses on, admiring his father's ability for a half-century to live two separate lives (an "authorized" and an "edited" version of self), and the fortitude it took both to remain silent about the witnessed horrors and to withstand the toll such silence necessarily exacted (117). An elaborate dance of pursuit and retreat characterizes the narrative, the desire to elicit the story abutting against the resistance to full disclosure.

I don't want to soften the hard edges of the father-son relation during the course of their collaborative investigation. Mark alludes to his own anger, since even though the father has protected his family from the terrible secret he has betrayed them and made himself a stranger. Mark's resentment battles with his sympathy for the horrors to which his father was continually subjected and the vigilance he had to maintain. But as the interrogator presses on, fearful of what he will hear, he is doubtless aware that the more he learns the more estranged from his father he may become. Given his desire for rapprochement, it is a dangerous game.

What must it have been like for Mark to listen to and then recount the story of the father's story? Each man struggles to give life to the experience—one reliving the past, the other shaping the narrative. For each one, in different ways, telling and listening must have been a continually painful experience. Over the years the father had made light of his past, recounting seemingly

frivolous stories about his childhood as if such storytelling were a safety valve
and not a plunge into a harrowing experience. The father is a natural racon-
teur, and hinting at his adventures in the war was his way of ingratiating himself with the family. As Mark urges him onward, Alex gives up the comforts
of denial or half-truths. And as Mark listens he identifies with the anguish
that recall brings his father: "I was…worried about my father's emotional
state. It seemed as if he were driving himself to the gallows to be hanged by
his past. I was overwhelmed at the thought of the toll—the inner terror—his
silence must have taken on him" (135). He is no less concerned for the effects
of the story on himself.

So unsure is Mark about his father's truth claims that subsequent, disturbing encounters with a historian and with a fraudulent Holocaust memoir
cause him at least temporarily to question the older man's assertions. First, a
Holocaust scholar at Oxford skeptically attributes the fantastic story of boyhood rescue to false memory syndrome—the father's desire to make sense
of things and "a way to describe the indescribable" (171). No boy of five
could have stayed alive in the forest, the historian claims, and no Nazis would
have kept a Jewish boy alive. The father, he tells Mark, wants to view himself
as a victim of fate to exaggerate his own innocence and to account for an
otherwise guilty survival, the truth of which he had to hide. Denial of having
taken charge of his survival would assuage his moral conscience since, the
historian argues, his father may be refusing fully to face up to his complicity,
perhaps because he killed Jews. Thus he has manipulated the story to make
himself seem a passive sufferer. In this reading, an unreliable tale is the product of a terrified subconscious.

Second, Mark reflects on *Fragments: Memories of a Wartime Childhood,* Benjamin Wilkomirski's scandalously fabricated memoir of his time in Auschwitz
as a child, a text the historian implies may be analogous to the father's story for
dissimulation and deception even if not deliberately and consciously so in Alex
Kurzem's case. Wilkomirski's powerful narrative, which garnered numerous
prizes when first published, has since been exposed as a fraud, though the author
has never ceased protesting its truthfulness. Not only was Wilkomirski not
Jewish, he grew up in Switzerland and had no experience of the Holocaust.
It's not clear whether Wilkomirski was consciously attempting to commit
fraud for self-aggrandizing purposes or had somehow so absorbed the Holocaust into his life (he has read thousands of books on the subject and seen
hundreds of films) that he genuinely believed he had been in the camps. As
a result of the historian's allusion, Mark is tormented by the possibility of his
father's self-deception. The specters of doubt and Mark's living with even
a modicum of uncertainty impel him to undertake research to authenticate

the story. In the midst of recording that story, he begins a quest to determine its authenticity: to see if he can identify the father's village, bring to light the two mysterious words, and learn his real family name. Much of *The Mascot* is a tale of authentication, both to assuage the son's anxieties and to give the father the story *he* needs—another act and expression of collaboration.

Before I turn to the research father and son conduct in partnership, I want to say more about the problem of memory for Alex Kurzem. When Mark notes that he and his father struggle for the truth of the father's memory, it can mean several quite different, equally valid things: that Alex seeks to repress and Mark to cajole him into unrepressing; that Mark wants a more reliable form of memory than the father is willing or able to strive for; that Mark encourages the father to remember in an unmediated way since the father's memory-system may have been shaped by what the Latvian soldiers instructed him to retain in order that he deny their anti-Jewish activities. Karl Lobe, the Commander of the battalion and according to historians a war criminal responsible for the murder of tens of thousands of Jews and thus the member of the battalion most vulnerable to postwar reprisal, in a letter to Alex warns him *not* to remember because memory's inherent unreliability might inadvertently lead to the betrayal of those who had protected him. Against that admonition the father eventually determines to remember, if only through the eyes of his long-ago childhood. Nevertheless, Mark is not convinced that Lobe's warning is the only factor shaping his father's memory.

Like the suppression of the narrative itself, the fear of memory constitutes another abnegation of self, and without memory the father's identity is compromised. Paul John Eakin has argued that "narrative is not merely *about* self, but is rather…a constituent part *of* self" (*Living Autobiographically,* 2); by the same token, autobiographical memory is not just a means of reconstituting experience and reliving the past but is itself a central part of one's identity. We are in large measure what we remember about ourselves. Thus another meaning, perhaps the most basic one, emerges from the struggle for the father's memory: to ensure that he is as fully constituted a self as possible.

This is why recent neurological research that appears to make possible the editing out of unwanted memories with a drug that blocks the production of a substance in the brain necessary for retention of information is so potentially disturbing. Erasing memories is tantamount to erasing part of who we are; if we no longer remember, our life-story, indeed our very self, is incomplete. This is science doing what Alex Kurzem's Nazi rescuers demanded of him, and why we might regard Mark's mission of memory-arousal as a rescue operation supplanting that of the Latvian battalion's original saving of the child. A common experience of victims of trauma is that if they recall and narrate their past they speak not from the present but from a past they appear to relive; at the moment they recount the remembered experience they appear to be "back there." Instinctually recognizing that possibility may be what prevents Alex from easily remembering. Even within the safety of the Jewish Holocaust Museum and Research Centre in Melbourne he cannot speak easily of his Jewishness. He resists as much as reveals, embarrassed in front of other Jews for having denied his truth as both child and adult. Merely to acknowledge his Jewishness seems to precipitate him into a situation of danger, forcing him to reexperience a predicament that nearly cost him his life, where he had to conceal his identity not only from others but also from himself. His son calls this a condition of "self-obliteration" (248). It is no surprise that memory can be an accursed thing for the father; if the past is shameful, why strive to recall it? And yet if he does not—and he seems to recognize this intuitively—his very self is imperiled.

The repressed traumatic past is obviously too painful for Alex Kurzem to recall, even under relatively benign circumstances: recall and confession are acts he is unable to perform, even in the presence of those at the Center who attempt to help him bring his war experiences into the open. This is true in part because of his guilt about a betrayal of his Jewishness, or perhaps from a fear that other Jews will regard his childhood actions that way. It is apparent that only the gentle but firm encouragement of his son—someone he trusts not to betray or condemn him—will allow him to remember without a devastating process of re-traumatization, always a danger for those who seek to express a traumatic past. His difficulty in representing that past has little or nothing to do with an ability to write. In order for remembering not to reassert the original trauma and to foreclose further speaking about it he requires the presence of an interlocutor or mediator whose sympathetic listening and compassionate understanding are beyond dispute and whose filiation is equally unquestioned. The willingness of that other person to become a partner and to take on the role of inscribing that experience in language is fundamental to the story getting told.

Recall his troubled statement: "I don't want to remember anything of what happened to me.... But the bigger truth is that I am more terrified to forget." The focus of this doubleness is an object and the repository of his memory—his briefcase; it is one of the few possessions brought with him from Eastern Europe and the storehouse of his photos, newspaper clippings, and other documents that constitute a personal archive. Mark has a lifelong recollection of his father tightly clasping the briefcase to his chest, as if it were both the embodiment of his secret life and a life preserver, though as we shall see the father also regards it as a sign of death. When Mark was a child his father would dip into the case to retrieve a photograph, but would never reveal the real story behind the image, only use it to refer to an innocent boyhood adventure. No one is ever allowed to look inside the case, which is kept under lock and key; it always goes with him. "[H]is air of mystery gave the case an almost totemic power over our imaginations" (7). The case is a material substitute for an absent past, a depository of memories, or perhaps itself a memento; it is also the sign of ambivalence, representing both a desire to cling to a past and a barrier to sharing more than its oblique traces.

When he begins his narration, Alex declares to Mark about the case: "It's your inheritance" (18), implying, in a way he's not fully conscious of, that his legacy to his son is the secret life with all its affliction, a veritable pack of woe. Mark initially perceives the case as a treasure trove of unexplained riches, mere enchanting stories, but as the story unfolds with its ominous resonances the briefcase becomes a Pandora's box. "I resented it and felt an inexplicable disgust toward it and even toward my father. I shrank away, wanting to escape from both. . . . Was there something even darker, if that was possible, than what I had just seen [a photograph of his father in the SS uniform]" (26)? At one time the briefcase had felt magical to Mark, but now it seems utterly malign; he would bury the case if he could, but that is no more possible than that he will ignore the story once it begins to seep out of the box. "Case closed" is not to be. The concealed contents of the case become a metonym of the father himself, and even he comes to see the case as "a bit of a curse." His otherwise innocent statement "I never know what I might find in it" suggests he cannot predict what haunted meanings and memories will proliferate from each keepsake, nor how, once the story is out, the family will ultimately regard him (117).

In *Archive Fever* Jacques Derrida claims that without a sense of future emptiness, especially the threat of the death drive, archives and "archive desire" cannot exist (19). Memorials to the past and gestures toward future preservation both depend on and attempt to counter the inevitable obliteration of memory, and of self. There's an interesting question whether Alex's mementos represent a defense against forgetting or, because they torment him, an unconscious death drive. At a number of points in the narrative he tells his son he wishes he were dead, or that he should have died rather than live with an ongoing sense of shame. Alex's personally accumulated archive is both painful evidence of his past and a bane he has transformed into comic raconteurship. We are never quite sure if his archive represents an affirmation of his life or a gesture toward suicide.

The inadequacy or possible unreliability of his father's memory convinces Mark to carry out a program of research. Secrets and silences persuade him of the need to authenticate the gradual revelations, the most pressing of which is to corroborate Alex's recollections about the battalion's movements with a discoverable historical record. Consultations with historians and a genealogist specializing in eastern European Judaic culture produce only tantalizing possibilities of verification of the boy's wartime activities. Mark even visits Commander Lobe in Stockholm to procure facts, an encounter that not surprisingly yields little but suspicion. Complicating the search is that Alex is confused by a plethora of conceivable names for himself: those given by the battalion, by his adoptive father, and by vague memories of his childhood surname. Each label establishes a different identity. Research turns up "facts" as uncertain and varied as the father's multiple names. Increasingly as the story accumulates, questions about its authenticity also multiply. Mark's outer narrative implicitly interrogates Alex's inner one, each researched finding unable definitively to validate the father's account. As more unearthed "evidence" falls into place, however, the father relives his past in torturing detail, almost dissuading Mark from further investigation and convincing him to leave family secrets buried. And even when the father has learned all he can about his childhood he is still rueful: "But the truth is, my story is all that I have" (395). If the Latvian soldiers who had "rescued" him had also "stolen him from himself" (386)—robbed not just his natural boyhood and his security but his very identity—then telling the story is as close as he will ever come to gaining back that identity.

A turning point comes through a woman from the Jewish Holocaust Centre who identifies "Koidanov" as the former name of a village the father must have come from; she writes for more information to a historian friend at the Holocaust research center in Minsk, the major city of Belarus. The Minsk historian reads the letter inquiring about the village of Koidanov and shows it to her publisher, who coincidentally is in her office when the letter arrives. The publisher, one Erick Galperin, had grown up in that very village, and his Jewish father, Solomon, had had a previous family that perished in a massacre in that shtetl. He urges Alex Kurzem to come to Minsk to track down any people still alive who might remember him or his family; and since Alex resembles a photo of the man's father, he thinks there's even a possibility that he, Erick Galperin, is Alex's much younger half-brother. The final section of the memoir explores that possibility, the search for origins undertaken to answer the question of Alex's anguished cry: "I don't know who I am. Will I ever know" (291)?

Just before the trip to Latvia there's a disturbing doubling of the inquiry. In Oxford an Israeli intelligence agent and his daughter seem to have learned something of Alex's story and, because of the presence of war criminals in Australia, they press Mark for details of his father, suspicious that the latter may be involved with Nazi sympathizers. At the same time someone—a Latvian? the Israeli intelligence agent?—breaks into Mark's parents' house in Melbourne, ostensibly searching for incriminating photographs they fear the father may use against members of the old battalion. There are multiple inquisitions, and the father becomes the object of investigation even as he conducts his own. Secrets and inquiry abound, spreading out from the original action, crossing time and space; the shadow of surveillance is everywhere. It begins to seem as if the Kurzems conduct their research not only to ease Alex's conscience and help him reclaim an identity but also to counter the implied accusations of others. The trope of discovering roots runs parallel to a game of counterespionage. As Mark notes in a crucial footnote: "accusations against my father were made public and never retracted; the resulting damage to his reputation distracted us from our pursuit of the truth...and...my father and I had to fight for the truth of his memory" (275).

The family travels to Minsk, met by Erick, and then to the village where the father was born. They discover the house in which he grew up—aided by a neighbor who remembers it as Solomon Galperin's place and by Alex's memories of significantly relevant details. Alex is introduced to an elderly couple who had known him as a child and survived the war; the man had engaged in partisan anti-Nazi activities with Alex's father. Unbidden, they mention the father's best boyhood friend, named Panok. "How could a man with only those two mysterious words—'Panok' and 'Koidanov'—have found his way home nearly sixty years later to the room where he had slept as a child" (341)? As the truth of the father's story begins to be verified, piece by piece, the *fact* of the revelations becomes as astonishing as the original story itself. The intermittent guilt Mark has felt in pressing his father into the torment of memory begins to dissipate in the face of manifold confirmations and coincidences and of Alex's astonishment that a momentous piece of his past indeed remains. Although he tells his son that the flood of recollection is almost more than he can handle, Mark's ethical doubts about forcing and uncovering the secret give way to the father's wonder: "It's been a long way home, but it has been worth it. We have found each other now" (354). At this point both father and son unquestionably acknowledge their Jewishness.

By way of bringing this discussion to a close, I want to cite a splendid paragraph regarding the ambiguity of evidence from an autobiographical essay by Carolyn Kraus. She is concerned with the problem of whether documentary material she unearthed from her father's past necessarily lends credibility, let alone truth, to the story.

> I had followed the frail private documents, dug through the dusty public records—and if they hadn't banished the shadows obscuring my father's . . . and ultimately my own story, they'd at least yielded flashes of insight and glimmers of substance, of corporality. But now as I seek to convey the truth behind my family history, my zeal for unambiguous answers has cooled, replaced by a steadier faith in meandering narrative. After all my dark nights of the soul, false starts, bewildering journeys, my final task is like any other writer's: to drag the chaos of life out of the shadows and wrestle it into a story. (268)

And so it is for Mark Kurzem. What do the photographs of his father, or the yellowed newspaper articles, or even a brief Nazi propaganda film in which the child Alex appeared and which father and son discover in the Latvia State Archive of Audiovisual Documents, ultimately reveal? Are they indices to or signs of "the truth," or must Mark *construct* "the truth" from them? With all the evidence in place, the secrets unlocked and the connections made, mysteries still remain, and Mark is compelled both to let them abide and, as best he can in conjunction with his father, to "wrestle [them] into the story." Who are the faces in photographs unearthed from the floorboards of his childhood house—family members, and if so which ones? Did the father witness executions of Jews? Why had his life been spared by the soldiers? How had the child managed so successfully to conceal his Jewishness? How much can his memory of events sixty years earlier be trusted? Are all his impressions subject to confirmation? Why had he remained silent as an adult, safe in Australia? We want to believe that the past will speak definitively through documents, images, and authentication by others. But Mark, who not only tells the story of the story but shepherds his father through the morass of disclosure and resistance, finally must accept the absence of conclusively verifiable evidence. Does it matter if every "memory" is necessarily true? "There was no resolution, no absolution, no closure, no moving on, no getting over it. . . . Only an accommodation of the past" (396). As he concludes the work, he inherits the uncertainty and the mystery that his father lives with, a mystery which *is* his father. This may be the inevitable legacy of all participants in family secrets.

While Mark accepts, however ambivalently, his role as detective, he comes to realize he can no more unearth *the* truth than his father can. Mark attempts to reassure his father that the little boy was too young to have had any control over his actions and encourages him to make peace with the mysteries of the past. The "evidence" in the briefcase tells ambiguous stories; and if Alex can say "the truth is, my story is all that I have now," Mark, a co-storyteller, can say no more.

It seems appropriate to conclude my account of the Kurzem odyssey with a final reference to Daniel Mendelsohn's *The Lost.* Mendelsohn speaks about the enormous effort that has put him in touch with a past and with the dead he had imagined were forever lost to anyone's knowledge about them. But though he may not literally have rescued them, in painstakingly retrieving their stories he gets close to them in unexpected ways. Still, Mendelsohn understands there is necessarily a lacuna between what he discovers and what must have occurred (what he calls "the eternal conflict between what happened and the *story* of what happened"), a lacuna he acknowledges but will not allow to dishearten him since secrets ineluctably persist.

Because it is one thing to have lived the story and quite another to *write* the story and organize it into a whole, the written narrative will never be *the* story; but it is all the narrator can achieve—and that is a great deal. I am convinced Mark Kurzem believes with Mendelsohn that "if you look for things, if you search, you will, by the very act of searching, make something happen that would not otherwise have happened.... [T]o search for a while in the debris of the past [is] to see not only what was lost but what there is still to be found" (486-487). That final present tense is crucial: the searching for the secret has been the significant thing, and the searching goes on, not because Mark believes he can obtain definitive answers, nor is unable to live with his father's and his own ambiguous narrative. It goes on because his relation with his father is forever changed by what they have experienced, *together.* Freud believed that the purpose of analysis was to get the patient to construct a narrative that was not necessarily "true" but efficacious. In achieving filial closeness and understanding, the Kurzems' mutual storytelling accomplishes that end.

In *Maus* Art Spiegelman constantly laments that his experiences as an artist and a son pale before his father's ordeal in the camps. Nothing he experiences by way of victimization at his father's nagging and attempts to exercise control over Art, let alone Art's mother's suicide, can come close to his father's suffering, and as a result his demand for the father's story alternates with guilt for plunging the older man into dreadful memory. Though Mark Kurzem seems largely immune from Spiegelman's self-laceration and even feelings of bad faith, he does, as we've seen, display moments of ambivalence about coaxing the story from the man who needed the protection of silence.

No such reluctance, however, marks the next figure in this chapter. In Michael Skakun's gripping memoir the son appears to gain profound closeness to his father as he reveals—with the father's cooperation—a story of an extraordinary former secret life. Perhaps because it is a secret the son has known all along, at least in some form, the narrator never distances himself from the father nor becomes a character in his own right. This gesture of narrative self-effacement enables the son to express sympathy with his father's life-threatening predicament and his extraordinary solution. Fascinated by the psychological and religious catastrophes as well as by the sheer threats to survival his father faced and overcame, Skakun's suspenseful tone mingled with his understanding of the emotional complexities of the secret life help him forge a bond with the father, one implicit in the very nature of his storytelling.

Into the Belly of the Beast: Counterfeiting Identity for Survival

Michael Skakun's extraordinary Holocaust memoir of his father, *On Burning Ground: A Son's Memoir* (1999), is substantially unlike any other work I treat in this book, insofar as the central secret at its heart is not one that was completely unknown to the son and author. There is no midlife discovery of a previously hidden truth (the writer knew some of the facts from an early age), no detective work to uncover a buried parental life (the father was forthcoming with his story), no revelatory documents (all relevant evidence was lost or destroyed), and no moment when the son refashions or revises his own identity in the face of a newly unearthed subterfuge (from early on he felt joined to his father).

But Skakun's text is worth discussing as a powerful account of perhaps the most astonishing of all secret lives included here. His father Joseph, a mild-mannered, young Polish Jew studying for the rabbinate on the eve of the Nazi occupation of Poland and the slaughter of virtually the entire Jewish population of his native town of Novogrudek in Belarus, escaped the killing and managed to hide—like Alex Kurzem, first in forests, then with false papers in several ghettos—subsequently obtaining a birth certificate from a friend that allowed him to pass as a Muslim Tartar and thus to account for his circumcision in a way that would not be an automatic death sentence. Armed with this new identification, he eventually did the most unimaginable and, to his conscience, troubling thing possible for a Jew: he joined the Waffen SS after undergoing a personal examination in the headquarters of the Gestapo.

On Burning Ground is a detailed, suspenseful story not just about the complex means by which the father choreographed his concealment and his survival, but of how identity—in his case *multiple* identities—may be understood, questioned, or ratified through a deliberate and often terrifying act of "moral improvisation" (3). There are several references in the text to the biblical tale of Jacob wrestling with the angel, and it's clear that the father (here referred to as Skakun) constantly wrestled with himself and with Jewish law as he went deeper into the enemy camp and took on the external identity of the enemy itself, struggling to cling to his pious Jewish self even as he had to suppress all manifestations of his religion and his past.

At the outset of the work Michael declares, "For as long as I can remember, I have been the confidant of a man's conscience. When I was a child, Father sat me down and recounted a story of terror that defied all logic. He conveyed it with such vivid emotional conviction that it became the substance of my life, until it achieved an immediacy as palpable as my own skin" (3). Michael first heard the bold outlines of his father's story at six or seven. Roughly once each decade, appropriate to his age, he was to learn more in complexity and depth, especially of the ethical dilemmas and the moral dimensions of his father's actions in relation to Judaism. (I sense that Skakun could hardly wait until Michael, his only child, was old enough to hear and eventually to understand the entire story of survival, a story that of course allowed Michael as well as his father to have life.) In his forties, roughly at the age most of the writers in my study undertake their memoirs, Michael began to narrate the story he had been gradually gathering over the years. There were no sudden or shocking disclosures, yet to write the account he sounded his father for details of his war experience and for the older man's remembered responses at every turn in his history. There is little in the work comparable to Spiegelman's self-conscious depiction in *Maus* of the process of probing a resistant older man and painstakingly assembling the story of his survival; nor is there much concerning Michael's relation to his father, either as a child or as an adult; and there is nothing whatsoever about the father's attitude toward having his story made public. Nevertheless we can glimpse all these matters between the lines. I draw on an interview I conducted with Michael Skakun—one of only two times I have spoken directly to an author in this study concerning his or her work (the other is Louise Steinman)—having felt a special need in this case because the text is relatively devoid of the process of acquiring and composing the story or of explicit analysis of the writer's own self as he situates it in relation to his father.

Michael's reluctance to intrude, even to insinuate himself into the story is important for what it reveals about the nature of the story itself. The author's voice *is* present, especially in the first of two prologues, when he tells us briefly that his father often related the story to him after morning prayers at the Brooklyn synagogue that housed the yeshiva from his native Novogrudek, recounting his past "sometimes in a cry, choking with pain" (6). Michael's narrative is based entirely on what his father had revealed to him, and though the story is in the third or "biographical" person, in effect Michael cedes narrative authority to his father. Unlike so many survivors of the Holocaust who, especially in the late 1940s and 1950s suppressed stories of their experience, whether out of fear of others' disbelief or reluctance to awaken and dwell on memories of horror, Skakun, having lived a life of secrecy, lies, and illusion-spinning, needed to talk openly. True, much of the book centers on Skakun's continual need for silence during his dangerous masquerade, lest, in the course of maintaining his multiple false identities and incarnations, he might say something that would expose his truth. Speech-lessness was the necessary condition in which he conducted his plotted exis-tence, and taciturnity is a dominant motif, especially concerning Skakun's vigilance in conveying nothing to others of his emotional life let alone of his strategies for survival. Nevertheless, the very narrative gift he exhib-ited when he invented lineages, origins, and identities and turned them into life-saving stories he demonstrates to his child at the Friday Sabbath table when he recounts his European past. Silence and expressiveness are the twin coordinates of his life. It is his history of solitude that brings about an almost Newtonian reaction: the compulsion to speak, significantly on the Sabbath, a time according to Jewish custom for restoration, which in Skakun's case led to the recitation of the story.

But because for so long Skakun could not speak in his true voice, his son narrates the tale in his father's voice as a kind of surrogate or proxy speaker representing his father's erstwhile hidden self able at last to come into the open. Since Michael hardly speaks of his relation to his father or of his responses to his father's account, that absence of self, paralleling his father's self-effacement during his wartime experience, becomes something like a secret homage to the father in the form of narrative ventriloquism. As the father had to be invisible, in the writing the son becomes analogously imper-ceptible, assuming an absence that endows his father with a newly minted presence and guarantees that Michael not overshadow the older man. Speak-ing out was a freedom that Skakun, not unlike Alex Kurzem, had forced himself to deny; and Michael, in a project similar to Mark Kurzem's, gives his father back the voice the older man had necessarily suppressed.

The elder Skakun's own father had, ironically, come to New York in 1906 only to return to Europe four years later without having made a success;

because the grandfather had told his son tales of an America that had disappointed and defeated him, Michael wished to hear tales from *his* father, as if to continue a family tradition of storytelling and to foster an explicit dialogue between two generations, an implicit one among three. Skakun's eventual voyage of survival to New York after the war (he spent some time first in Israel, where Michael was born) reenacts more successfully his own father's early twentieth century voyage of defeated hopes; at the same time Michael's narration casts an eye back to Europe much as, in reverse, his grandfather had cast an eye back to New York in order to relate tales to Michael's father when the latter was a boy in Poland. *On Burning Ground* is a multigenerational memoir, with the author locating himself within a complex family narrative. The meaning of the subtitle, *A Son's Memoir,* is double: the work is both *Skakun's* memoir composed by his son and *Michael's* memoir as the ear for his father's speech, the father free at last to claim and give voice to his story through his son. Speaking about his father's continual need for vocal caution, Michael cites what appears to be a maxim from Novogrudek: "If people were born with two ears but only one tongue, it must be for the reason that they should hear twice and speak once" (205). It is a statement that applies not only to Skakun's verbal cunning but as well to the son's careful listening. Crafted speech depends on crafty hearing, and in this sense the son imitates the father.

In our interview Michael reported that his father was glad for the book to be written; there was no hesitation about going public with his story, no resistance in the name of privacy, no concern that having himself exposed in print would violate confidence, and no fear that the story might not be believed. In a curious sense since he was so used to living false identities, he had worried that until the story became known others might steal it from him, and so was eager for the story to be divulged. To be sure, he was wary that the saga could be misread as a collaboration with the Nazis and an act of unforgivable apostasy, and this apprehension no doubt played a role, as we shall see, in Michael's decision to emphasize the father's piety at each moment when the latter's conduct appears sacrilegious.

The narrative proper begins with the Nazi roundup of Jews in Novogrudek, the murder of Skakun's mother, the young man's temporary reprieve from the killing, and his decision to flee into the surrounding forest followed by what will be the first of several extraordinary pieces of luck enabling him to appropriate secret and fraudulent identities. He finds a book dropped by a German soldier with a page containing an official stamp and imprinted swastika that will grant the bearer travel rights to Warsaw. Of course the Warsaw ghetto would ultimately be no haven for Skakun, though going there ironically turns out to be a step on the road to freedom via a German foreign labor program in Berlin and eventually the offices of the SS.

The crucial aspect of the early pages of the memoir concerns his mother, and his guilt at not following her to death. Skakun's mother hovers over his dangerous life and over his son's account like a guardian angel: "his mother's radiant life…allowed him to pass deeper into the iron web without being crushed" (135). He regards her not only as a protector but as the voice of conscience to which he appeals in the face of moral doubts about his actions. He makes her the auditor of his secret life, perhaps a projection of his unconscious, to whom he appeals both for validation of his authentic (former rabbinical student) self and for forgiveness. The maternal absolution he seeks is for escaping what she could not, but also of course for what might appear a betrayal of faith in his public denial of Jewishness. Skakun's continually asserted reverence for his mother suggests an allegiance to family and piety in the face of shame for filial and religious treason, as well as an anticipation of accusations from readers condemning his "collaboration," accusations that proved unsurprisingly common. As a result the details of Skakun's story are interlaced with protestations of reverence: When he makes his way through the forest escaping the shots of Nazi patrols he thinks about great religious leaders and yeshiva study; when he contemplates going to the Vilna ghetto he hopes there will still be synagogues when he arrives; and the closer he moves to "the maw of the beast" the more he claims to be "true to his native grounds" (3, 132). At the moments of greatest narrative tension—during the numerous showers he was forced to take on his way into Germany and in Berlin, and especially during several examinations for admission into the Waffen SS—Skakun silently prays and harkens back to his prewar life as a scholar of Orthodox Judaism. It seems plausible that granting his son permission to write and publish the book is Shakun's expiation to his mother and to his faith, a request for forgiveness and a sign of his "stigma of conscience" (221).

It is relevant to speak briefly of the specific Jewish tradition in which Skakun was raised because it provides a clue to the severity of his guilt and the possible origins of his remarkable improvisational skill in framing identities for survival. Skakun was educated in the Mussar movement. Originating over a millennium ago and developed in nineteenth century Eastern Europe, especially among Lithuanian Orthodox Jews, it is an ethical, educational, and cultural movement whose program helps its disciples overcome internal obstacles to spiritual enlightenment and holiness and promotes the desire to live according to Jewish law and the commandments. Of course Skakun, in the light of his education in pietistic Judaism, feared that his joining the

Nazis, even if countenanced by Jewish law as a necessary life-saving measure, was a violation of everything in which he was schooled. But at the same time Mussar, especially as it was practiced most famously in the yeshivas of the town of Novogrudek where he was raised, developed characteristics in its students that enabled Skakun to survive. Mussar encouraged a confidence that one could overcome any obstacle standing in the way of desired goals. The program espoused a belief that life is a never-ending struggle against complacency and stressed hypervigilance lest one make mistakes; as such, it demanded a constant struggle against weakness. A nineteenth-century movement leader, Yosef Yozel Horowitz, speaks of jolting the soul to withstand life's trials.

Mussar emphasized diligent striving and the development of all necessary strategies to accomplish one's ends. Above all it advocated a strong will and a belief in one's ability to carry out that will. Mussar enables Skakun to assert an authentic self even as his secret identity appears to subvert it; he needed to convince himself he had retained a true self at the very moment he seemed to be—even to himself—profoundly *in*authentic.

According to a modern interpreter, Novogrudek Mussar "was an all-consuming fire, its teachings were flames, its atmosphere electric. The image and terminology of fire and conflagration are omnipresent in its literature" (Levin, xviii). The "burning ground" of Michael Skakun's title refers not just to the scorched land of Holocaust Europe nor to the ravaged soul of his father but also to the searing teachings of Mussar, which allowed Skakun to undertake unprecedented acts.

Skakun's identity might seem problematic given that he performed a series of multiple and conflicting selves. But paradoxically those false identifications served to shore up and enhance a genuine and fundamental sense of who he was.

Early in the work his son quotes Paul Valéry: "I believe in all sincerity that if each man were not able to live a number of lives besides his own, he would not be able to live his own life" (12). Valéry suggests that we not only have the ability to inhabit multiple selves but that such a capacity allows us to experiment with our lives, to expand and deepen our sense of self. Of course Skakun carried out this skill under extreme pressure; reading the saga we come to admire the dexterity that exemplifies a human power of mimesis, one that testifies to self-expansion. I do not mean to imply that each secret self Skakun enacts represents in its specificity who he really is (Michael says his father "vandaliz[ed] a whole line of strange and foreign lineages"). Rather Skakun's self-transformations reveal a capaciousness of character, an art of improvisation and invention enabling him to incarnate a fuller self (11–12). Because Skakun's life literally depended on living other lives, "secretly craft[ing] a new identity," Michael is correct in representing his father's ordeal as "the darker meaning" of Valéry's statement. And though he claims his father's mask was "so tight-fitting that it became nearly one with his life" (4), we know that pretending to be the other is an imitation, not finally an identification. Still, we should understand that seeing his father as "a performing aerialist with no safety net" (11) attributes to him a power in which secrecy and the ability to spin illusions are less aberrations than essential human traits he carries off with mastery.

On Burning Ground employs several images crucial for figuring Skakun's secret identities. When he fears that Sergei, a Russian laborer working with him on the farm outside Berlin, has suspected some kind of duplicity, even with his Muslim identification papers Skakun's situation seems precarious, impelling him to volunteer for the SS to escape further suspicion. Sergei "had deciphered the palimpsest's faintly visible underwriting" (187). The metaphor of the palimpsest suggests the multiple layers of identity, each of which continues to exist while others are layered on top of them—what his son calls his "marvel of incarnations" (117). The palimpsest of course represents layered identity as strata of writing, though there is no writing until his son inscribes him in a book. Skakun fears his original identity and name will be written on the wind. The palimpsest implies that identity is never singular; Skakun's case is an extreme example under the pressure of secrecy of the multilayered forms the self may take. Skakun actually inhabits two clusters of triple-identities: Polish-Lithuanian-Tartar and Jewish-Christian-Muslim. Before assuming the Muslim self, in order to work outside Vilna's ghetto walls Skakun had passed as a Christian, learning the gestures and habits, as well as the rituals and customs, of a Polish peasant; when he borrows and retains the birth certificate of a Muslim friend allowing him to gain a German passport and eventually to enlist in the SS, he familiarizes himself with the history and religion of Islam, especially with the Osmanov family lineage since he is appropriating Stefan Osmanov's name and identity. The palimpsest is an especially appropriate image for his dissimulation since each "writing" is replaced by another, although traces of the original remain, however indistinct. Skakun's Jewishness, which forms the original ground and cannot be erased entirely, is the suppressed identity he fears will bleed through but that he must retain even if written in invisible ink.

In fact the Tartar Muslim identity is not so alien to Judaism as it might seem. In addition to the shared ritual of circumcision, Michael refers to "the cross-fertilization of cultures" in the court of the Tartar Genghis Khan, whose descendents in Poland battled Teutonic knights. Skakun himself recalls that in Novogrudek his grandfather was friendly with a Tartar spiritual leader who felt linked to Jews and told him: "Don't forget, my good friend, we share many things in common....We are...people of commentary, and believe just as adamantly in revelation and law. Didn't Mohammed preach that the Torah was to be revered and was integral to Islamic revelation....?" (111). As a boy Skakun had memorized lines from the Friday Islamic prayers, and his son notes that the first systematic work on Jewish ethics, which influenced the Mussar movement, was written in Arabic in Muslim Spain. These parallels and links "in the communion of faiths" partly put Skakun at his ease as he practices and rehearses his new identity by "reminding himself of the similarities between his ancestral faith and Mohammed's" (118), and though the story of his newly adopted identity is somewhat strange to him, it is not entirely so. At the same time—and this accounts for the SS officers' sympathy for Skakun's claim as "Stefan Osmanov" to be a Crimean Tartar—the Nazis saw Hitler and Muhammad as fellow charismatic warriors; in fact the Crimean Tartars had been Nazi collaborators, and Hitler had declared, "I am going to become a religious figure. Soon I'll be the great chief of the Tatars....Among the Tatars I shall become khan" (121). Skakun adopts an identity both foreign and familiar. This doubleness suggests his ability to live within secrets, and it validates Valéry's apothegm about multiple selves making possible greater authenticity.

As he awaits the SS examination, Skakun "restitched the weave of his false identity into a pattern as sinuous as that of an oriental carpet" (192). In taking on the mantle of an eastern Tartar from Russia, he has "become" oriental, ironic in that unlike his fellow Jews who move deathward toward the East, he has journeyed westward into the very heart of the enemy but toward safety and life. He dwells on "the arabesque of a new identity," as if the intricate pattern of the carpet were replicated in the sinuosity of selfhood; since the questions of any Nazi interlocutor will be similarly "sinuous," he must be a match in psychological dexterity for their suspicions and insinuations (109).

Two further metaphors square with these notions. One is the border crossing ("into the unknown, a frontier he feared he would never be able to recross" [203]). The problem is not just the crossing but the *recrossing*: Will he get back, as it were, to the original writing inscribed on the palimpsest of the self? The borders are not merely geographical but existential: Will his secret life make authenticity impossible to regain, and will he be forbidden to assert his Jewishness? Finally, since the pseudo-Osmanov's identity is "the central act in the drama of his survival" and the crucial aspect of his "shifting scenario of otherness" (178, 191), the entire masquerade becomes a piece of theatre with props (the birth certificate); a chorus (the voices of his ancestors); rising action, climax, and a denouement; entrances and exits (a series of journeys in and out of forests, ghettos, work camps, farms, and official offices); rehearsals and performances (repeated practicing of elaborate deceptions, confrontations with Gestapo officers regarded as a form of playacting); and scenes of dramatic recognition (at the moment he is being examined for admission into the SS a shaft of sunlight falls on Skakun's blond hair, making it more golden than normal and ironically convincing the examining officer of his Aryan blood). Even the book itself has a theatrical form: it begins with two "Prologues" and concludes with two "Epilogues."

Much of the work consists of Skakun's strategies and plans for passing—as a Polish Christian peasant, a farmer, a Muslim Tartar, and ultimately as a man eager for service in the Nazi regime. He dons false masks and false names, learns to impersonate, and realizes he must go beyond mere study of his personae to "incarnate" them (an ironic term given how he learns and prepares if necessary to assert his belief in the Incarnation). The drama emerges in his desire to seal off the self as "hermetically...as a sarcophagus lid," to crush his past and to breed "Yiddish, the language of his childhood sentiment,...out of his bones" (126, 150), while at the same time attempting to be true to who he is despite the perilous tangle of identities. When a Ukrainian friend calls an oppressing Nazi "our Jew," Skakun wonders at "the irony of a Ukrainian yokel calling a Nazi a Jew in front of a Jew masquerading as a Polish Tatar" (152). When he makes a point of speaking Russian with Poles and Polish with Russians so he can pass himself off as either depending on circumstances, we perceive how much the world he inhabits is a labyrinth of deception and concealment.

The turns and twists of identity persist in an even more ironic fashion when the Russian army arrives to free Germany from Nazi domination. Skakun views the Russians as liberators, but he still carries his Waffen SS papers for insurance in case the tide turns against the Russians. Were the Russians to discover those papers he risks being shot as a spy. Tempted to announce to the Russians his Jewishness—an act he initially imagines as a cathartic relief after so much deception—he realizes some soldiers may be anti-Semitic, and if he were to reveal his true identity and the Germans returned in strength, he would surrender the protection he struggled so hard to obtain. "His triple identity still had a ways to go" (211). Persistent danger and the fear he might misread the situation always leads Skakun to necessary mistrust, vigilance, and subterfuge. No single identity provides guaranteed safety; he is trapped not so much inside any one as in the continual play of charades that threaten to keep him off-balance.

The result of Skakun's ordeal is a constant longing to return to the past, for he clings to a reverence for the lost paradise of his Novogrudek childhood despite its death-haunted aftermath. He regards the Novogrudek ghetto as a memento mori, a sign of what is at once irretrievable and unforgettable. Like the exile, Skakun knows the past is an unrecoverable country, but because he cannot dwell *in* it he cannot cease dwelling *on* it. The text vacillates between a shadowy future and a haunted history.

Earlier I said that Michael suppresses his own voice to allow his father the unrestrained speech Skakun necessarily avoided during his ordeal. But I want to qualify this statement. While never speaking *for* his father, Michael in effect speaks *with* him, and even *as* him: "He conveyed [a story of terror] with such vivid emotional conviction that it became the substance of my life, until it achieved an immediacy as palpable as my own skin." And again: "[T]hrough his recitation I became a party to his grief" (3, 6). The son is outside and yet inside his father's story, as he acknowledges both his likeness to and distinctness from the other. Their separateness does not preclude mutual recognition.

In this regard another comparison with *Maus* may be relevant. As I've noted, Spiegelman is acutely aware of having been spared the Holocaust, and that whatever his difficulties of career or paternal relationship, they pale next to anything experienced by his father; and he is guilty for that difference. By contrast Michael does not address differences in suffering, but joins with his father in the only way he can—as an act of solidarity and communion, identifying with his father's grief and intrigued by Skakun's conscience as much as the father is consumed by it. Unlike with Spiegelman, we never sense any detachment by Michael from his father, never perceive a stance even slightly outside him. It is as if the writer were a kind of alter ego, or perhaps a companion living alongside his father. The son's voice *is* his father's voice. Perhaps the most vivid statement of a shared role is his comment: "Both of us lived in the subjunctive, imagining what might have occurred had the end of the war come later. For many years *we* sifted through a grim inventory of possibilities" (232, my emphasis). "The subjunctive" raises not merely a question about the "what if" of the war ending much later, entailing the greater possibility of his father being expected to carry out unthinkable actions against fellow Jews, but more broadly speculation about the ultimate effect on Skakun of his life of secrets and the effect on Michael as their repository and transcriber, especially as one who has identified so fully with the story.

Of all the children writing about parents in this study, no other seems so faithful a confidant as Michael. I want to conclude by speculating briefly about one of his literary interests as a way of understanding his fascination with his father's story. *On Burning Ground* makes several references to Melville, and though Michael never finished graduate school in English, he had planned to write a dissertation on Melville, who remains his favorite American author. Melville's last novel was *The Confidence Man* about a protean Mississippi River gambler who lives secret lives, taking on and shedding countless disguises and incognitos. Could an attraction to Melville stem from his admiration for his father, a man of great self-assurance who confidently took on, maintained, discarded, and took on again a series of aliases, and whose skill in conning others and in becoming a con man for his life allowed Michael, in whom he invested his confidence, to have his own—as writer of that life?

If Michael Skakun, in telling his father's story, seems almost novelistically to enter into the consciousness of his subject, writing with a point of view virtually indistinguishable from that of his father and resistant to even a trace of irony let alone cynicism, Helen Fremont, the author of my next selection, is torn between respect for her parents' Holocaust ordeal and a puzzled, even chiding attitude toward their continual attempt to retain their secret. Fremont makes a great effort to gather the story of their past and to retell it with sensitivity and sympathy, but her self-interest as a daughter who needs to sort out her own role in the family is nearly as important as the desire to retrieve and translate her parents' past. Though she may not come to any settled beliefs about her self, she demonstrates the way that the pursuer of truth cannot be fully separated from the object of her quest. In her account we see the melding of autobiography and biography, but the writer's own resistance to introspection somewhat undermines the yield in knowledge. Could it be that Fremont's parents' conflicting and confusing signals regarding their religious identity, so different from Joseph Skakun's assured one, has ironically kept Helen from searching herself as doggedly as she probes her parents?

Probing Secret Conversions:
Helen Fremont's Anguished Inquisition

Many studies have appeared in the past quarter century analyzing the difficult relationship of Holocaust survivors to their children. These studies focus on a wide range of issues: the children's inheritance of their parents' sense of vulnerability to external forces; the children's shame regarding perceived parental humiliation and degradation; their guilt for having led a privileged life while their parents had suffered so much, or conversely their resentment for being reminded of that disparity; their discontent at the parents' suffocating closeness or their affectless detachment; and the burden of having to represent the future and a new life in the face of threatened annihilation.

But when the so-called second generation confront parents who, unlike Joseph Skakun, have repressed or falsified their wartime experiences, the desire to grasp that experience and expose secrets or misrepresentation can lead to unsettling and explosive confrontations. Of all the family circumstances that involve a history of parental concealment and their offspring's impulse to question, investigate, and pierce the armor of that secrecy—or to create a coherent explanation from stories that seem inconsistent and suspiciously distorted, even untrue if not deliberately deceptive—few raise such profound ethical, relational, and identity problems as those set in the context of the aftermath of the Holocaust.

It is relatively uncommon, however, for Jews who survived the Holocaust by veiling and changing their religious identity during the war to continue in their adopted religion long after and to pass on that religion to their children, refusing to acknowledge their identity as Jews. Madeleine Albright may be the best-known example of this phenomenon. There are relatively few memoirs narrating such revelations; perhaps the best among them is Helen Fremont's *After Long Silence: A Memoir* (1999), which touches on many of those complex parent-child issues. Its significance, however, lies in the way it examines parental efforts to hide their religion—during and after the war, even in the safe haven of the United States—and their two daughters' dogged attempt to get at the truth, however disturbing that discovery may be both to themselves and to the parents. The circumstances leading to the Fremonts' secrecy may have been less dramatic than Skakun's, but the aftermath and the process of revelation is more troubled. This text is an example of life writing in which the profoundest questions of identity are raised: What is your real life, what is mine, and why have you withheld the truth about both issues?

In their thirties, Helen and her sister Lara (a lawyer and a psychiatrist respectively), convinced that their parents' story about their past contained some falsifications if not outright lies, began to inquire about the family history. The parents, who spent the war years in Europe and eventually moved to the American Midwest, were nominally Catholic and reared their daughters in that faith. The mother had converted largely to protect the identity of her older sister who during the war had married an Italian count and, taking on his religion for pragmatic purposes, escaped from Nazi-occupied Poland to Rome. The mother, who also fled to Rome during the war to join her sister, barely escaped incarceration and death in Auschwitz by a variety of hair-rending escapes using false papers and false names. The father spent six years in a Siberian Gulag, and, when released at the end of the war and reunited in Rome with the woman who had been his fiancée six years earlier, he agreed to protect her and his future sister-in-law's identities by also becoming Catholic.

For years both daughters were suspicious that their parents had betrayed their histories and denied their Jewishness. Their adopted religion seemed superficial ("It was as if they had read the *Cliff Notes* on Catholicism" [14]), mere form without substance, more fiction than conviction; they were oddly Catholic, always leaving church before Communion. Conversant with many details of Jewish traditions, they explained them to their daughters as if to the manner born. The daughters themselves felt most comfortable with their Jewish friends. Frequently at social gatherings every other person in the room was Jewish, many of them Holocaust survivors; a Jewish family friend even told the girls their parents were Jews, though initially Helen and her sister were more intrigued and skeptical than convinced.

Arriving in Michigan in 1950, Fremont's parents had changed their last name and acted much as they were forced to during the war: with silence, cunning, and evasion. Fremont grew up with the story of her parents' separation and reunion, but not with the years in between. The parents' story "tied a knot in their tongues at the end, and the war remained silent; the intervening six years could never be spoken" (8).

Inauthenticity appeared at every turn; even among fellow Jewish immigrant-survivors the parents continued to falsify. As Fremont begins to probe their past, the more adept the mother becomes at resistance and narrative transformation, stubbornly holding to an invented story that increases in its magnitude and in the teller's determination to be believed at all costs. Her parents appear addicted to the falsified past, with all the defenses and lies that characterize addiction. Even the father's six hundred-page unpublished memoir about his war years in the Gulag makes no mention of religion, his own parents, or his Jewish family. Fremont suggests the father wanted to tell his daughters when they turned eighteen that they were Jewish, but when the mother checked with her sister in Rome who vetoed the idea, both parents stayed silent. As labyrinthine stories metamorphose into other stories ("layers upon layers of secrets, thick lead shields against the truth" [207]) and the fabrications became more practiced, it grows harder for Fremont to interpret correctly. This is especially frustrating and maddening when she senses she's been given glimmers of fact and truth, as if she were being invited in and shut out at the same time, a victim of fictions that keep her off balance.

Eventually the sisters undertake to assemble the "jigsaw-puzzle past" (21). They discover, after research at the Yad Vashem memorial in Israel

and the Holocaust Memorial Museum in Washington, D.C., and extensive correspondence with Holocaust witnesses still alive in Israel, several of
whom remember their parents, that the Bocard's (the parents' adopted name
in America) were in fact Jewish. The daughters receive pages of testimony
proving that the Nazis had gassed both sets of grandparents in 1943—contrary
to the Bocards' claim that their parents were random victims of bombings.
The text shows how the sisters arranged slender bits of information, testimony from libraries and museums, even from street maps of prewar Polish
towns. To conduct their research they also returned to the towns where
their parents lived before the invasion, interviewing anyone who might have
remembered them.

As a lawyer used to probing witnesses' statements, Helen is positioned
to examine evidence with meticulous precision, and as a psychiatrist given to
analyzing and assessing resistance, Lara is positioned to be skeptical in the
face of evasion. If Helen's story of the unflagging investigation begins with
the realization that her parents' friends are all Jewish survivors, her suspicion becomes an *idée fixe* as the Jews she meets suspect her parents' alleged
Catholicism. Helen realizes her mother's stories of escape make sense only if
she is Jewish. Evidence piles up: A rabbi in Israel whom she contacts sends
documents attesting to the parents' Judaism; the Red Cross discovers a rabbi
in the family, a survivor from her father's Polish village living in Chicago,
who identifies her father as Jewish; proof arrives from libraries, museums,
and from other survivors. "Consumed by our need to know" (107), Helen
plunges ahead, speculating until she puts together as many pieces of the
genealogical puzzle as she can. Undertaking the research is as rewarding as
the definitive finding. Though unraveling lies is a dangerous business, the
desire to speak truth to evasion overcomes all prohibitions, whether external
or matters of conscience. But the relative paucity of documents is cause for
the sisters' frustration, and they fear that a dearth of concrete evidence will
make it easier for the parents to remain silent and in denial, absent from their
own history.

The parents' silence created confusion for the daughters when they were
young, inevitably forcing them to invent their own versions of history. But
it also has the temporary effect of enjoining them to their own silence, as if
the family secret had to be preserved at all costs, their reticence about the
parents' fabricated past matching the parents' own. Even in family therapy
the secret is preserved, part of a fifty-year vow the mother had made with
her sister to keep their true identity secret. Ironically the gap in consistency
and coherence is a version of the emptiness the Nazis had tried to make of
Judaism itself; instead of pride in a narration of survival and heroic resistance

to extermination policies, "the Secret" entails both parents' refusal to admit even that they *are* survivors.

When eventually confronted with evidence about their Judaism the parents stonewall: "What difference does the past make?" the mother cries. "You are who you are today, that's all that matters! Forget about the past! Look forward! Live for today!" (45). The daughters continue to meet resistance or silence: "[M]y parents were still in hiding...all the underground tunnels in our house were not just figments of my imagination" (22). More disturbingly Helen's aunt, at one time an active Zionist raised in a Polish Orthodox Jewish home, responds to the revelation with indignation, accusing her niece of acting like the Nazis, as if uncovering and exposing her identity threatens to replicate the very threat that the obfuscating disguise was designed to thwart. Fremont images her aunt's evasion as a wall built brick-by-brick, as if her mind had become ghettoized, cut off from history and truth. The aunt provides a great negative example of truth-telling: Her grief is so great that she "eventually banish[es] herself from her own memory" (104). The younger sisters' research attempts to counter the willed amnesia of the sisters from the older generation, but even when pieces of the mother's memory gradually emerge, she herself remains skeptical of her daughters' quest for knowledge, cynically describing the "roots" phenomenon as "just another American fad" (45).

Only after continual pleading from Helen and her presentation of decisive evidence do the parents grudgingly and fragmentarily acknowledge the truth, and only after long silence does the mother eventually weave the story of her falsified roles. A dialectic between revealing and concealing runs through the work, exposing the naiveté as well as the determination of the researchers. Fremont gradually provokes her mother to speech, but it takes years before either the teller or the writer can arrange the shards of the account into a coherent narrative. The text is an exercise in what André Aciman has called "speculophilia," the compulsion to speculate about what happened when access to the truth seems impossible to determine.

So driven is Fremont to compose a coherent explanatory narrative that the reader is left wondering how much of the story is given by the parents, how much is put together from external evidence, and how much, particularly in its transitional threads, is woven together by the younger sisters. As a result, we have a collaborative account, yet one that depends on the parents' resistance to historical accuracy and the daughters' compulsive insistence on authenticity, if not always on verifiability.

After Helen suspects she and her sister have been deceived and the true stories begin to emerge, the parents gradually begin to acknowledge their identity as Jews and the children begin to think differently of themselves. But it is difficult to know what a Jewish identity means to Helen. True, she gains a new sense of the past whose legacy she has inherited, recognizing herself as a figure in a family history; she has indeed been a child with a false past as well as a kind of belatedly displaced person, someone like a person without a country. And yet she never explores her own identity in the book. While a reader might well assume the realization of her Jewishness would be central to her newly discovered self, she doesn't tell us if she begins to read books on Judaism, goes to synagogue, or feels particularly Jewish, and if so how. She appears more interested in her relation to her family than in any newfound religious identity as such. There is no "homecoming" pride in being Jewish.

Rather, the moral center of gravity is on the effort of Fremont's detective work—founded on her desire and her claimed right to know—and on the acts of exposure and re-narrativization of the past. The book is not as much a vehicle for self-discovery as we might presume and wish; only in the most generalized sense are the *secret* lives of the parents represented in the *inner* life of the daughter who writes those lives. It may be that Fremont's resistance to deeper self-reflection, ironic in its analogy to her parents' own reluctance, comes from her focus on relationship rather than ego. Family and not self is her overriding concern. This seems to me less an evasion than a point of view resulting from her perception that she has lived in a context of familial inauthenticity. But even though Fremont does not probe her inner self, her resourceful detective work in the face of familial opposition and her establishment of a new identity do create a linkage to the parents rather than a break from them. As each new discovery leads to further ones, as in the revelation of aunts and uncles shot in forests and gassed in camps, uncovering secrets creates deeper closeness. She defines herself as ineluctably tied to others and to their history. For this reason alone we might excuse what appears to be a kind of bullying, a refusal to relent when the parents attempt to halt or at least to slow down the process—often painful for her parents—of insistent unraveling and exposure of the past.

Fremont does want that story to become her own. "And strangely enough, on the page I begin to recognize myself in my parents" (344). Her initial innocence is replaced by an immersion, as historian, biographer, and autobiographer, into a world she never experienced but insists on knowing about and sharing. In writing her memoir she recognizes that the collective history is fraught with the personal, and vice-versa. And as each revelation leads to the next one ("If you open one door, a thousand other doors creak open" [166]), both sisters appear to grow closer to their parents and frozen emotions begin to thaw. It is this renewal, or rather a closeness experienced for the first time, that validates Fremont's enterprise.

During the course of her research Fremont crucially admits a secret she herself has long harbored, revealing to her mother that she is a lesbian. It's as if a family disposition to denial had been at work in Fremont as well, until she decides to come out even as she pressures her parents to openness. "Their secret was their armor, but it was a mask of silence imposed on all of us. Was it possible to be loyal to them and to myself at the same time?" (342). Whether Fremont wants to level the playing field and show that she too has a hidden identity, or whether her decision to reveal her own secret becomes a strategic move to convince her parents that speaking truth is a virtue, is not certain. Though the episode hardly figures as a dominant theme in the text, and it naturally pales for danger relative to the parents' war experiences, the disclosure serves as an instance of the unburdening of family secrets and as a model for the honesty she has attempted to elicit from her parents. Given her mother's initial resistance to Fremont's declaration and the mother's attempt to portray her daughter's particular sexuality as temporary, Fremont's burden is to define who she is (a Jewish lesbian) apart from how her mother conceives of her. But typically Fremont does not explore this matter at length, never plumbing the depths of her sexual identity. That story is placed strictly in the context of the dynamics of family secrecy.

If Fremont's motive is largely to re-create a more authentic family, we need to examine what we might call the ethics of inquiry and enforced admission. Fremont's project can awaken an inquisitorial guilt for causing further anguish to those bent on concealment. As we've seen, in flushing out the family's secrets Helen can seem like the enemy, not a figure seeking reparation, as she claims. Pushing her parents into revelation can be devastating, for telling them she "knows" they are Jewish can seem more like an "accusation" (42) than a revelation to bring relief after a lifetime of denial. Her investigation may indeed have the unwanted effect of dragging them back into the nightmare they have tried to escape through the concealment. Awakened memories haunt and terrify her mother, and in a statement that poses not only generational but cultural difference, Helen admits the treacherous (in both senses) nature of her sleuthing: "[We] were playing with fire, stepping right into the flames of the Holocaust with our goofy American gumshoed sneakers. Hot on the track of our discovery, we were dragging her back across the burning coals" (48). The word "goofy" of course suggests how different, if not alien, she can seem from her parents, how aware she is that her detective work might easily and dangerously strike the wrong chord. Her investigation may even represent a desire for power, forcing the parents to unearth what they had buried and threatening their psychological armor.

Proficient at lawyerly record keeping, Fremont becomes obsessed not only with exposing their secret but also with establishing the veracity and coherence of the narrative, as well as establishing the reasons for the deception. She basically subdues her mother into agreement, and on July 4, 1992, she gains her independence from doubt, beginning the story that lasts several years and occupies half of her text—a story of flight, disguise, deception, concealment, and self-invention. Unlike more typical Holocaust discoveries that start with children spotting numbers tattooed on a wrist, this one must be coerced, ferreted out, pieced together, and interpreted, especially since obfuscation was the very practice with which the parents became so adept and to which they necessarily became accustomed if not addicted.

Though her questioning must feel to the parents like a lack of gratitude for having been sheltered from the most precarious aspects of Judaism as they understand it, one of the tragic ironies of the parents' silence is that for a long time it keeps Helen from sympathy for their suffering. Their secret deprives her of an opportunity for deep affiliation and connection to a past that is hers as well. How can Fremont truly empathize with her parents unless she gets memories from them, given her belief that their story is in some sense her own? As Eva Hoffman puts it: "Sometimes for the children too...there is a deferred mourning—for those perished relatives, for our parents' hard lives, perhaps for ourselves and the inchoate sense of loss we were bequeathed" (184). Given the absence of parental openness, Fremont is denied any awareness of what was going on *in them*. So her project attempts to forge a bond with the past, with her parents' role in that past, and with the dead.

Fremont never appears to castigate her parents' deception. Indeed there's a begrudging admiration, especially of her mother's ability continually to reinvent herself. There is something like a detective's fascination for the double-dealer he is bent on exposing, and some of the mother's canniness is alive in the daughter as she deconstructs false stories and replaces them with new ones.

A "slippery figure" (9), the mother is skillful at making up stories, spinning diverse, often contradictory tales, taking on new identities, and inventing herself to suit the occasion. With each new self she inhabits she must forget the previous one; with each new role she becomes what she plays, the self identical with its performance, whether the Catholic sister-in-law of an Italian count, a Polish office worker, or, most astonishing, a young Italian soldier riding to Italy in a train full of *soldati*. Names, religions, nationalities—each is temporary, a "label to be peeled off and reapplied, like a picture pasted on a crate of fruit" (300). Fremont's mother may not strictly speaking be a *survivor* in the sense of someone who escaped alive from the camps, but she survives one treacherous situation after another, from prison to prison, from one official's interrogation to the next, shedding parents, friends, and her own past as she goes. She learns to shape herself into whatever role is necessary; impersonation and concealment come to her as second, third, and fourth natures.

Since *After Long Silence* presents three conjoined stories—of the secret, of the investigation, and of the revelations—I now wish to raise a central question about the parents' secret and the fiction-making it demanded: Why did they persist in the secrecy long after it would seem to have served any useful or necessary purpose, and when the reasons for concealing it had ceased to be materially relevant? Their returning to Judaism, so many years later and an ocean and a continent away, would not have adverse consequences for the mother's sister still living in Rome, however disturbed she might have been and indeed did become when her niece informed her that she had ferreted out the truth.

When Fremont raises the question she never finds a fully satisfactory answer. A family friend speculates that Fremont's parents denied their religion to protect the children, but this doesn't make much sense to Fremont, even though there *was* anti-Semitism in the 1950s American Midwest. Her parents grew up with dangerous enemies, and Fremont acknowledges there's some rationale in their joining and continuing to identify with Christians, who were once their persecutors. Identification with the aggressor is of course a well-known phenomenon. Fremont understands how distrustful her father was, even with his friends: "He would never let his guard down, sacrificing his connection to others for safety" (342). Secrecy was his shield, and if it enveloped his offspring in the network of their deceit, he was willing to assume that risk. The mother is more blunt: "[A]fter what I lived through, I decided it would be irresponsible to be Jewish and have children. If I wanted children, I could not be Jewish" (343).

These reasons make some sense, but I want to speculate further. It may be that the parents were so adept at invention and deception they became unwilling to surrender a disposition that had seen them through difficult circumstances. A reluctance to admit their Jewish past may have resulted from how brilliantly they functioned as artful and canny ersatz Christians. People get used to keeping secrets, proud of their ability to frame and hold on to them. Deception had given them power, and the secretiveness they practiced in Europe was an engrained habit they continued to practice in America. They did not regard their alias and their invented past as imprisoning so much as guaranteeing freedom.

If secrets and evasions have their uses, so does forgetting. Lisa Appignanesi, author of the memoir *Losing the Dead,* about her Jewish parents' wartime experiences evading the Nazis, argues that "Sometimes it's better not to have memory" (108). The virtues of forgetting, inadvertent or deliberate, are often undervalued, and they certainly played a vital role in Fremont's parents' lives. The truth of who they were went underground, as if nostalgia even for their happy early childhoods threatened to resurrect a past they needed to repress. Maintaining their "conversion" was a way of putting and keeping the past behind them. They consciously and deliberately repressed the past to avoid retraumatization.

Refusing to acknowledge their Holocaust experience is a kind of psychic numbing, as if going back to their Judaism would have reawakened old wounds, subjected them to hopelessness, and caused them to dwell on grief, death, and mourning, if not made them suspicious, even paranoid, about their new American world. Taken to the extreme, one might wonder if they had internalized a Nazi dislike of Jews, even absorbing the discourse of the oppressor, thus causing them to "kill" the Jew within. Less dramatically, their reluctance to reclaim their Jewish identity or to tell their children the truth might have come from a sense of shame, humiliation, or guilt.

Their anguish may also have kept them from telling their story, as if in the narrativizing they would invariably relive the experience. Eva Hoffman suggests, "The unspeakable and the unimaginable . . . may have initially had to do as much with the literal inadmissibility and inexpressibility of the survivors' anguish, as with the nature of the events themselves" (47). Perhaps Fremont's parents did not want to be forced to tell their stories to an uncomprehending audience of Americans, lest they seem like emissaries from an alien world.

Fremont is aware, as virtually all writers are who expose family secrets, of the difficulty of establishing narrative coherence: how to tell the story so it makes convincing sense, captures as best one can the truth of the past (as it is both told and reinterpreted), and validates the role of the writer in composing the story. Fremont is self-conscious about her function in structuring a narrative that at best is a second-hand account that "will never [be] just the way it was" (166). As she slowly and painfully gathers the details, she knows that gaps remain and "certain topics remained taboo" (50). We cannot be definitively certain, nor apparently can she, that she is not making some things up as her mother had. Can we know for sure that the story Fremont tells, a story her mother reluctantly told *her,* is true or accurate? Is she creating as well as researching? "Stories always change for a reason. The truth lies somewhere between the reasons and the stories" (243). Is it possible that what Fremont says about her mother's stories applies as well to her own?

One of the most interesting aspects of her narrative is the story of the story, as she not only assembles "facts" but shows her mother painfully and fitfully narrating the war and her activities while at the same time showing herself in the act of renarrating to us the stories her mother told to her. Inevitably mysteries remain; often it's impossible to make coherent sense of clues or to piece them together. Her mother had learned to change stories, to play the chameleon or Proteus the shape-changer for her life; inured to secrecy and dodging the truth, she not only forgot what is accurate but was unable fully to surrender the evasion and equivocation crucial to her survival. Even fifty years later, as she relates the stories, she continues to shift ground; Fremont is left raising questions, speculating no less than I have about motives, forced to weave her own connectives into an otherwise disjunctive sequence. "Where was my mother when...? Was she dressed in...? Was she meeting...? Where were...? Did they...?" "It was Zosia [her aunt] who warned them, *I think*" (183–184, my emphasis). Fremont is aware that her mother, even after she agrees to speak about the past, will sort through and tell only what she wishes. Her daughter must be satisfied with lingering doubts, if not ignorance, about many matters. The memoir is obliged to follow the mother's often murky, hesitating, incomplete, and sputtering tale, as the story "unfolds and then folds again and again" (166). Because she seeks to find continuity in a weave of fragments, Fremont must be as inventive as her mother had been. It's a delicate matter both to give her mother control of the story and at the same time to be the master interpreter of secrets without usurping the narrative—or her parents' very identities.

In an "Afterword" published a year later in a new edition of *After Long Silence* Fremont describes an extended family gathering, including many cousins who came forward after reading the book and recognizing the story. Fremont brings forth a box of documents, containing a pile of her mother's letters from Poland to America in 1939, just months before the Nazi invasion, and more letters from her written from Rome. The survival of these letters is a metonym for the survival of the parents, who depended on secrets that are finally surrendered in an act acknowledging a generational continuity the Nazis could not deny. Fremont's records are as spare as the evidence of how exactly her relatives died. Minimal documentary evidence is barely sufficient; only in league with parental memory, finally offered up in all its equivocations, memory lapses, and defensive strategies, can it allow Fremont to achieve the life writing that satisfies her desire to gain a fuller sense of the relations through which she has lived.

CHAPTER 2

Deciphering Enigma Codes

In this chapter I group five works about fathers, but unlike those in the first chapter, these fathers were dead at the time their children wrote about them. Because the children could not interview their parents as the previous investigators did, these writers are especially aware of the dangers of misrepresentation. Because the fathers portrayed in these texts deliberately misled, lied to, or generally concealed their lives from their children, the latter seem anguished about whether they are accurate in their assessments of the parental lives, particularly what they regard as the reason for the fathers' harboring their secrets. The writers seem acutely sensitive to the fragility if not the inaccessibility of truth, and even more so to the temptation to assert what we might call an epistemological power over the parents—a control of the information about the past.

In the texts discussed in this chapter we witness a kind of biographical rivalry, for the authors regard the stories as much their own creation as the possession of the parent. The writers continually correct, revise, censor, augment, or outright demolish the claims the secretive father has made about his life. In the act of restoring him to textual life each writer engages in endless speculation and hypothesizing, sometimes even resorting to forms of fiction in an effort to resurrect the parent's motives. The writers seem torn between wanting and not wanting to know, between a passionate desire to learn and an anxiety about what will be found. While the need to know seems fundamental to these projects, there's frequently a corresponding instinct to sabotage the entire enterprise.

I call this chapter "Deciphering Enigma Codes" after Germaine Greer's discussion of her father, who helped crack a major enemy code in World War II. I see the fathers in this chapter as purveyors of secret languages and the investigative children as code breakers, voyeurs, or spies. For a variety of reasons, the parents needed to protect themselves and therefore either presented a false view to the world or receded into silence, uncommunicativeness, and unknowability. The children engage in what Greer regards as a type of military campaign or hunting expedition, searching for a father who seemed hell-bent on throwing any pursuer off the scent.

In *The Shadow Man: A Daughter's Search for Her Father* Mary Gordon sets out to learn about her long-dead father, only to discover that he was not a Catholic as she thought but a self-hating Jew who became a rabid anti-Semite, wrote articles extolling Hitler, and wrote for and edited a pornographic magazine. Gordon's discoveries plague her to the core, and she attempts, not always successfully, to confront the demons of a daughter's love for the man she has come nearly to despise; yet she cannot help feeling what amounts almost to a quasi-incestuous love for him. In her work she tries to understand why he has erected a series of counterfeit identities and endlessly falsified claims, but more crucially why she continues to hold him in such high, near-romantic regard. In the course of her interminable investigation of his evasive life she expresses profound ambivalence for her project, revealing a need to get closer to him and to repudiate the man who has become such a problem for affiliation. Germaine Greer's *Daddy, We Hardly Knew You* makes the cryptograph a metaphor for her father's enigmatic personality: He has concealed the truth about his birth, his parents, and numerous other facts of his life. Although Greer expresses continual guilt about her search (like Gordon she worries that the dead should be left alone and fears that her implacable inquiry has betrayed her father), at the same time she relishes a rivalry with her father in their elaborate game of hide and seek. Mike O'Connor, in his extravagantly titled *Crisis, Pursued By Disaster, Followed Closely by Catastrophe: A Memoir of Life on the Run,* inquires why his parents were always fleeing, whether from authorities or from the extended family which the son had never heard about nor met. O'Connor views not just his parents but also the entire family as a coded secret, and it takes all his investigative energy to solve the riddles that constituted and defined their existence.

We might regard families and their secretive lives as archives, and in *Omaha Blues: A Memory Loop,* Joseph Lelyveld explores reams of documents and problematical evidence as he attempts to interpret not so much a single dark secret but his parents' lives generally—lives that can never be fully known by the son and that trouble him for their undecipherable mysteries. Unlike Greer, confident she will gain the knowledge she pursues, Lelyveld is mordantly resigned to the ultimate unknowability of others' behavior. Michael Rips is even more pessimistic regarding any clarity concerning his father's behavior and identity. In *The Face of a Naked Lady: An Omaha Family Mystery* Rips writes what might be called a surrealistic memoir, in that the stories, memories, and rumors he puts forth as evidence seem bizarrely unreliable and often preposterous, so given is he to reproducing surmises, gossip, and obscure hypotheses, all of which substitute for rational inquiry into the father's secretive activity.

O'Connor and Lelyveld are investigative journalists, used to trafficking in archives and tracking down subjects who are frequently devious, furtive, unreliable, or otherwise difficult to know and apprehend. Their professional expertise makes them ideal researchers as they subject their parents' lives to the same scrutiny, evidence gathering, and study they would give to anyone within the scope of their radar. The other three writers are not investigative reporters by trade, but in their capacity as novelist (Gordon), scholar (Greer), and lawyer (Rips) are accustomed to undertaking research, working in public records and depositories, or making up stories that depend on an empathic imagination, all qualities we find in these interrogations.

Another theme unifying these five texts is the writers' discovery that the secrets have dominated not only the parents' lives but their own as well. The imperative to understand, while it may be somewhat different in each case and not without a countervailing reluctance to discover the worst, predominates because without knowing who the parent has been they cannot know themselves, so profoundly do they feel their identity is a function of their relation with the other. Writing the accounts of how they learned what they did—whether through research or always-fallible memory—is partly therapeutic, but whether they fully come to terms with how they have been affected if not injured by the secrets is never certain. The writers veer between reconciliation and a residual bitterness at their findings, expressing both affection and resentment.

Shadowing the Furtive Father Beyond the Grave: Mary Gordon's Ambivalent Inquiry

Mary Gordon's *The Shadow Man: A Daughter's Search for Her Father* (1996) is the most comprehensive depiction in autobiography I know of a writer's effort to come to terms with an emended view of a parent, one arrived at through a painful process of unearthing concealed facts about her father's enigmatic past and persistent and prolonged detective work. Gordon, a New York novelist, was raised a devout Catholic and revered her father, who died when she was seven. *The Shadow Man,* written in her forties when she felt the need to learn more about her father, is the story of how she discovered the lies, deceptions, secrets, and reactionary politics that constituted his life, discoveries that lead her to revise her estimation of him. Her text implicitly undermines the hagiography of David Gordon she wrote as a child, but the adult work is a complex wrestling with her emotions rather than a recantation of her early and ongoing adoration.

Writing about her inexplicable father, Gordon expresses a profound ambivalence, a continual gyration between a desire for closeness and a need to split off from the man to whom, after thirty-five years and her scandalous findings, she still feels uncannily close. In the act of decoding the father, the specific revelations notwithstanding, she claims an emotional affiliation that her rational self seeks to reject. Gordon's project sends her "on a journey of discovery and loss, of loss and re-creation, of the shedding of illusion and the taking on of what might be another illusion" (xiii). The drama of Gordon's work emerges from a realization that the father of her memory is no longer a viable one and a counter impulse to deny that realization; from evidence accepted and evidence refused. Most powerfully Gordon moves between accepting him on his own terms and inventing him as a figure she can reconstruct in the face of her uncertainty or his monstrosity. One way to deal with the man of mystery is to re-create him in her own cherished image; discovering him anew leads to her desire—with all the erotic implications of the term—to possess him: "Having lost him, once [in death], twice [through her findings of his authentic character], I will have him forever. He is always with me, always mine" (xxiv).

The Shadow Man is an account of how one discovers a familial past when it is inaccessible to memory. Losing the father as a child, she finds him again through her investigations into his writings and his character, though he is a very different man from the one she worshipped. Much of her quest and the book that results from it repeatedly raise the question: Can an act of memory represent the "real" father? But Gordon's own identity is so closely entwined with his, she can scarcely feel assured about the "real" daughter either.

Gordon believes that as a child she was adored by a father who lived only for her. And of course she prefers the beloved father of childhood memory to the "new" father of adult discovery. Significantly her memories of him constitute a kind of "entombment" in an anachronistic vision of the man; that memory and her desire to retain the false view become a "mausoleum" (xvii), the images of death symbolizing a dead-end representation that has become increasingly congealed into fiction.

Gordon conveys a belief that had the father written his own life, it would have been pure fabrication; only a perspective from outside can convey even a trace of truth about him. David Gordon invented an identity as a native of Ohio, a Harvard graduate, a student at Oxford, and a successful businessman. But the truth, which Mary learns as she researches his life, is that he was born Israel Gordon in a shtetl in Poland, had a working-class childhood, never finished high school, converted from Judaism to Catholicism, concealed an earlier marriage and the children from that marriage, and was constantly unemployed. He became a right-wing propagandist, a virulent anti-Semite who extolled Hitler, and edited and wrote for a pornographic magazine. *The Shadow Man* is a work of both readjusting his image and rediscovering herself as separate from the father. When she concludes, "David Gordon is a man I cannot know," her sense of self-knowledge threatens to crumble as well. Gordon's project is not simply to uncover the scarcely known father she originally regarded as charming and glamorous, but to confront and shed her illusions about him *and about herself,* especially to change her idea of herself as the father's creation. At the outset Gordon says of him, "I did what he wanted me to do" (xix); one function of her writing is to break his hold over her. But her initiating motive is her need to know a man who turns out to have been more secretive than she could have imagined. To find him anew is to get back to the lost and furtive father, but also to gain control over him, perhaps even to possess him again on her own terms and in the process to see him though not exclusively through her eyes.

The paradox is that the more she discovers through her investigation the more she wishes her work and its findings undone, for the verifications are always distressing. So long as he is "unverifiable" she can persist in the earliest childhood fantasies that produced her great faith in him, a faith that grew over the thirty-five years following his death. But when she "verifies" him she loses that faith and so must unverify him once again by imagining and inventing a renewed, beloved father. Because her discoveries threaten her fantasy relation to him, she must retrieve the fantasy by desperate measures that allow her to forgive. She conceives of her search as not that of a revengeful daughter who discovers dreadful truths but as that of a daughter who has lost her father and desperately wants him back. Toward the end she declares she has given birth to her father, by which she means she has reinvented his image to regain him on acceptable terms.

Everything she discovers stems from what she calls "the insufficiency of memory" (164); because her memory is as untrustworthy as the father himself, she turns to empirical research to capture the secretive past, making the process of detection central to her project. Working in archives suggests to her that memory always pales in the light of hard evidence. Her text is the autobiography of her investigation as much as it is a revised life of her father.

She first examines his writing because it seems a stable source of truth. She believes that if she finds enough of his words from the past and writes her account of her discovery, David Gordon will rise from the dead. This is not a mere cliché expressing what biographers do for their subjects but an almost magical, godlike act of resurrecting the dead so as to join with him once again. But the more she searches in the documents of his life, the more she feels like "a detective in the department of magical realism" (xxii), plummeting into a world whose laws make no rational sense. She gradually and then radically revises her image of the man as she discovers his pornography in the Brown and Yale university libraries, his vitriolic anti-Semitic essays in the Columbia Library, and his articles in support of Mussolini, Hitler, Franco, and Father Coughlin (the leader of the anti-Semitic Christian Front) in the New York Public Library. If the man she remembers is nothing like the man who emerges from the archives, both their identities are subject to emendation, his as the godlike hero, hers as the dutiful acolyte.

Gordon struggles with a problem I am concerned with throughout this study: memory versus research. In her case it's less a matter of the failure of memory than of memory traces from her childhood betrayed by newly detected truths arrived at through the investigation. Gordon's memory cannot stand up to the newly discovered truths, so she invokes what she calls "the angel of erasure" (104), a benevolent creature who would correct the "errors" she hopes her findings might be. Her desired forgetfulness turns against everything life writers necessarily cultivate. Gradually she becomes an unwilling researcher, drawn to her discoveries but at the same time wishing there were no trail to provide an evidentiary basis for David Gordon's past.

She tracks him down first in the National Archives for the Northeast Region in New York; then in Cleveland, where she visits local libraries, scans city directories, high school yearbooks, synagogue records, and local histories of Lorain, Ohio, his hometown; she consults a Jewish genealogist who puts her in touch with long-lost family members; she searches in government offices, examining death certificates and wills. Gordon's memoir is a torturous saga of blind alleys, false leads, tantalizing miscues, the discovery of outright lies and of a family she didn't know she had.

Searching for the father in all the places that appear to contain his truth leads, after all the dead ends are tracked, to the final place that is no less mysterious: the coffin. Her text is filled with cartons and containers: the box containing back issues of the pornographic magazine her father edited, *Hot Dog: A Monthly for Regular Fellows;* old newspaper records in "the morgue"; a section of necrology files in the Case Western Reserve Library; records in city offices as hushed as a tomb; and the last box, David Gordon's old coffin in his new grave. Gordon discovers her father's grave at the burial site of his wife's family and decides to have his bones exhumed and reinterred in a cemetery of her own choice. Digging up the past is no empty metaphor. We might expect that she would transfer his remains to a Jewish cemetery, but she realizes such an act would violate the concealment he desired; instead she has him reburied in a Catholic cemetery closer to her home, so she might keep an eye on him. It is a curious act of both love and appropriation. With all the troubled connotations of the term for her, Gordon's act of exhumation and reburial of her father's bones is a figurative form of *resurrection.* Many historical figures have been reinterred as a marker of their changing political reputations; just so we might consider David Gordon's reburial as his daughter's symbolic gesture of reclamation and repatriation, analogous no less to her desire to repair the reputation she believes her unsavory discoveries may have undermined.

But long before that act, because the revised David Gordon is so unimaginable to her, she reaches the point biographers often speak of when she wonders if she can go on with her task. Given how hateful he now appears to her, she wonders if he is even worth exposing and "digging up." This is not so much an ethical issue but a matter of her own stomach for the enterprise. But she presses on, in part because she cannot bear not to find *something* that will enable her to maintain the older revered image, the devotion she is unwilling to surrender; in part because she has a fascination for whatever horrors may lie in wait.

"This is the story of my reluctance, of my flinching from the loss I knew would follow the truth" (93). Gordon composes a work she half-wishes she did not have to write, and her reluctance is evident on every page. The anguish emanating from her research is doubled in the act of writing, and one feels it throughout her text. There is little that seems like catharsis, only the pain of reliving a scarcely bearable past. As a devout Catholic and writer, Gordon must have been aware of an issue of literary genre with ironic implications: if the most traditional autobiographical form is that of crisis and conversion, Gordon writes a text that we might call the crisis *of* conversion—both her father's clandestine conversion from Judaism to Catholicism and her own struggle *not* to convert her love for him to shame or to hatred.

Gordon's narrative constantly reflects her ambivalence about her father and her project. She obsessively seeks information about the man who disappeared from her life so many years earlier, even as she realizes that the new information will disgust her. The story of discovering his true identity is long and detailed, and each clue becomes the instrument to probe a cherished but increasingly obsolete conception of the man. As she investigates she declares, "I am losing my father" (84). She refers to her project as "a journey of discovery and loss, of loss and re-creation" (xiii), and that loss extends not only to the father but to the stability of truth she had counted on. As every revelation brings forth a new, disturbing version of her father, Gordon's world disintegrates. "I feel nauseated and the ground below me seems unstable." The crisis is epistemological: She can no longer discern the difference between his lies and her creations: "[T]hese ideas were the things I based my life on, scenes I played over and over to place myself in the world, to give myself stature and protection" (127). Her past has become vertiginous.

Gordon worries that in undertaking the role of scholar, critic, historian, and detective, she herself may have become the criminal, murdering the father in her mind and again in print. She quotes from a poem by the Russian Marina Tsvetaeva the very line that Germaine Greer will use in her memoir of her father: "Love is no detective." There are moments in Gordon's text when she feels it would have been better *not* to know nor to reveal so much forbidden knowledge, that she ought to leave him in peace and disregard what he worked so hard to conceal. Gordon's guilt arises from both her growing excitement and her dismay in the face of the accumulating revelations: "What was I doing digging in the archives? What was I looking for, and was my search in any way an act of love? Was it a vengeful act, like the uncovering of Noah by his drunken sons?...If I had loved my father above all things, would I have turned detective?" (160). But the image of the father's nakedness, perceived here by a daughter, has disturbingly erotic aspects, as we shall see in a moment. She confesses what feels to her a sin in exposing the father even as she effectively cajoles him into admitting a self he has hidden. The text functions as a twin confession, in which she is both a priest-figure provoking his startling revelations and a sinner guiltily acknowledging her treasonous exposure.

Her way to combat that guilt is to make a dramatic narrative move. Thus the heart of her quest involves an attempt to see the world through her father's eyes, and this entails her identifying with his needs and fears as a young man, imagining her father's view of the world, and assuming his anxieties and desires. Just as he had made the young Mary into a "partner" or an apprentice, training her to do as he wished, robbing her of any self but that of his "shadow," so now the dutiful daughter tries to shadow him or even to "become" him by taking on his identity and fantasizing the motives for his actions. She attempts to understand not only why he converted from Judaism but especially how a Jew in the 1930s and 1940s could celebrate Nazism. Gordon concludes that her father turned against Judaism and invented a refurbished Gentile image to protect himself from the anti-Semitism prevalent in his childhood and early adulthood, to transform himself so as to succeed in Gentile America. As Annette Kuhn argues, secrets that don't fit into a desired family narrative tend to be edited out or altered (2). David Gordon had "murdered his past" to be accepted; Mary Gordon's project is to revise that past and reinvent her father's character (analogous to what the Gatsby-like Gordon had himself done). Explaining his deceptions becomes a way both to understand him *and* to gain power over him by making him into a figure whom she has conceived.

There's a powerful moment when, in the Brown University Library, she locates a box of pornographic magazines called *Hot Dog* that he edited; she locates the very issue that at twelve she had discovered in a closet at home lodged between the pages of a volume of *The Catholic Encyclopedia*. "Nothing is unrecoverable" (74), a realization that is at once the historian's relief and the daughter's torment.

There's another moment when she struggles to disbelieve the truth she confronts. "Facts nose their way into what I thought was the past like a dog sticking his nose under a lady's skirts." Facts are at best unwelcome, at worst obscene. But there is more. "How I resent the insidious, relentless, somehow filthy nudging of these facts. Yet I cannot ban them" (125). Gordon's use of the Yiddishism "nudging" suggests that the truth of Israel Gordon's Jewishness may itself be cause for some distress, the "filthy" fact that nudges its unwelcome way into her feeling for her Catholic father. I am not arguing any anti-Semitism on Gordon's part, but her identification with her father is so palpably strong that she appears to lament the father's repressed identity that returns with a vengeance and that she cannot easily assimilate to her idea of him. Both his Semitism and his anti-Semitism challenge her revered image.

She feels the need to revise him back into the cherished father she knew, and this impulse is tantamount to her taking back the narrative, to own the father exclusively, "created by me, untouched by history" (120). This leads to her fantasy of having given birth to him: "He has become my child" (184). She also imagines she is a police artist, capturing his face by piecing together eyes, mouth, and other parts, as if she were gradually bringing him into being. But she wonders if she is bringing him to light only to kill the persona David Gordon pretended to be.

Gordon laments: "We have lost our dead. They are no longer ours" (146). She fears she cannot control her father's image, that David Gordon will slip away from her, so unfathomable has be become. How to get him back? By somehow making his identity dependent on her faithful representation of him. In an almost vampiric gesture she seeks not simply to impersonate him but to be *absorbed* in him. As if imitating Catherine Earnshaw in *Wuthering Heights,* she cries out, "I am David Gordon" (171).

Gordon wants to preserve an inviolate past, one embalmed in her memory and not subject to vicissitudes or contingencies. But holding to such fixity is hard work, demanding an active resistance to newly discovered truths. When she states that "it is only by my efforts that he stays alive" (224), I take her to mean not just that she brings him before the reader but that she has resurrected him in his purified, remembered state.

Her desire to keep him alive and her belief that only her effort can accomplish that feat stand in sharp contrast to her feelings about her mother. When Gordon researches and writes her book, her mother is in a home for the elderly, suffering from severe memory loss. The mother remembers little about her husband or their life together, which relieves Gordon who fears that otherwise the mother might misremember and skew her daughter's attempts at revision. The mother's dementia actually removes any threat to Gordon's solipsism.

Because the mother has no remembered past Mary is scarcely interested in her: "I turn my back on her. And go off, as I always did, with him" (227). While Gordon is free to reinvent her dead father, her mother has the stolidity of inert matter; she simply cannot be made over. In her mind Gordon says to her mother with brutal frankness: "I have never lived a day not wishing my father was alive.... I think regularly about the desirability of your death" (241). I would argue that we are made uneasy by the daughter's obvious Electra complex working here and throughout the memoir. Gordon has inserted herself into the family romance, and her visit to the home for the elderly expresses triumph rather than remorse.

The last section of the work is a discussion of the bureaucratic red tape and family resistance Gordon encountered trying to move her father's remains. Her quest for permission is nearly as elaborate as her search for his identity. Given her supervision over the process of dis- and reinterment, she again achieves control over the father. She claims love as the motivating factor, by which she means a desire to assign him his proper name (he had been buried in a grave bearing her mother's family name). But disturbingly, "like a lover I wish to lie with my beloved for all eternity" (261). This final act is the concrete embodiment of what her entire book has done: unearthed a past, renamed its principal figure, and reassigned him to a new identity. Death and transfiguration have enabled Gordon to give an afterlife to her father in her text, a revisionary enterprise if there ever was one.

One of the disturbing aspects of her quest is the continual reaffirmation of an almost desperate, erotic adoration of her father: When she sees his photograph on his pornographic magazine, identified by a pseudonym (symptomatic of his many false identities), she cannot help saying "I'm so in love with the beautiful young man" (70). She manipulates the reader, makes us into accomplices if not voyeurs of her secret (love) life, one that can seem as darkly disturbing as David Gordon's own. Her obsessive search and her writing about him ensure she will possess him: "He is always with me, always mine" (xxiv). Here then is the rooted conflict: She wants to revivify her father, but largely to reaffirm a fantasy that in so doing he will somehow be grateful to her and acknowledge that she has been the only person he has cared for all along. "I'll do anything to get back a father I can love" (76).

And yet Gordon understands as well as we do the excess of her gestures, both the funerary one depicted in the closing pages of her work and her expressed desire for her and her father to be each other's exclusive love. She quotes Theseus's fifth act speech from *A Midsummer Night's Dream* about the lunatic, the lover, and the poet and sees herself embodying all three parts: a lunatic confusing the actual with the symbolic, a lover confusing the proper filial role, and a poet confusing the impulse to re-create the man with the impulse to put him finally to rest. However much she claims her love for him, she cannot cease from expressing a desire for domination, a discursive power reversing the father's protracted hold over her.

Gordon's project expresses a complex blend of power and adoration, exposé and redemption. She has made David Gordon into her own creation, an endlessly dichotomized being: Jew and Gentile, European and American, liar and truth-teller, lover and hater, proud figure and figure of shame. There is no glee in her exposure, and no pleasure in outing a scoundrel. Her sorrow is evident, but her vampiric love for him almost trumps that sorrow. When she reburies David Gordon it is to bring him closer to her, not to give offense to his remains. She has shadowed him like a detective, and he is the shadow-love she carries with her. And yet, in one final turn of the screw, the memoir also seems to be an act of anger for his betrayal of the past. Francine du Plessix Gray once declared, "I write out of a desire for revenge against reality" (246). Gordon writes from no less similar motives.

Nancy Miller speaks of "two poles between which memoir writers come to grips with the loss of parents and the pull of their history": forgiveness and resentment. Gordon expresses both sentiments, but in addition a third one: a possessive love that goes beyond mere acceptance or understanding, certainly beyond any conventionally therapeutic desire to forgive and move on. Miller also notes that when we put the memory of the dead on paper there is often a "tension between what is documented and what is remembered, and that tension between these two modes of accounting for the past is part of what makes [such] works affecting and interesting" (*Bequest* 5, 17). But even as Gordon wrestles with how to evaluate the sinister revelations she has uncovered, it seems as if her egotism has transcended memory and fact. She manipulates us into applauding her struggle, yet she may have confused claims of ancient love with displays of present power—*over* him, even as she purports to be *with* him. Her father's secrets may have provoked deeper feelings than she ever imagined.

Gordon leaves me very troubled about her love for her father. That love is initially defined as a childhood reverence that lingers despite later findings that threaten to undermine those feelings, but as we have seen she represents the reverence as nearly incestuous. Perhaps the extremity of her adoration compensates for the guilt her project entails. But if Mary Gordon expresses guilt as well as ego, Germaine Greer, the author I turn to next, exalts feverishly in her victory over her father. Uncovering his secret and deciphering his puzzling self validate her power in a game that pits wit and wiles against his passive-aggressive subterfuge. As Greer's account of her triumph unfolds, we witness a strong feminist whose prowess and perseverance overcome any residual guilt she might feel for attacking the core of his fraudulent identity.

"Love Is No Detective": Germaine Greer's Guilty Hunt

If Mary Gordon seldom seems aware how she needs to dominate her deceased father in the course of reaffirming her love for him, Germaine Greer knows full well how her present relation to *her* father is built on her control, power, and the authority of a commanding narrative tone. The title of my discussion, taken from Greer's memoir of the search for her father, could easily have been inverted—"Detection Is No Love"—for her quest to learn about the covert older man could hardly be confused with affection let alone with love. Given Reg Greer's hurtful indifference to his daughter throughout her childhood and his subsequent distance from her, possibly born out of a fear of inadvertently disclosing his past, Greer regains mastery through the acquisition of knowledge about him he had attempted to conceal.

Daddy, We Hardly Knew You (1989) depicts Greer's two-year search to learn about the family of her dead father, whose life was a deliberate exercise in forgetting and fabrication. For a man who ostensibly hated deception, ironically her "father's whole life was a lie" (60). The biggest lie was that he spoke of himself as if he had come out of nowhere, and he remained mute and evasive about his origins. "He was a man without a past," she laments (6). The less Greer knows about the enigmatic man the more determined she becomes to learn all she can about him. He had almost never spoken of his past, and what he did say was often full of contradictions. Greer realized she knew virtually nothing about him though she thought he was English and born in South Africa before immigrating to Australia, that he was "posh," and had been a journalist and a war hero. Each of these stories turns out to be a fabrication. At his death, Greer, like Gordon, sets off on a long, torturous odyssey to discover what she can about his origins. Her findings confirm if not increase her sense of power and her self-confidence.

As a young child growing up in a suburb of Melbourne she tried to get close to her father, but he remained distant: He never hugged her and he never praised or encouraged the work she pursued, ignored her budding talent for writing. And he told her nothing definitive about himself or his past. Having left Australia and her family when she was eighteen, she returned years later to find him dying in a derelict hostel, indigent and ignored by his wife.

Pouncing on any available clue, tracking every shred of evidence she can find, she investigates his employment and genealogical records, civil documents from Tasmania to the Australian mainland to England, as well as military archives from India and Malta, where he was posted during World War II. She examines electoral rolls, parish records, his war medical files, boat passenger manifests, and marriage and death certificates. She turns up his Royal Air Force forms and his repatriation file, but no birth certificate—the absence of which will prove to be crucial. The acknowledgment page of the text is a compendium of her sources: archival offices in Tasmania and Queensland, public libraries throughout Australia, newspaper rooms and public record offices in Victoria, bureaus of population censuses and surveys in London, general register offices in Ireland, Veterans Affairs offices and Probate offices in Melbourne. In addition, Greer travels up and down Tasmania and mainland Australia, interviewing people who may have had the slightest contact with her father. As a literary intellectual she is at home in libraries and places of research, but she becomes increasingly frustrated, for in countries that normally document such things with care there are simply no birth records of the man. She writes letters to Greer families in every English-speaking country, hoping for information about Reg Greer's origins, but it's an exercise in futility: "I knew Greer history from the plantation of Ulster to yesterday. . . . I was a Greerologist, a Greerographer, a Greeromane" (239).

Her conclusion, verified by documents from a Tasmanian orphanage that she procures after searching through mountains of evidence, is that she and her father are not Greers after all. "Reg Greer" was really Eric Greeney, and his stories were all fictions, especially that he came from a respectable, wealthy family, instead of being a poor foster child. His foster mother had rescued him from an orphanage and adopted the young child. She was a working class woman, the illegitimate daughter of a domestic servant and granddaughter of convicts, and Greer's father was ashamed of his adoptive parents. In addition he made no effort to learn of his biological mother.

According to Greer everything about him proves to be fraudulent. He had faked his English background, his war record, his newspaper career, his name. Even his body was an assemblage of artifice: false teeth and dyed hair.

Though the Greer family motto is "Be mindful of your ancestors," her father had either invented his own or simply refused to talk about them. So when his daughter, code-breaker of parental secrets, finally runs him to ground, "closing in on our quarry"—employing the hunting image that runs throughout the text—he becomes an adversary she has captured in a war of feints, evasions, and counterthrusts (239).

Ironically, during World War II her father had attended a school for breaking codes, eventually working on the team that cracked "Ultra," the name for the intelligence resulting from decyrption of coded German radio communications. It was a perfect task for a man given to deception and the custodianship of secrets. Greer is never sure whether the Secret Service turned him into a "Deception person," or, being that kind of man, he was admirably suited to the work. Leading a double, triple, quadruple life, he deceives not merely genealogically but universally: he is a full-service pretender.

His daughter turns out to be a code-breaker of parental secrets. She dedicates herself to "[d]igging my father out of his grave" (98); when her leads or guesses prove false, she is driven to a greater frenzy of inquiry but also of guilt. Each provisional image of her father turns into a metaphor for her violation of his privacy; thus an army medical record elicits an image of him naked before the examining doctors, which in turn becomes a figure for *her* trying to strip him naked. Pleading "anxiety neurosis" to get out of serving in the army, he is scrutinized by the hospital "much the way that I have ferreted away in the archives for verification of his autobiography" (193). Greer speaks of "digging up the dead with my nails" (310). But the cost is high: As she pursues her obsessive search, she thinks of King Lear and declares, "O Papa, I would be your Cordelia, but I'm afraid I shall prove a Goneril or a Regan" (107). The reference is appropriate because she suspects she has tracked him down not from love but as an act of revenge. She worries that she is as despicable as she claims he has been: "I am a bounder's child. The blood of bounders runs in my veins." But such an admission never causes her to desist.

Is she doing all this as an act of writerly vengeance on a dead man who can no longer answer back? Early on we learn she has a book contract to launch her investigation: Is there bad faith in her undertaking, a motive ultimately self-serving, and if so is her quest for the father's (and ultimately her own) identity compromised and ethically suspect? Greer's work raises important considerations regarding the reasons for undertaking such a search and for writing its story, and she implicitly questions the propriety of both undertakings. I will return to the ethical issues shortly.

Daddy, We Hardly Knew You begins with Reg Greer returning home to wife and daughter from the war, when he seemed a "speechless wreck" of a man, a "zombie" who appeared utterly "broken" (9, 13). Because her earliest memories of her father before he went off to war were of a handsome, distinguished man and because he was radically different when he returned, she wonders as she thinks back to the earlier period in their lives how her father came to be so distant from her and the family, so seemingly without an inner core. Was Reg Greer brainwashed by the Allies, "debriefed by [mind-emptying] shock therapy," or was he perhaps "a criminal, a traitor, a sexual deviant?" "It seems a mad suspicion, but once it has been entertained I have no choice but to investigate it" (13, 14). As a profound skeptic Greer views the world as a thicket of deceptions, labyrinthine evasions, and paranoia-inducing impediments throwing the quester off the scent. The impulse behind this suspicion-laden text is best characterized by epistomania, her compulsive desire to know everything.

Daddy, We Hardly Knew You is obsessed with uncovering, revealing, and decoding. Each new revelation exposes further concealments and presses Greer into a more complex narration of discovery and resistance. As Jon Thompson has written about detective fiction in *Fiction, Crime, and Empire,* any "doubts about the possibilities of successfully finding the concealed clue to existence" (and I'd add "to *an individual's* existence") are in tension with a desire to decode that clue and to confer an order upon it (112).

Typical of such biographical quest-narratives, the more difficulty Greer has finding the true father, the more she focuses on her own dislocation and unstable identity, whether she frames it by an uncertain nationality (Australian or English), or by not knowing her own ancestry: "I was suddenly chilled by the sense of not belonging, of never having belonged anywhere" (33). She also wonders what she has inherited beyond his face and his genes. Her genealogical doubts in turn excite her passion to know. Greer is not one to resist inquiry, speculation, and analysis; as a literary critic as well as a feminist social historian, she is by profession an unmasker. But while the prospect of knowledge justifies the search, the process of searching is equally enticing to her. Since she suspects her father's whole life has been a lie, she is fascinated both by the hope of discovering the truth and by the inquiry itself, which, for several years, virtually becomes her identity. It is not simply that she gives herself over to the search, but that she cannot be sure who she is until she has found her father. I would venture that there is even a thrill in the prospect of triumphant revelation and its attendant exposure. In this regard the work is *her* story more than it is *his*. Despite the fact that we are left hanging until the end of the work about Reg Greer's real identity, and that that is precisely what we have required and awaited as narrative closure, the *subject* of the quest is more predominant than the *object*. Like most detective stories, the emphasis is on the method of investigation rather than the final result, however much the disclosure is the goal of the quest.

We might think of this inquisitional text as analogous to *The Odyssey*, with the female Telemachus figure out in the world attempting to verify the pseudo-autobiographies her father has scattered among diverse peoples. Everywhere she goes she encounters the conflicting, impossible-to-reconcile life narratives he has told. She nearly drives herself crazy in the process, confused about the validity of her project, enmeshed in the web of fantasies he has spun. Her language points to the violence implicit in her disruption of the father's carefully constructed surface: "My hand was on the plough, and the apparently solid ground was already gashed. There could be no stopping until it was all laid open. Time then to tend the wound" (109). Who has wounded whom? Given that so much of the father's past as Greer tracks it down takes place in various theaters of war, it is significant that her quest is realized as a brutal assault on his body. Like a warrior armed with accumulating evidence gathered from her expeditions that increasingly resemble military campaigns, Greer is always embattled, and her rivalry with the father centers around which one will have the true and definitive story. Germaine Greer the biographer must tell the authentic story that Reg Greer the false *auto*biographer has concocted.

This same combat inheres in her dislike of the Australian male as a type and in her loathing of patriarchy, which such a figure represents. As a self-exile to England, Greer has always had an equivocal relation to her native land, but her national identity figures in her search. Several Australian values seem relevant to the father's identity and the difficulty Greer has in tracking him down. First, the reluctance to ask too many questions about another person as well as frontier habits of reticence and respect for private matters suggest the importance of stoical silence over unseemly inquiry. (Tasmanians are completely free of that most un-Australian thing, an identity card.) Second, the national history of a convict past encourages the freedom to make one's life over, to be whatever one can imagine, desire, and achieve; thus the father's self-invention might be prized as an escape from the rigidity that convict identity would have imposed. In Australia, you can change your name and marry, vote, and open bank accounts under the new name without officially registering the change. Her father had taken on multiple identities—Robert Hamilton, Eric Greeney, and Reg Greer among them—and the act, easy enough to accomplish Down Under, can be read as a genealogical defiance of the convict history that threatened to saddle succeeding generations.

A recurrent motif in this agonistic text is the father attempting to throw Greer off the scent. A myth guides the search—Greer calls it "the primal elder's curse"—her witty characterization of the repeated notion that just when she gets close to revelation, something unforeseen happens to hamper or impede the quest, such as sudden misleading information or unexpected resistance by those who had previously promised cooperation (218). The phrase "primal elder's curse," taken from *Hamlet* and rife with ominous biblical overtones, is meant to distinguish Greer's undertaking from that of a mere casual interest in family history, a commonplace "roots" phenomenon. Like Hamlet, she inquires for her very life, and in her reading of the project her ghostly father regularly appears to hinder the task. But the curse may also be Noah's—on *his* child Ham for having witnessed his nakedness, an image that recurs throughout the text. (Is Greer punning on Ham and Hamlet here?) When she invokes a kind of commandment, "Thou shalt not uncover the nakedness of thy father" (109), her phrasing of the forbidden act suggests how dangerous she perceives her own enterprise to be. As she embarks on a collision course with what she regards as her father's deliberate dodges and premeditated equivocations, she represents her task as a serious game in which not only his genealogical identity is at stake but her own, as well as her credibility as a truth teller. The father has cursed her both *with* and *to* ignorance, and she must fight to regain the high ground of authenticity.

But it is a risky venture, and she fears that when she discovers his true identity she may wind up not forgiving his deceptions but blaming him the more. Though she undertakes her investigation to get back to the dead father, believing that knowledge may reestablish a severed bond, at the same time she worries that her discoveries might corrode her image of him.

Why indeed is she searching for the father? Early in her quest, when she goes to India to interview people her father had encountered during the war, she meets a woman who is genuinely perplexed about Greer's task: "Why do you go so far into it?... Why do you want to know so much about your father? He borned you, that is the great thing." (98). Because this woman's question counsels the same "curtain of silence" Greer's father had drawn around himself, the same "exercise in forgetting" (6) he had made of his life, that question profoundly haunts Greer's story. It inevitably becomes the reader's question as well.

Greer's struggle with her mother provides a clue. One of the epiphenomena of her investigation is a continual battle with the mother, not only over the truth but also for the right to search for it. Greer claims to have gleaned more about her father than the mother ever knew about him, though of course there is much about the marriage she could never possibly learn. Greer describes her mother as a self-absorbed, infantile woman (at seventy her greatest interest, according to Greer, is working on a lifetime tan). At times she supposedly harbors her own notion of her husband's past and at others expresses utter indifference to it. Greer perceives her as a sadistic wife; when he was quite elderly her mother threw out his possessions and coldly committed him to a hostel. The mother seems both a protector of family secrets and Greer's rival for keeper of the flame. No one is more adamant in her objections and resistance to Greer's questions, and Greer seems convinced that the mother constructs as many impediments and evasions as the father himself. Greer insists on her own version of the father if she can uncover it, not her mother's: "I wanted to find my own father, not my mother's husband" (110). Greer's Electra conflict with the mother thus becomes a crucial justification for the quest, and Greer struggles with her as much as with her father.

An emblematic moment captures Greer's ambivalence about the quest. Immediately after learning that Reg Greer is really Eric Greeney, and that he was adopted and had falsified his origins, casting off all connection to his foster family, she is suddenly filled with guilt at what she has done. Greer studies her face in a mirror, and for several pages she and the face engage in dialogue, alternately criticizing and justifying the three-year-long investigation in a manner reminiscent of Nathalie Sarraute's double-voiced self in her memoir *Childhood,* where the autobiographer splits herself into a rationalizing "I" and a reprimanding "you." The face accuses Greer of selfishness and revenge, implying that the father all along felt his precocious daughter was trying to blow his cover and so understandably kept his distance out of self-protection. Greer's doubts about the enterprise emerge most forcefully in this scene of self-accusation: "Love," says the face, "is no detective" (247).

So how might we frame Greer's justification for the investigation? Why indeed *has* she searched for the father, and what gain does she realize? I want to ask if there is a motive beyond an archetypal need to know one's origins and to know one's father, especially since there is no doubt that Eric Greeney *is* Greer's biological father. The paternal identity is a gap, an emptiness that needs to be filled. Like Australia's vast untracked interior, Reg Greer is an absence, a vacuum that arouses a certain horror in his daughter. The impulse to search is not merely a natural instinct but derives from the nature of the father–daughter relation. He commands power over her by virtue of his enigmatic self, and she seeks to diminish that power by asserting an equivalence: her knowledge versus his obfuscation, her "scrutinizing nature" versus his "charade" (311). Greer and her father are rival biographers, or rather her "biography" is a form of detective nonfiction that functions as a corrective to his autobiographical fiction. As "detective" she asserts authority over a forger of identities, a maker of fraudulent accounts she subjects to revision.

In writing a book that is ferocious, obsessive, and passionate in its desire to expose, Greer is well aware that her motives may be tainted by hostility. She must know that his disaffiliation from his foster family is a common impulse of many adopted children; but she is more interested in attack than complex understanding. "Liar! Liar! Liar!" she hurls at him, as she finds yet another piece of evidence to complete the puzzle. When she finally crows, "Reg Greer was about to be flushed from his cover," the hunting image implies her superiority over the father. Her next response is one of gleeful triumph, as if exposure and ridicule were doing the work we'd normally assign to mourning: "'Gotcha!' I kept saying to Daddy. 'Gotcha! Didn't lie quite enough, did you?'" (239, 245). If this sounds like a little girl playing a game with her father, we might speculate whether Greer regains a childhood lost during his absence.

Like Mary Gordon disinterring her father, Greer speaks of "digging up the dead with my nails" (310), a vampiric act for which she cannot forgive herself. But whatever guilt she feels is mitigated by the thrill of betrayal that replaces any felt interdiction. I choose the term *betrayal* from Philip Roth's novel *I Married a Communist;* though he's speaking of the public betrayal of friends and colleagues during McCarthyism, Roth's words regarding the way exposing people produces a covert gratification are relevant to Greer's more private project: "You retain your purity at the same time as you are . . . realizing a satisfaction that verges on the sexual with its ambiguous components of pleasure and weakness, of aggression and shame. . . . Betrayal is in this same zone of perverse and illicit . . . pleasure. An interesting, manipulative, underground type of pleasure . . . in which there is much that a human being finds appealing" (264).

There is indeed a seductively aggressive, even sexual energy in Greer's search for her father, realized in the battle with the mother and in the several references to stripping him bare and gazing on his nakedness. Her search for him is much like a romantic quest to know and connect with the loved object, and then to dominate him. As she engages in the game of spy and counterspy, her language becomes more charged, and her voice grows more fervent. What appears like espionage becomes a kind of erotic frenzy, and her guilt at the possibly illicit nature of her quest to get close to him cannot be severed from an almost incestuous excitement with her dogged process. She has "ferreted away in the [hospital] archives for verification of his auto-biography" (193), dwelling on such details as an appendiceal scar, another scar under his chin, his slight scoliosis, his narrow chest, and numerous other bodily features.

The father believed he had escaped his past only to have it uncovered, like Oedipus. But because Reg Greer, unlike Oedipus, deliberately obscured his origins, were he alive at the publication of his daughter's book might he not regard Germaine as a monster child, an Antigone who would not keep the family secrets?

If the ethics of Greer's action are problematic, she recognizes it as such and makes her consciousness of the problem an integral part of her account. Greer may doubt the purity of her undertaking, may turn against herself for unearthing a father who wished to be concealed, even may turn the aggression she has felt toward him against herself. But she defends against such self-laceration by justifying her quest in the name of investigative honesty, becoming the self-appointed heroine of truth telling. Reg Greer is dead and thus as immune from hurt as she is from his retribution. I suspect, in addition, that given Greer's history of transgressing traditional ethics as evidenced by her frequent attempts to outrage readers and to contravene normative cultural views, she might not ultimately worry much about the propriety of her search. The ethical question about outing the parent who has made a choice let alone a career of concealment never becomes a paramount one for Greer.

Greer's text, for all its narrative drive and investigational persistence, leads us to an overwhelming question: Can the truth about a parent ever be known by the investigating child? Because so much of her tracking focuses on gene-alogy, we are inclined to think that such information, when finally divulged, is sufficient. But that seemingly "objective" data is hardly all Reg Greer is, and the more his daughter tries to give us a full tallying, the more she recognizes an inevitable insubstantiality—not just of his motives but of his very iden-tity. It's crucial, I think, that she begins with the "distant, speechless wreck," "the grand ruin which was his mind"; but for all her careful detection of his heredity, she never fully solves the issue of mind or of character. Hence her mordant pronouncement, "Daddy is still unknown to me, more unknown than ever" (81). Does Reg Greer get lost in all her record hunting, and is this disappearance inevitable given his evasive behavior? Or is his identity ulti-mately less important than the ego of the investigator and the pride she takes in the persistence and the cunning of her pursuit? Such are the unanswered, perhaps unanswerable, questions her text inevitably raises.

If Greer's tone is finally one of triumphalism, Mike O'Connor, the next subject, is more modest. As an investigative journalist he knows how difficult it is to arrive at definitive truth, and rather than crowing over bagging his prey he is grateful for what he manages to discover. And rather than attacking his father's behavior, he expresses a sympathy for an understandable secrecy and compulsive privacy. Whereas Greer focuses almost exclusively on her father with brief attention to her mother, O'Connor looks at the influence of parental secrecy on an extended family; we see how his entire family becomes an archive of secrets, a fortress of self-imposed constraints. In shedding light on this prison house and on his own past, O'Connor recognizes that the kind of inquiry he practices professionally may have a significant payoff in personal terms.

Family on the Lam: A Son Running After Secrets

Crisis, Pursued by Disaster, Followed Closely by Catastrophe (2007), Mike O'Connor's memoir whose title comes from his father's witty report of a failed business deal, puts the reader in virtually the same position of uncertainty the author had been for much of his life. The answer to his questions about the origins and meaning of his parents' secret life is not disclosed until the end of the work, and the arc of the text replicates O'Connor's gradual and painstakingly delayed discovery of the family puzzle. The work's title of course echoes Winston Churchill's celebrated definition of Russia ("a riddle, wrapped in a mystery, inside an enigma"), and captures the interlocking conundrums that constitute O'Connor's parents' bewildering actions about which he knew nothing until well into middle age. The memoir slowly untangles a series of knotted concealments, as O'Connor the investigator gradually realizes that his parents' inscrutability can be understood only when their extended family begins to reveal its collective dark history. Like O'Connor, we learn the truth only after following a complex process of detection.

Two-thirds of the work comprises a detailed description of the youth and early adulthood of O'Connor and his two sisters, in their increasingly isolated family. The last third focuses on his elaborate investigation of the secret that had driven his parents to be continually on the run, fearing threats—real and imagined—of law enforcement and other intrusions into their carefully constructed closed world. A reluctant O'Connor had put off for years any inquiry into the recesses of his parents' life, though his capacity for tenacious fact-finding and research came naturally. As an investigative reporter for CBS, NPR, and the *New York Times,* working in Central America, Kosovo, Bosnia, and Israel, detective work has been at the heart of his professional life:

> I was probably the most aggressive reporter when it came to hunting for government deception or looking for people who felt cheated. Or looking into secretive groups....I was driven by wanting to find the secrets and then tell the public about them. I was relentless in looking for what had been concealed—

But then he adds: "except when it came to the O'Connor family mystery, which I tried to put out of my mind" (188–189). It is reasonable to surmise that the burning questions about private mysteries led to his becoming a reporter, as if inquiry into public issues substituted for inquiry into his family. It's apparent that the career was both an escape from dwelling too much on the family concealments and a commitment to discovering patterns in formlessness, something he learned as a child within the family and that enabled him to be at once detached from and fascinated by figuring out the seemingly inexplicable.

The inspiration for the inquiry comes from his younger sister and their discovery of a previously sealed container: a cigar box belonging to his mother filled with important family documents, a diary, and photos, all of which at once raise the prospect of knowledge. But at the same time they arouse his anxiety concerning what he might learn, for O'Connor's parents, intent on keeping their children from knowing their secret, drilled into them a lesson about not attempting to gain forbidden knowledge. And there may be a more personal reason for his reluctance to pursue the clues. As John Lanchester says in a memoir about *his* parents' secrets, *Family Romance,* "The things you don't know are very often the things you have chosen not to know" (10). O'Connor's long-standing resistance to learning too much is a form of self-protection, but from what? I suspect it's not from the sheer facts regarding what happened to cause his parents' incessant and apprehensive flights, as much as from what those discoveries will reveal about his parents' inner lives. More important, he seems to fear that the discoveries will force him to reconfigure his relation to his parents, even after their deaths. Perhaps the greatest worry is how he will come to think of himself. Having achieved a kind of independence from his parents, particularly from his father, embarking on research about them may threaten to pull him back into the familial morass, profoundly unsettling the equilibrium that escape from their conflicts has brought him.

The description of life with his parents unfolds as a series of events bewildering to the child, mostly involving precipitous moves back and forth from America to Mexico. Border crossings figure as the most terrifying of the experiences. (We will eventually learn that national borders are the source of much of their trouble). Do the parents have the right papers? Will they be questioned by guards and custom officials? The most normal procedures at the Texas–Mexico frontier become practices in evasion and fraudulence. On several occasions the family flees to Mexico, after no more than a day's deliberation, abandoning a house full of possessions in desperation to avoid what O'Connor terms mysteriously "the Danger" (xi). This menace recurs whenever something appears to interfere with the parents' security. On one occasion the father is arrested for a minor infraction of selling items without a license. On another the mother is summoned to a court hearing for a minor auto accident. After each incident the family runs, settling uneasily into the new country, evading the authorities. After Mike, as a teenager, runs away from his home in Monterrey, Mexico, to Los Angeles and is arrested for hitchhiking on a freeway, his father fears to pick him up lest he himself get into legal difficulties. When Mike gives the police his Monterrey address, the family, again fearing involvement with the law, flees Mexico and moves to California. The text comprises a series of sudden flights, the motives for which make no more sense to the children than to the reader. Early in the work O'Connor describes his father's work as a door-to-door salesman: With no forms "that might find their way to the authorities," it was "a portable trade, dissolved in one town and remade in the next before anyone would realize he was gone" (6). That work made it easy for him to be a stranger and for the family to conceive of itself as fluid, rootless, tenuous. The parents stay on the run for over twenty years. Though O'Connor, as he narrates the history, gives us ostensible reasons for their fugitive status, not until the end of the work do we learn the truth. For decades (and for many pages) the real reason is "shoved away, pushed down a well" (34).

The slightest disturbances create shock waves of apprehension: a policeman who visits their house to welcome them to town, a man at a rodeo who looks with seeming suspicion at the father. "The Danger" permeates everything; as a child O'Connor senses the inchoate dread without being able to define it, let alone to know its cause. He describes what I'd call familial claustrophobia, in which the sense of danger increases even as the family builds impermeable walls of secrecy against an unwelcome invasion from the outside, something they regard as an always-threatening violation—but of what the child cannot say.

Even more distressing than fear are the endless deceptions that characterize family life. The father tells lies at border stations to avoid detection, deceives potential buyers regarding the roof repairs he sells, and concocts schemes for getting rich though most of them are built on a tissue of falsehoods. The mother is evasive about her English past: "There are things we don't talk about," she says (76). O'Connor himself absorbs the tendency to prevarication, spinning increasingly blatant falsehoods during his Los Angeles escapade; he tells fictions to friends to corroborate stories about his parents he knows to be distortions, justifying the lies to keep "the Danger" at bay.

Only gradually does he feel disgust with his parents' evasions and his own falsehoods, as he struggles to understand the outside world in the face of his family's frustrating opacity. His adolescent desire to be independent of them takes on special urgency, and, in a prophetic transition to his future career, he turns from reading novels to history and politics, eschewing fictions for facts and "truth."

A recurring motif in the memoir is O'Connor's awareness that the family does not seem to include any uncles, aunts, cousins, or grandparents—an anomaly for Irish Catholics. There is no family history to speak of, or rather, none that is spoken of. In the absence of any mention of relatives, he narrates a pervasive feeling of isolated oddness, while the family of five coheres around its fear.

The last long section of the work forms a narrative of patiently conducted research and often shocking revelations, as O'Connor exposes secret after secret. If he is to uncover the fundamental mystery of his parents' lives he must gather and verify facts, a process that will take him to terra incognita; that is, to the family he never knew he had. Confronting walls of evasion and silence, he alone bears the burden of discovery and its deepest emotional consequences; he alone can put all the fragments and clues together to shape the story.

The process begins after his mother's death in 1997, when his younger sister, Fiona, who has urged him to search out the truth, casually mentions the existence of two half-brothers and a first wife of his father, all living in the Boston area. John O'Connor, Mike's father, had abandoned his first wife and two young sons during World War II, and had joined the Canadian army where, on his way to Italy to fight, he met, fell in love, and had a child in Germany with Mike's mother Jess, a British citizen who was with the Entertainments National Service Association, the British equivalent of the USO (United Service Organizations). When he decided to leave his first marriage his traditional Catholic parents were stunned with disapproval; they would be even more shocked to learn that their favorite son had returned from the war with another woman and a new baby, Mike. O'Connor's first theory for parental flight is that his father was on the run out of shame for that desertion. Initially, he is dubious about investigating further: "I thought, *this is the crap you get when you go looking into the past.* Suddenly I had two brothers" (200), a sentiment vaguely echoed by his father's sister, Aunt Eleanor, the family matriarch, when she resists divulging too much. Questions about the family's past exposed "tragedies that only became worse when people tried to exhume them" (204), another instance of the motif in these texts of unburial.

O'Connor learns that in the late 1940s both the INS and the FBI were looking for his mother; he eventually discovers that those agencies had embarked on a decades-long search for father, mother, and even for Mike himself, wanting all three for questioning. His mother had attended left-wing political meetings in Boston, but could this innocent fact be sufficient reason for law enforcement organizations pursuing them? And why for baby Mike? As more mysterious clues surface, O'Connor slowly overcomes his resistance to the search and his investigative instincts take over.

He meets his father's family in Boston, an experience unnerving, embarrassing, and yet enlightening, which further convinces him to pursue a serious search. He examines FBI files procured through the Freedom of Information Act and, when they yield nothing of importance, he tracks down buried and all-but-forgotten files with the help of ex-federal agents and an ex-CIA operative. After extensive interviews with his newly acquired extended family, he elicits secrets from them as if he were confronting a recalcitrant political group or government, slowly piecing together the following story.

In 1947 his grandmother and an uncle pursued John O'Connor to his Boston home, found his English bride and baby Mike, and demanded that she immediately return to England with her baby. When she refused, they contacted the INS to begin deportation proceedings, after which the fledgling family decamped for Texas. Meanwhile John's sons by his first marriage were fed a lie—that their father had been killed in World War II, their mother now a war widow. This deception held for many years, and when John O'Connor died in 1973, he was buried in secret while the first sons remained ignorant of their father's real death. When O'Connor learns about these deceptions, he feels a bond with his half-brothers, mutual victims of unforgivable falsehoods, some from a cabal of aunts and uncles, some from a conspiracy of his father and mother.

As if he were uncovering a tale of international intrigue for a news organization, O'Connor journeys to England (his mother's birthplace), Canada (his father's), Germany (where his father had run a refugee camp immediately after the war), Israel (to learn more about the camp), and Mexico (to interview business partners of his father). He discovers that his mother's brother was a member of the British Communist Party, though his mother was simply a Socialist with a pacifist strain. When in Boston she attended meetings at the liberal Community Church, which would hardly seem a dangerous thing to do, but two phenomena merged to put her squarely in the radar of the FBI and INS. The church's pastor was under investigation for possibly subversive activities, and J. Edgar Hoover demanded his agency produce damning evidence against the clergyman, the church, and its parishioners despite the fact that little such evidence existed. The church was infiltrated by an undercover agent who was a source of false information regarding right-wing organizations, and an FBI investigation produced largely trumped-up testimony. In an atmosphere pervaded by national hysteria about the Soviet Union and its recent acquisition of the atomic bomb, the Korean War, the Communist Revolution in China, and rampant McCarthyism, the FBI went after anyone they could, however insignificant a threat they posed to national security, and O'Connor's mother fell into the trap; her being on the run inevitably added to her seeming guilt. In addition, she had entered the United States after the war, illegally posing as John O'Connor's wife, a "crime" discovered when O'Connor's grandmother, attempting to preserve the integrity of her family, exposed her new daughter-in-law to the INS. No wonder O'Connor says about his parents, "Paranoia was part of their DNA" (249).

One of the dramas of O'Connor's research, and of his text, following a pattern common to such investigations, is his intermittent resistance to continuing the search for the secret of the secrets. His commitment to the process runs up against a fear of what he will find. "A part of me wanted to sabotage this mission" (253). But O'Connor differs from other reluctant discoverers such as Germaine Greer and Mary Gordon in that his initial resistance involves a physical revulsion, including an array of symptoms. About to drive into Mexico to interview people who had known the family during their several sojourns there, he cannot bring himself to cross the Laredo bridge, frozen with panic at the spot where his father had often lied his way across. He experiences migraines, blurred vision, loss of concentration, and nausea. While interviewing his father's one-time business partner, O'Connor's right hand suffers temporary paralysis; he simply cannot write, as if his body unwills what his mind struggles to accomplish. He has broken his parents' implicit injunction not to ask questions, in effect betraying them by a quest for answers he was not meant to have.

The way out of this impasse for O'Connor is, paradoxically, to delve further. As he gathers more information, O'Connor's attitude toward his parents gradually shifts, most likely as the depression and anxiety that accompany his search fade. While his primary goal is the accumulation and analysis of information, a crucial secondary objective is to see if he can revise his attitude toward his parents. Forgiveness is too much to expect, but he does gain something like acceptance, at least a tolerant understanding of the impossibly difficult choices they faced.

Nevertheless, for all the assiduousness of O'Connor's search and the wealth of information he unearths, something seems missing from his account. He never learns about his parents from the inside—what they felt, how they talked to each other about their life, what sense they made of their lives, what they perceived as the emotional consequences of their decisions. O'Connor cannot get into their skins, nor can he tell the story he might have imagined they told to one another. How could he? Such a narrative could only take the form of something close to fiction writing, and we have noted the journalist's innate skepticism about fiction: "I was less interested in literature and more in facts…because there was something in my own life—our secret—which was covered in lies" (152). So the imagined story about their story remains an untold one. Even the parents' few extant remarks in letters and memos are necessarily subject to their son's suspicion or mistrust, given how they edited their comments for public consumption. O'Connor can hardly accept anything they might say as unequivocal truth; hence his reliance on documentation and interviews.

Can we imagine his parents *not* being displeased at the discoveries made by their son? Is there any way they might *not* feel he has been prying into forbidden corners of their lives? And should O'Connor be concerned with such matters, or is his curiosity alone sufficient justification for the research? A possible answer to such ethical questions comes at the conclusion of the text, when O'Connor attends the funeral of his Aunt Eleanor in 2001, midway through his investigation.

Eleanor had been one of the father's sisters who, if not precisely approving her brother's adulterous relationship with Jess and their child, at least gave help to Jess in Boston, disagreed with her own mother's intervention with the INS, refused to give the FBI information about the O'Connors' whereabouts, and generally protected their secrecy. It is not surprising O'Connor attended that funeral. There he meets for the first time Helen, his father's first wife, mother of his half-brothers. That meeting and a subsequent one at her apartment form the climax of the work. In a kind of symmetry that seems almost too fortuitous, their meeting becomes the opportunity for O'Connor to close a circle: "I was doing what my father had never done. I'd gone back" (284).

I want to emphasize in this "reunion" two things. First, O'Connor forgives his parents, an unspoken sentiment echoed in Helen's forgiveness of O'Connor's father. Second, and tied to this familial intricacy through Helen's surprising acceptance of Mike as her "other son," is a discovery every bit as important as the historical and biographical facts he has uncovered—namely, the sheer importance for O'Connor of family itself. In a belated revelation, he acknowledges and celebrates not only the fact and presence of the larger family he never knew but also the importance for him of its acts of sharing and reciprocity, however flawed such gestures may be. Of course there's a marked irony in his comment that "A strong, comforting wall encircled everyone, all together" (281). He has known about such walls.

O'Connor's book shows how deeply embedded in complex family relations secrets can be, how fiercely they are held onto once enlisted in the name of protection and supposed benefit. For the O'Connor clan, secrets had a tendency to grow and proliferate, and when one part of the family split from the other, an entire new cluster of secrets sprang into action, driving further wedges, creating borders the crossing of which present threats to safety, and setting up new barriers to understanding let alone to relationship. In O'Connor's case his parents' secrets had so hardened into the norm he became inured to them, believing it easier to live with them than to undertake the difficult work of exposure or risk the revelations that would threaten whatever accommodations he had made. For this reason he waited many years, convinced that his well-being depended on *not* knowing too much, even as he ironically replicated one aspect of his parents' life; namely, a tendency to "run," as an international journalist moving from place to place, refusing a settled permanence, more comfortable on the road than at home.

When the impulse to press on with his investigation takes hold, O'Connor needs to clarify just what he means by sufficient evidence. So let's return briefly to the cigar box containing documents assembled by Jess O'Connor, the opening of which inspires her son's quest. The opened box reveals not so much a host of secrets but mere hints, a tantalizing array of incomplete signification. The contents of the box constitute a kind of tease, opening only to possibility, not to certainty. Like an archive, it is merely a starting point, not an answer; data, not a solution. As an assemblage of temptations, it can only entice to further search and create a longing for more knowledge—or perhaps, as is temporarily true for O'Connor, for less, even for forgetting or obliteration. Like so many repositories of artifacts, there is less in the box than meets the eye; what is *not* present is of greater import than what *is*.

Of course what O'Connor searches for is *in the family itself,* rather than in archives or in documents. Or, put another way, the family itself becomes an archive, a repository of memory, a treasure trove of material that slowly, painfully yields up its buried secrets. But the family archive is a perverse one in that it frequently misrepresents history, distorts facts, and causes its members to mis-remember. The overseers of that "archive" are the family matriarchs (O'Connor's grandmother and aunts), but they are like misleading archons, controlling the information to shape the history as they wish it to appear, or rather *not* to appear, in order to hold the family together. As the lynchpins of family history, the secrets they protected along with the constant vigilance they exercised served to prevent the possibility of divergence from within or intrusion from without. As so often with family secrets, the insiders are torn between concealing and revealing what they know, and the outsiders (like O'Connor himself) show both a resistance to inquire and an impulse to probe.

Secrecy is power. The family decides what to know and who will know it. By constructing truth and controlling information, they create a tolerable family identity while preventing the family from being defined by others in unwelcome ways. Each O'Connor "branch" has its own secrets, and each maintains them for its own private and particular needs, closing in on themselves to maintain solidarity and to preserve a form of sacred privilege.

At the end of the work the two sides of the family come together in harmony. But not completely. As I suggested earlier, there is much that is never fully and openly dealt with, nor even mentioned. The title *Crisis, Pursued by Disaster, Followed Closely by Catastrophe* hardly promises redemption; the titular bleakness speaks not only to the nature of O'Connor's past but implicitly to the inevitable disappointments of his search for answers. O'Connor knows that the gains of inquiry cannot possibly divulge everything he ultimately wishes to understand. Mysteries remain, and though he seems to accept them, at the conclusion we sense both his desire for closure and a frustration with all he will never know. O'Connor reenters his past, but that return is ineluctably incomplete; some secrets remain sealed in vessels stronger than any cigar box.

Still, the persistence of undiscovered truths hardly negates the primal satisfactions of O'Connor's quest, including his painstaking assemblage of the available information, careful narrative exposition, and continuing speculation. Joseph Lelyveld, to whom I turn next, is also a journalistic investigator who realizes the impossibility of recovering a complete account of the past. When Lelyveld writes about his parents, who resist full disclosure of themselves in what they've left behind by way of evidence, clues, or intimations, he appears both to lament the foreclosure of information and to recognize the necessary limitations of knowledge. Whether his father's difficult experience in the McCarthy period inhibited the son from a fuller inquest is a question we might ponder in both these texts.

A Scavenger in the Archives: The "Memory Boy" Tracks His Parents

In his memoir *Omaha Blues: A Memory Loop* (2005) Joseph Lelyveld, who spent his career with the *New York Times* as a foreign correspondent, managing editor, and executive editor, has chosen a biographer's approach to representing his parents rather than a detective's way (though he might call it the investigative reporter's way). There is no single dark secret to ferret out so much as several lives to explain and represent. Actually there *is* a specific revelation, one made indirectly to him by his younger brother Michael: that the brother was the son not of Joseph's father but of a lover of his mother during the course of his parents' marriage. But the exposure of that secret is not the climax nor even a central revelation toward which the book is leading. Rather, the work demonstrates Lelyveld's thirst for knowledge generally about his covert parents. Young Michael's paternity is less crucial to the narrative than the problem of how to characterize the lives of Joseph's parents and their motives for action. The book focuses on the effect their often unaccountable, occasionally surreptitious behavior had on him as a boy and on his increasing difficulty in fathoming them with the perspective of decades. When lives under scrutiny are secretive, memory can often be of little help. In the course of Lelyveld's search for knowledge about his parents and himself in relation to them he raises doubts about the reliability of his memory and about the accuracy of any putative understanding at which he arrives.

Lelyveld's father, Arthur, was a well-known Reform rabbi, Zionist advocate, and spokesman as well as activist for civil liberties. His mother, Toby, was an actress who, feeling restricted as the wife of a rabbi, left her husband and two young sons to attend Columbia University where she studied English Renaissance literature with the man who eventually fathered her third son. After many restless years in which she sporadically abandoned and returned to her family, Toby Lelyveld eventually divorced her husband to pursue the life of a teacher and scholar.

Memory and its constantly defective operations are at the heart of the work. As a child Joseph Lelyveld's parents called him "the memory boy" (3), but ironically he can no longer remember what they meant by that; the memory of his memory has faded. But this forgetting is not accidental nor a product of aging; rather the forgetting is deliberate, an "acquired skill" that encourages him to shed his past so as not to be stuck in it, a dissipating that allows him, as he puts it, to get on with his life. The former "memory boy" strives to be a memory-less man: when his father in old age sends him a packet of love letters between himself and Lelyveld's mother, which the father had long since hidden away, Lelyveld summarily disposes of the letters, unwilling to read them. It's unclear whether he fears contaminating his memory with alternative truths or whether he is simply not ready to learn *any* truth. He then characteristically forgets *how* he had disposed of them. But jettisoning a significant past appears to be the eventual spur to a renewed desire for knowledge, and not long after he discards the letters, while his father lies dying, Lelyveld "go[es] scavenging" in the basement of his father's Cleveland synagogue through a trunk whose existence an acquaintance had mentioned; inside the box of effects Lelyveld finds "mounds of clippings, report cards, speech notes, typed correspondence, and family mail," eliciting in its cumulative effect what he calls the dangerous "genie of reminiscence" (4, 8). But so resistant is he to disturbing his memory, or perhaps to filling the cavities of deliberate forgetting, that he stuffs that genie back inside and has the trunk removed to his home where he lets it sit unexamined for another six years. As with Mike O'Connor, exploring a past either forgotten or unknown threatens to bring forth demons. Too much knowledge seems a curse.

So what does finally move Lelyveld to revive and question memory and to undertake memoir? The key to resurrecting his family's past and his role in it comes via a desire, in retirement from the *Times,* to write not about his parents but about a family friend and mentor to the adolescent Lelyveld named Ben Goldstein. It is this lengthy investigation into a complex story and its central figure that ultimately gives rise not to a biography of Goldstein but to the family memoir in which Goldstein plays a significant role and which includes a detailed account of the process of Lelyveld's investigation. We see how indirect all of this is: You get to a history of the family via an outside figure, and that history cannot be understood without a self-conscious exploration of the way that history was attained.

Ben Goldstein was also a rabbi and a younger colleague of Lelyveld's father whose work for a long time the latter encouraged and supported. Arthur Lelyveld was a forceful champion of the disenfranchised, but Goldstein was far more radical; in the 1930s he was effectively ousted from his Alabama pulpit when he preached against low wages for workers, spoke out forcefully on the "Negro question," and in a Yom Kippur sermon publicly defended the innocence of the Scottsboro Boys (the case concerned nine young blacks on death row who were accused—falsely as it turned out—of raping two white women who later recanted). The Jewish community of Montgomery, aware of its vulnerability in a conservative southern city and sensitive to accusations they were disrupting the traditional southern way of life, could not afford to have the leader of its congregation perceived as a rabble-rouser. In addition Goldstein was likely a member of the Communist Party, and there were allegations he was linked to Russian agents, including the KGB's main operative in the United States.

After a stint in Hollywood distributing Soviet films, Goldstein, now Rabbi Benjamin Lowell (he took his second wife's name), became an assistant to Lelyveld's father, who by that time was the director of the Hillel foundation, the Jewish student organization. But eventually Arthur Lelyveld fired him, probably, Lelyveld concludes, to avoid tainting his own work by association with Goldstein, who had defended the Nazi–Soviet pact. A considerable portion of the book examines the complex story surrounding Goldstein's politics and Rabbi Lelyveld's tormented decision to end their professional alliance and personal connection. Arthur Lelyveld was no conservative: He vigorously opposed Joseph McCarthy and, following the deaths of James Chaney, Andrew Goodman, and Michael Schwerner, traveled to Mississippi during the Freedom Summer of 1964 to register black voters; in the course of his work the elder Lelyveld was badly beaten by white supremacists. His son follows in exacting detail—some pertinent documents were in the trunk, others became available through diligent research—the process by which his father arrived at his difficult decision to end his association with Goldstein, analyzing how his father made his decision and why. He speculates about both the justice of the accusations against Goldstein and the link between politics and personal relations.

The detailed and intricate story and the quest for the "truth" about the Goldstein "case" makes us wonder why, in a family memoir, he is given such seemingly outsized recognition. In a *New York Times* review of *Omaha Blues,* Cynthia Ozick has correctly stated that Lelyveld *as a boy* was hardly concerned with or even aware of Goldstein's politics; "Ben" was appreciated and beloved for his attentions to young Joseph, especially for taking him to baseball games. The *political* Goldstein was beyond the boy's interest or his ken. As Ozick writes, "the Ben who takes over and sets the tone of this narrative is only partly in Lelyveld's memory loop. He is pre-eminently in Lelyveld's research loop." The newspaper man's investigative impulse does indeed take center stage: When he tracks the relation of his father to Goldstein and its historical and political context, Lelyveld turns to government files, newspaper stories, letters, committee reports, court records, and interviews—traditional sources on which a reporter depends and which, in this work, take the place of memory in more conventional life writing. Significantly Goldstein, like so many intimate figures from Lelyveld's past, became for him "a story to be reported someday" (159). It is understandable that when memory is fabricated, deficient, or absent, Lelyveld would turn to documentation, and much of the Goldstein saga shows the power of the writer's reportorial and investigative skill.

Nevertheless, memory is not entirely absent from the work. Calling memory a "loop" suggests that for Lelyveld when memory functions it does not move in a linear chronological fashion. He keeps looping back to half-remembered events even as he discovers new facts about the past; as he merges memory with research, he tests and judges the past from both personal and archival perspectives. He wants to believe in the accuracy of memories, perhaps to justify his early nickname, but as he conducts his research into the secret lives of his parents he acknowledges if not the invalid nature of memory then at least its insufficiency as a determinant of truth. What he remembers having felt or experienced as a child may be so distorted or inadequate that it invariably generates a false or at least compromised reading of the past. He is continually saying in effect, "This is what I remember, but this is what I have newly found out. Can they be made to harmonize and if so, how? Or are they too much at odds to yield any definitive understanding?" Much of the text finds Lelyveld wondering why he has harbored a particular memory, how it has created what he regards as a mythic view of his past, and to what use he has put that memory.

Memories "loop" around the researched disclosures, each accession to the past negotiating with the other, neither one fully conclusive as evidence, neither one a guarantee of authenticity.

> I think of this [book] as a memory loop...; a particular circuit of memories that I feel driven to retrace and connect, where possible, to something like an objective record or the memories of someone else, in hopes of glimpsing what was once real. I say they form a loop simply because that's the capricious way they unravel in my mind. (18–19)

His own memories may be undermined or at least qualified by the memories of others, which he finds in external accounts of his past. And much of his own past comes back to him through a history originally inaccessible to him. His ignorance of material to which his mind can't even begin to "loop" back makes his interpretations highly subjective, if not inevitably defective.

The heart of the work involves his parents' marriage and the questions he raises concerning its secrets and its gradual demise: Did his father fight against his wife's desire to be away from the family? Did his mother feel guilt for abandoning her family? Were her inability to embrace motherhood and her detachment from her family signs of independence or of a mental problem? How badly bruised was he by his parents' troubles? In the course of his search for at least approximate truth, he recognizes the futility of understanding the past as purposeful or designed by its participants with logic. Much of what he discovers, or at least acknowledges, is that the past is haphazard and unplanned, and if he denies that fact he will reconstruct the past as if it had been premeditated, possibly overdetermined. He also recognizes that what he thought was true at the time may not necessarily have been so. For instance, as a boy he had been sent to a farm in Nebraska with Seventh-Day Adventists (his father was frequently away on business, while his mother was off to graduate school in New York); he has vague and inchoate memories of abandonment and misery, or that is how he retrospectively imagines he must have felt at the time. But when he delves into a cache of his childhood letters in his father's trunk and reads one he sent from the farm, it appears he was quite happy. A small matter, perhaps, but one indicative of how evidence can collide with reminiscence, setting Lelyveld on the road to ambivalence about the past and skepticism regarding any definitive reading of it.

In the course of these shifts in recognition and understanding he becomes preoccupied with returns to places that were crucial, even traumatic sites: the Nebraska farm to which he was sent and the family house his mother continually abandoned. Going back to these places is like revisiting memories themselves, for these locales, no less than his memories, form "a layered series of narratives of [my] own family" (51). And, in keeping with the mysteries and secrets of his childhood, the revisited sites are never as he had remembered them. Lelyveld's book emphasizes the way he continually revises the understanding of his life.

Lelyveld's own motives often baffle him as much as those of his parents. Why, for example, did he go to Mississippi to do a story on the Freedom Summer of 1964? He thinks it was because his father had been seriously beaten there and a photograph of him that appeared in many newspapers moved the son to follow in his father's footsteps. But after some research he concludes he went only because a *Times* editor sent him to do a story. The exact mix of internal and external causes is always mysterious, and the accounts of motivation necessarily remain murky. Lelyveld's blend of memory, useful forgetting, and error is ineluctably convoluted and confounding.

He explores a past that may not have happened as he believed it did because, as a boy, he was confronted with too much secrecy, denial, and misleading information. To protect young Lelyveld from the messy facts of their marriage, his parents ensured that his childhood would be filled with quandary and doubt. As a result he needs to impose an order in which he could believe. His *self*-exploration, because it cannot be detached from the parents whose behavior and motives he could not possibly understand as a child, focuses on his ignorance and the anxiety it produced. In a way it was fortuitous because Lelyveld's childhood uncertainty and later desire to unravel the loops of memory may be what made him a reporter disposed to skepticism and incredulity. In excavating material on Goldstein, he necessarily "look[s] for clues to my sometimes puzzling self; my own history, my own character." Each tentative revelation about others opens the door to stories about himself. There may only be "stories but not the whole story," an "itinerary" rather than a coherent narrative, memory fragments that may or may not add up to a satisfactory self-portrait (17). Lelyveld, like a good reporter, obsesses about the editing and revision of memories thought to be clear but, with hindsight, appear to have been erroneous, incomplete, or misleading.

Out of the suspicions in his boyhood he builds a story rife with distrust, especially of conventional interpretations and of elegant, excessively logical narrations. Merely to narrativize his life and the lives of his parents is, in his eyes, to risk imposing misleading structures. Transparency is not easy to come by, and any given hypothesis is subject to doubt and further scrutiny. To invoke Michael Kimmelman's phrase about Janet Malcolm writing on Gertrude Stein, Lelyveld constantly displays "the anxiety of disclosure," (6) inclined to challenge if not to discredit himself as narrator as well as anyone who gives him material for his story. He takes no one at his word, including himself.

As he retrieves from his father's trunk and reads letters from each parent to the other, many from hotels across the country, Lelyveld gradually pieces together a story of their complex itineraries and their tortured way of keeping one another in the dark about their future. And as he tries to fit his memory of abandonment and fear into a narrative of flight and resettlement—to Manhattan, Brooklyn, Queens, Omaha, and Kansas City—and into the interstices and inconclusiveness of the complex saga of their vacillations, Lelyveld remembers having posed endless, unanswerable questions: Will they get divorced? Have they already done so? Where would each parent wind up? Where would he? As he reads the letters he calls on each of the major figures in his life—father, mother, and Ben Goldstein, as well as his reportorial self—"to fill in the gaps in the lost narrative" of his and their lives (85). Each stab at exploring the mystery of his parents' lives is "an attempt to round out and perhaps put to rest an early chapter of my own life." But the research, however much he trusts it to clarify matters, cannot dispel the secrecy and uncertainty of everyone's actions. The father remains opaque to his son.

The more he remembers, the less he knows; the more intriguing his past, the more speculative he is forced to be. But his journalistic self balks at the possibility he may be creating a fictionalized past, or at least one too neat and coherent. He invokes Ben, but might as well be talking in his head to his father: "because I wanted to know you, not create you, I had to resist the idea that I might summon up, through an act of imagination, your sense of your life, then lodge it in a fictional persona bearing your name. So it was as a reporter and scavenger in archives that I sought you" (87). He distrusts imagination without solid, indisputable research to stand behind it; otherwise he may be left only with "fictional persona[e]" (87). And yet he comes to acknowledge the inevitable ambiguity if not unknowability of others' behavior, the subjectivity if not the solipsism of his interpretations. This realization is what makes his book so absorbing in both its capitulation and its resistance to secrets.

Given such uncertainties we make up stories that become memories because they fit convenient narrative lines, having been unconsciously but deftly censored, rearranged, and augmented. The most poignant instance of this phenomenon occurs when he thinks back to his father's distress over having to fire Ben Goldstein, whose refusal to come clean about his Communist affiliation compromised his father's work with Hillel. Lelyveld believed his father "had acted on clear principles," but as he reflects on the past he notes: "I don't think that's how it felt to him" (149). Now he realizes his father probably anguished that he was becoming more like the witch-hunters and the House Un-American Activities Committee than he ever imagined. The son is tempted to hold his father responsible; but even as the "memory boy" gives way to the "re-memory man" he never argues that revised memory represents the definitive interpretation of his or others' lives.

Lelyveld's memories most commonly concern separation and reunion, loss and return, torment and idyll. It takes him years of "scaveng[ing] in archives" and questioning his parents to accept the facts of their complex marriage, their breakup, and the truth of his youngest brother's paternity (though his mother's life, with its frequent breakdowns and three suicide attempts, remains a mystery to him, her secrets never fully explained). In effect he recognizes that the family he grew up in is the family existing only in his memory. In keeping with a text that examines how we know what we profess to know, Lelyveld is less disillusioned by his mother's infidelity than by his feeling of having lived in illusion and misplaced belief, of having harbored a story that turned out to be at odds with reality. It might not be a stretch to argue that *Omaha Blues* centers more on epistemological betrayal than on his mother's marital betrayal. Living in a world of secrets creates a sense of fragility no truth can fully repair. And the questions that any reporter might pose never cease: What was going on? What did his mother understand? What did he suspect? What clues were in the air, and were any of them false ones deliberately planted? There are also questions directed to himself: What do I feel about all this? Will sure-fire knowledge open up old wounds better left scarred over? Does performing a "reporting job on [my] childhood" effectively numb the pain that emotional memory virtually guarantees? The problem of how much to ask, suspect, speculate about, and feel is the abiding issue of *Omaha Blues*.

Has all the probing violated his parents' wishes, even implicit ones, not to be held up to a reportorial light? Do his mother's evasions make it clear she would have regarded her son's digging into her past as intrusive, unseemly, or unethical? Perhaps, but though Lelyveld conveys some anger at both parents' actions when he was a child and may not fully accept them now even as an adult, the book ends with two scenes that suggest reconciliation. The first is at his father's funeral, where, as he sits silently, a memory unsummoned arises of himself at three or four, running through grass on a summer day, calling "Daddy, Daddy, Daddy" (212). Whatever the feeling he expressed at the time—desire, joy, longing, anxiety—it was one he had spent a lifetime suppressing. The entire book is an attempt to get back to and to explore the significance of those words and emotions.

The second scene depicts the scattering of his mother's ashes on the Maine coast when, as he and one of his brothers open the contents of the canister, in a classically comic moment the wind blows the ashes back in their faces: "A fair portion of Mom was now in our hair and eyebrows. She clung to our shirts and our skin" (215). The brothers regard this scene as hilarious, the tone easing the possibility of an intimacy with the mother long denied. It also dramatizes, as metaphor, a realization that however remote and furtive she was and however elusive her truth and her story may have been, she is still there, all along absorbed into his being, unerasable.

Writing the memoir represents Lelyveld's attempt to disentangle family secrets and understand those mysteries, though as we've seen he can never be assured that his past will be fully or even satisfactorily explained. What he demonstrates, often intellectually, occasionally more personally, is that exploring family secrets with the twin instruments of memory and documentation became as significant as his career. The profession may have enabled him to get on with his life, perhaps even to escape from his boyhood past, but it also provided him with the means to explore and, however tentatively, to grapple with that past.

Joseph Lelyveld asks whether it is possible to know another and, if so, how. But Michael Rips, whose memoir *The Face of a Naked Lady: An Omaha Family Mystery (2005)* is the final work I consider in this chapter, stakes out an even more radical position. Rips, after thoroughly investigating a father who led a secret life unknown to his son (or to anyone else), a life completely incongruous with everything he appeared to be, suggests the limits of autobiographical inquiry. He enlarges the search for his father to a more general problem raised by the genre of life writing. Yet although he represents as skeptical an attitude about filial inquiry as any writer in this book, Rips is sufficiently intrigued by his project and fascinated by his (non-) findings not to withdraw from the search in the face of its inevitable futility. Though he discovers he knows virtually nothing about a person with whom he believed he was intimately acquainted, he nevertheless conceives the search itself to be worthwhile, and refuses to scorn memoir for its limited payoff regarding knowledge of both the self and the other.

The Naked Lady's Face and the Detective's Effacement

Even if writers investigating secretive parents don't always discern to their satisfaction every aspect of the secret-holder's identity or the reasons for their furtive behavior, the process of detection usually enables the investigator to discover some traits previously unknown or unsuspected. Speculation may substitute for certainty, or suspicion for conviction; but even when the findings remain provisional the writer may reach a tentative conclusion, however unclosed the "case."

Michael Rips's *The Face of a Naked Lady: An Omaha Family Mystery* illustrates a radical uncertainty about achieving definitive knowledge, perhaps *any* knowledge, of another person. It is a work that poses the questions: "What can I possibly know about someone else?" and "How can I conceivably know that I know?" Of all the works I examine, it is the one expressing the greatest epistemological doubt. Although the book received a respectful and even admiring response when it appeared in 2005, this strange text nonetheless puzzled everyone who wrote about it. Rips once clerked for Supreme Court Justice William J. Brennan Jr., and is an attorney who occasionally practices criminal litigation. He felt compelled to learn and write about his father when, soon after the latter's death, he discovered a stack of paintings of a naked black woman, each one initialed and painted by his father, that had been stashed in the older man's closet. Norman Rips owned a factory that manufactured optical equipment and eyeglasses, and as far as his son knew, had never painted in his life. Intrigued by the canvasses that suggested an unsuspected life, Rips set out to investigate the man who had always presented a bland, unoriginal, and utterly ordinary face to the world: "if he had an emotion or thought that was individual to him, it lacked the power of emanation" (2). Because the Republican and middle-class midwesterner— and the Omaha where he resided—struck Rips as conventional and colorless, a fascination with the possibility of a darker, perhaps ominous, side seems to have spurred his search. The memoir is Rips's attempt to uncover shadowy truths about his father, "the most vacant of . . . men" (12). But the quest and the "family mystery" remain essentially unsolved; Norman Rips went to his grave with whatever secret he carried intact. By the end of the book, it is not clear just what the father's secrets may be. In lieu of definitive revelations of character and motive, Rips narrates a story of surreal happenings, phantasmagoric characters, and dreamlike experiences—inexplicable tales that surround the father, intriguing and baffling the son who records a futile act of detection. Profoundly puzzled by his father, Rips subjects the reader to an equally enigmatic account, a whirligig of surmise that veers between reality and report, substance and conjecture, truth and appearance.

The problem for knowledge is not merely that the father's life remains inconclusive. Rips's resistance to clarifying the older man's identity results from his cynicism that life writing is ever capable of furthering knowledge, even of achieving clarity. As an investigative mode of inquiry and an instrument of detection, his work is frustratingly opaque because he does not believe in the logic of the genre itself. Rips regards such writing as unable to further an understanding of an Other because whenever he describes something apparently approaching truth his natural tendency to free associate and find symbolic analogies takes him further away from his subject.

Rips's investigation of his father quickly moves from questions about the identity of the black woman and his father's putative relation to her—the expected direction of the search—to a more general attempt at biography, reaching back to his father's childhood. We're never sure where Rips is heading in his search, or even why, but he is intrigued by almost anything that strikes him as a paternal mystery. Abhorring a vacuum of knowledge, yet seemingly resigned to that inevitability, he learns bits and pieces about his father's past, yet they never add up to much, remaining fragments that fascinate him exactly because he cannot make them cohere into an intelligible picture. The discovery of the paintings appears so troubling because they imply Rips has misunderstood his father all along; he wonders if the paintings point to a secret life more extensive than anything he can imagine, and if so whether he could possibly ascertain it.

The more he accumulates shards of evidence, if *evidence* is even the correct word, the further he ventures from the original investigation. "Attempting to locate clues that would lead me to the woman in the painting, I had slipped into my father's past" (39). "Slipped" suggests an almost unconscious process, something like a dream state if not even hallucination, the very opposite of the deliberate, ratiocinative procedure we associate with detective work. Such a dream state will be a clue to the tone and subject matter of the text, which is haunted by phantasmagoric happenings, surreal characters, and hallucinatory moods and associations. To cite one instance of this phenomenon, immediately following this statement about slipping into the past, Rips tells of receiving—out of the blue—a letter from a Michael Ripps (his own name with an additional *p*), who provides a lengthy and somewhat distracting history of the Rips (or Ripps) family going back to medieval Europe. Is this person the writer's doppelgänger? We never hear of him again, and his existence seems something like a version of, or metaphor for, the furtive father himself: shadowy, cryptic, and never fully explainable. What is this person doing in Rips's book, and is he also a metaphor for the investigation itself, an incarnation of untranslatable code and a reminder of an impossible goal?

We learn of the father's upbringing, which largely took place in *his* grandparents' hotel, which was in part a brothel; as a child Norman Rips cavorted with the prostitutes. His son does not connect this story, to which he returns throughout the text, to the paintings, and it is not clear if we are meant to. Are we supposed to be surprised that the quiet, placid man has this unlikely past? Or does this past somehow explain the paintings? There are many stories in the memoir that trail off, seemingly without point, certainly without connection to the father. Typical of such dead-end narratives, one concerns a cousin of Rips's grandfather who lectured a group of bankers about an invention of "reducing underwear" and an auction for the "underpants of the auctioneer" (61). The more these bizarre and seemingly incongruous stories accumulate, the more they resist our comprehension of the ostensible subject of the memoir. The narrative is itself an emptying out of meaning even as the investigator gathers an endless set of clues, none of which adds up to achieved understanding. This absence of conclusiveness is precisely the point about his baffling father, surprising to his son because he seemed a man utterly lacking in surprise.

In the course of playing detective, Rips goes to a real one who takes him to the basement room of a bar where there are surveillance cameras, another metaphor for the entire project. The private eye tells Rips he has a machine that "goes into your brain and reads thoughts you didn't know were there" (9). During their conversation six naked black women enter the bar, while a friend informs Rips that the detective knows the woman in the paintings and is protecting her and other black women the father had hired in his optical factory, one or more of whom were his mistress. "[I]f the woman in the painting was his mistress and was still out there, I would find her. And when I found her, I would find her children, my half brothers and sisters" (11). It is hard to know if this is an account of something that really happened, or Rips's fantasy, or a premonition of his discovery of his father's life in the brothel-hotel. And who can know if the "brain machine" is the detective's delusion or simply a figure for inquiry itself and thus for Rips's project. The encounter appears to go nowhere, and the same is true of countless others in the course of his inquiries. Rips's narrative, structured around incomplete stories that often seem irrelevant to his quest or phantasmagoric if not downright fabricated, circles around his father without arriving at definitive conclusions. The more people he interviews and the more he probes them, the less he actually learns about his father.

Rips gets plenty of help in detection, though the "evidence" he gathers is highly questionable. His mother gives him names to consult—friends and family—and the father's acquaintances suggest other people he might talk to; his network of plausible subjects to interview grows exponentially. Frank Williams, the detective, has a significant file of leads, so that Rips is both client and accomplice in sleuthing. But the more he searches without uncovering anything definitive, the more he concedes "the question of whether one can ever know the mind of anyone else" (149). This question lies at the heart of Rips's investigation, since an impulse to search, comprehend, and expose may be nothing more than a way to appear comfortable in the face of "strange and unsettling" ignorance, a pretext to give *ourselves* an identity we might otherwise lack. Were he to remain in the dark about a father who was inexpressive if not entirely vacant, Rips surmises he might begin to doubt his *own* existence, either because he had inherited that emptiness or because he was unaware of foundational truths about the family.

As the narrative plots his futile search, Rips crams his text with stories of odd characters—a man who roller-skates up and down stairs, a man who dresses in a fez and a brassiere, a skeptic who wonders if anything exists, and a man who straps an artificial penis to his boot. What are these persons doing in the narrative? They seem like diversions from the quest, yet they too function as shadowy enigmas enhancing the overall mystery. The question the reader inevitably asks is the one that haunts Rips himself: "What *is* going on here?" These marginal if not imaginary characters from Rips's past create an atmosphere of equivocation in which everything—especially meaning and veracity—is in doubt. Even those who compose a network of informants are no less incredible; while his father is the uncapturable object of the quest, everyone whom Rips enlists to aid him is equally hard to pin down.

The louche nature of his father's acquaintances throws Rips off the track, and yet they come to represent the father as his son gradually discovers the dark underbelly of Omaha and of Norman Rips's unexpected life. Even as each bizarre character appears to divert Rips from the object of his quest, they establish the father as far more complex and indefinable than his son realized. As an adolescent Rips himself spent time around such characters, drunks, and prostitutes, the very types his father consorted with as a young man. Such similarities are less part of a pattern of coincidence than of Rips's belief that "[W]e were all floating on the blood current of our ancestors" (148). Father and son in fact may not be so different. Even as a boy Rips like his father sought to become "a figure that could exist anywhere, never give offense, know exactly what to say so that people would ignore me, deferring to all semisolid objects, thoughts, personalities" (177). The "detective" is made of the same material—or perhaps immateriality—as the object of his search. Because he feels he himself has no continuous, stable self, he will never find an intelligible, forthright, and legible father.

Musing on an old friend from childhood, Rips learns that he had been institutionalized. He is shocked: "So insistent was I in finding continuity in him, in discovering a persistent essence, that I ignored what he had become" (129). He wonders whether continuity and consistency are indeed illusions, and if this is the case he may never discover a comprehensible father, only a succession of fragmentary "others" constituting a chain of incoherence. Since no one had seemed to Rips more *un*changing than his father, it is almost impossible for him to accept that his father may have had a kaleidoscope of secret lives. And this same instability characterizes the text, in its refusal of linearity, coherent logic, and cause and effect. Rips moves from topic to topic with little sense of direction and purpose, other than the general one of forming a portrait of the father that appears to lack any form. As de-centered writing, the text mirrors its subject.

Norman Rips, in the son's eyes, "was a man who could not be seen" (142), an appropriate way to describe someone resistant to scrutiny since, owning an optics factory, the acquisition of vision is obviously central to his life. His son remarks that occasionally "a lens would come through that was so clean, so utterly free of everything in this world, that it would vanish and it was in those moments that I came to appreciate the beauty of the invisible" (105). It is tempting to assume that his "invisible" father may be alluring to his son precisely for his nondetectability, his resistance to others' gaze. Even as Rips tries to look beyond surfaces, he is fascinated by the way his father escapes revelation, remaining outside the field of filial vision.

The father is a private man with little interest in the world around him, none in his children, "and none in himself." He abdicated all paternal duties, and even when he was with his sons he was altogether "transparent," by which Rips means not intelligible but empty (142, 72). If every gesture,

act, and attitude are strategies to prevent his being known, any retrospec-
tive attempt at interpretation is guaranteed to be thwarted, for his father has
ensured his opacity and continued secret life by surrounding himself with
characters bound to throw an investigator off the scent.

Throughout the text Rips shows his fascination with pursuits of all kinds.
A friend informs him about the disappearance and search for Weldon Kees;
Kees, also from Nebraska, was a poet, composer, jazz musician, photographer,
critic, and painter, who disappeared without a trace in 1955. He is thought to
have jumped from the Golden Gate Bridge when his car, with its keys still in
the ignition, was found near the bridge, though no body was ever discovered.
There was also speculation that he may have exiled himself to Mexico, as Kees
suggested to friends he might do. Rips surmises Kees did just that, eventually
returning to Nebraska and holing up in the very hotel where Rips himself
had worked as a boy. He even questions the old men there, hoping to find
Kees among them.

Anthony Lane, in a 2005 *New Yorker* profile on Kees, writes about him as
Rips might have about his own father:

> [T]he figure cut by Kees [in New York]... suggests not an insider but
> an intruder, somebody from out of town who may leave the party
> at any time.... It was as if the artistic look were surplus to require-
> ments; or rather, as if to don the outer crust of an insurance agent or
> an advertising man—to conduct himself like the steady Nebraskan
> citizen that Kees might have stayed to become—struck him as the sly-
> est of disguises.

Lane goes on to describe Kees in words Rips could well have used about his
father: "There is a spectral, somewhat Jamesian suggestion of a man who manages to be absent from his own life. Even as we sift the evidence of the poems,
the stories, and the correspondence, their creator is removed from the picture;
we are like homicide detectives, chalking a white outline around the space
where Weldon Kees used to be" (76).

To pursue the analogy a bit further, Lane tells us that rumors of Kees's
sightings have been occurring for years, in Mexico and in New Orleans.
"These apparitions are impossible to forget, yet what can they add to our
knowledge of a man who seemed, even when alive, like a dapper and dissatis-
fied ghost?" (80) So when Rips says "I had spent many years attempting to
follow my father into oblivion... [b]ut I may have been mistaken about him;
I may have been following not him but his well-dressed ghost" (177), we
sense that nothing definitive will come of this pursuit either. Like so much
in *The Face of a Naked Lady,* Rips's remarks about Kees provide us with only

a fragmented, discontinuous story. As Rips imagines inspecting the old men in the hotel, we scrutinize Rips scrutinizing his father, and, like him, wind up more in the dark than ever.

But no matter how baffled he is, Rips won't give up the chase because engaging in the quest is how he defines himself. Early in the book Rips recounts a biblical story his father had told the child about the Witch of Endor. Saul, wishing to consult the dead Samuel about his upcoming battle with the Philistines, goes to the Witch, who retrieves Samuel from the dead so that Saul may speak with him. Years later a woman Rips meets in a New York coffee shop mentions the biblical narrative, and as she begins to tell the tale, Rips hears the voice of his father finishing it. At that moment he knows he will embark on his search for his father, to "retrieve him from the dead" (8) and to find the black woman in the paintings. Such stories, involving a resurrectionary impulse, recur throughout the text.

Rips frequently quotes the philosopher Emmanuel Levinas to justify and define his project, stressing Levinas's obligation to respect the alterity of the Other and not confuse that person with one's own self. In refusing to regard the Other as an extension of ourselves, says Levinas, we acknowledge our necessary apartness as well as the specialness of the other. Rips notes that for Levinas the ethics of seeing and knowing the Other as distinct from ourselves is "a type of optics" (182). Rips, son of a maker of lenses, wants to view his father clearly, however difficult that may be. Levinas significantly terms interactive relations as "face-to-face"; as we face the other person, we recognize the countenance of the Other and the ineluctable mystery emanating from that face, existing beyond our appropriation or even our knowing. Rips might discover the woman belonging to "The Face," but what will he really know about this Other? And will his father's "face" be anything but similarly opaque?

As in any detective story, the missing person is located at the end (Rips thinks, but is not certain, that the black woman of the paintings had been given his name by Williams the detective). But predictably the woman reveals little about the father. She tells Rips she had been stabbed in the face by a lover, and that Norman Rips, fully accepting her scarred countenance, had fitted her with glasses. He then asked if he could paint her, and she agreed. He had painted not her face but "the face below her face and the face below that and the face below that" (191), representing in paint the mystery of being in that face.

What has Rips learned in this curious quest and its even more curious representation? Has he "painted" the face of his father? To be sure he learns things he did not know: that his father grew up in a hotel that also served as a brothel, consorted with gamblers and bootleggers, and wanted to be a writer. The clues to such accounts are straightforward enough. But what do we make of the inclusion of such bizarre findings as the claims that his grandmother was sucked up through a garbage chute during a tornado, a dead man fell through the ceiling of a coffee shop where his father often ate lunch, and Rips witnessed a neighbor having sex with a chicken while whistling "The Surrey with the Fringe on the Top?" Do these happenings help Rips understand his father, or do they rather suggest a world in which nothing is predictable, where anything can happen? And if so, then nothing about the father should surprise his son, though it's not evident there is any discernible pattern to the father's life. Rather than a coherent, well-structured story, Rips gives us a collage of disparate and incongruous incidents, above all a narrative in which it is almost impossible to tell what is real and what is fiction.

Rips's conclusion after all the clues, specific and oblique, are sifted is that his father had no autonomous existence. "I had spent years attempting to find him and had not. He had never wanted me crawling around in the grave of his self. He wanted me to find him elsewhere... in people rising and falling through space, in the woman who was stabbed in the face" (192). The clues, then, are in other people more than in the father himself. But why does Rips think the father wanted his son to discover him "elsewhere"? And could he really be found and discovered at all? Such questions may represent the largest mysteries of the book. Diverting his son from any definitive conclusions enables him, posthumously, to guard the secrets he chose so assiduously to maintain. By writing a work of surrealistic detection, Rips can never penetrate those secrets; yet in a sense, no less mysterious than his father's acts, he has managed to preserve, whether deliberately or inadvertently, something of that father's unfathomable identity.

The authority of the biographer to make sense of his subject simply disappears. It's unclear whether Rips finds this lack a serious disappointment or simply a generic inevitability. I sense from the tone of his work less a matter of regret than of bemusement, even a kind of pleasure in the irony of being a detective unable to detect, a cross-interrogator who faces both the other's and his own defacement. Unlike in the other texts of this chapter, where the identity of the writer is nearly as important as that of the parent, in Rips's work we learn as little about him as he does about his father. Life writing seldom offers greater indefiniteness, a guarantee of its own epistemological undependability.

CHAPTER 3

The Men Who Were Not There

Secrecy is one thing, but secrecy combined with absence is more radical still, at least as far as the children of missing fathers is concerned. There is an abiding melancholy in all four narratives in this chapter, first for the child's missed opportunity to know the parent, then for the awakened reminder of loss as each writer engages in the challenging and frustrating task of describing the indescribable, reconstructing a barely perceptible figure, and confronting evidence that is fragile and questionable. The persistent issue here is how to understand a father who has had only a tangential relation to the writer even though the writer argues for the centrality of that relation to his or her identity.

The initial work is by Paul Auster, who recounts in the first part of his memoir *The Invention of Solitude* a father so remote from the son, even from himself, that Auster can convey only the older man's nothingness. Because Auster fears he may have inherited a similar detachment from world and self, in the second part he strives to capture himself through narratives of other fathers and sons, lacking the confidence of a solid and expressible self except through representations of numerous filial relationships. In a different vein Louise Steinman in *The Souvenir* tells how she found a cache of her father's letters from the Pacific theater in World War II, letters that reveal a father far more exuberant, romantic, and dramatically present than the psychologically emaciated and distant one with whom she grew up. The Japanese flag in which the letters were wrapped becomes the clue to understanding what had happened to him. In the course of her detective work she slowly begins to piece together the missing elements, an undertaking that involves her in imagining aspects of his life she could not have known, but which, in their plausible inventions, bring her closer to him than she had ever been. Anna Cypra Oliver knew almost nothing about her remote father who killed himself when she was a young child. Her mother had forbidden all inquiry about him, and for many years the daughter repressed any desire to learn who he was and her relation to him aside from the mere fact of his biological fatherhood. In *Assembling My Father: A Daughter's Detective Story* she painfully and painstakingly "assembles" bits of evidence—photographs, journal entries, letters, interviews, and visits to places important in his life—as she embarks on an odyssey of discovery that leads inexorably to the site of his suicide. Finally I look at a film, *My Architect,* written and directed by Nathaniel Kahn about his father, the distinguished American architect Louis Kahn. Kahn simultaneously had three families and a child in each; Nathaniel, the youngest, seems to have suffered most from his father's periodic absence, and many years after Kahn's death decided to make a highly personal biographical documentary to understand the forces that drove Kahn to such remoteness. I analyze this work to see how filmic narrative, in ways different from that of written texts, explores the puzzle of another's furtive identity, particularly in relation to the child's own.

These are all compulsive works. The search to discover the father threatens to take over the lives of the writers, at least during the project itself. Oliver especially reminds us that the more remote and unknowable the parent, the greater the need to surrender herself to the search; while she conducts the inquest it *becomes* her life. By the same token these works are obsessed with accumulating evidence, as if material density could substitute for the body of the missing parent. There's a compulsion about acquiring information and meticulously assembling reports, rumors, photographs, tapes, iconic objects, interviews, journals, and the like.

The need to tell stories, even to make up fictions when necessary, helps these writers regain some control over the parent who had in one way or another deserted the child. I use the word *control* because the children are writing the life in the parent's stead, turning the tables by giving their own shape to a past the parents have obliterated into speechlessness and undermining the power the parents' absence had perversely asserted. In retreat these parents abandoned self-representation, leaving the task to the child. While this is not always the case (Louis Kahn certainly expressed himself in his buildings though he never spoke about the relation of his personal life to his creative one), what Nancy Miller claims for memoir writing occasionally holds: "When they...are gone, we can finally make them love us the way we wanted to be loved when they were alive. . . . You repair the old wounds and inflict some of your own—that's the storyteller's prerogative" (*Bequest,* 162).

At once gestures of love and subtle forms of revenge, these narratives allow the writer to reassert a self that might have been diminished or damaged by the parental absence. Oliver's mother alludes to the Noah trope, warning her daughter of the sin of betrayal for probing and exposing her father's life, but Oliver has her own ideas of betrayal and repudiates any charge of indiscretion by arguing the need to know him if she is to know herself. There's an opposing trope to the one of unseemly peering: resurrecting the dead. If the father deserted me, these children say, I will counter by giving new life to one who had all along retreated, either into obscurity, death-in-life, or familial disengagement. And we should not overlook a writerly pleasure in reaching one's own interpretation of the past and of the parent himself, as the child metaphorically takes the father's place by filling the void of absence with a subjective, even self-interested, portrait. In attempting to account for fathers who were deliberately unaccountable, these writers make tentative gestures toward reimagining the parents' past and thus their own, suggestively emphasizing multigenerational stories as if seeing across time might explain what seemed mysterious. Whether writing revisionist history is a legitimate practice in memoir or belongs rather to fiction is a debatable issue, but we can see the urgency of such writing in the case of children whose fathers were given to relational silence. What might seem like violating distortions may also be read as imperative acts of rehabilitation, posthumous closeness, and memorializing.

I don't want to overlook a sense of barely suppressed rage that runs through these works, sometimes just under the surface. It would be a mistake to regard these stories as representing simply a desire that things turn out well, what William Dean Howells once categorized as America's taste for "a tragedy with a happy ending." On the contrary, despite the pleasures of understanding what had been opaque and of making previously unsuspected connections leading to self-knowledge, these texts spotlight the troubled relation of the fathers' silence to their claims of family love. The writings demand we read between the lines to see exactly where resentment still burns even when reconciliation is the order of the day.

Sleuthing Amidst the Shards of the Past: Tracking Absence in the Austers

What does it mean to have a parent who, even when he or she is there, is not there? How do we describe absence, and what relation do we have to a parent who seems to be without a self, a victim of identity theft where the person is one's own thief?

I want to look at a text that describes what the writer believes is indescribable: a parent who seems to be without personhood, a phenomenon that is not merely intriguing but terrifying, in part because the son fears he may be no different from the invisible senior figure. If he has inherited a similar remoteness, tendency to secrecy, and insubstantiality, how can he understand let alone write about a man who appears to be beyond comprehension?

In Paul Auster's *The Invention of Solitude* (1982) his father Samuel, a landlord who owned buildings in Jersey City, does not merely *have* a secret, he *is* a secret. Auster attempts not only to uncover and describe specific secrets harbored by his father but to understand a man whose very existence was inscrutable, a kind of cipher or (dis)embodied mystery. In Auster's eyes his father was a man so transparent you could see through him, for Samuel Auster was a radical absence. Since the father himself appears to make no distinction between inner and outer life, Auster can portray only the mysterious surface, grappling with the problem of representing a man who was not there, a man without qualities.

The Invention of Solitude shows the young man sleuthing among his dead father's property, "ransacking the secret places of a man's mind" (11) to understand the figure who had seemed to lack any discernible relation to the external world, but also to discover his own uncertain identity, especially in relation to the enigmatic figure. "The world was a distant place for [my father], I think, a place he was never to enter, and out there in the distance, among all the shadows that flitted past him. . . . I [was] just one more shadow, appearing and disappearing in a half-lit realm of his consciousness" (24). Auster characterizes his father as an elusive stranger, but cannot help feeling he has inherited a similar disturbing emptiness, a disposition to absence and nonbeing. Auster's autobiographical work is the effort of a family detective both to restore as much as he can of his father's character and come to terms with his own problematical self. He hopes a coherent self-portrait will gradually emerge as he researches his father's life; he learns to "see" his father in order to define and then to represent *himself.*

But Auster fears his project of discovering and uncovering is doomed from the start because there is so little to see and so little to go on. He is determined to write about a man who not only concealed himself but, Auster believes, had nothing inside worth concealing. The difficulty with writing his father's story and hence, more important, his own, stems from a growing belief that there is no subject, no center to get a hold of. The father "did not seem to be a man occupying space, but rather a block of impenetrable space in the form of a man" (7). Auster is seized with "a feeling of moving around in circles, of perpetual back-tracking, of going off in many directions at once. And even if I do manage to make some progress, I am not at all convinced that it will take me to where I think I am going" (32). "For as long as he lived, he was somewhere else, between here and there. But he was never really here. And he was never really there" (19). The spatial swing of those phrases suggests a lack of grounding, or an emptiness poised between poles of tentativeness. Auster raises the questions that torment Conrad's Marlow regarding Kurtz in *Heart of Darkness:* How do you speak of another, especially when he seems to be only a shadow self? And how can you make a narrative of someone who seems to be an essential absence? If the father was a man "who never talked about himself, never seemed to know there was anything he *could* talk about" (22), Auster wonders whether he will be able to write about him. All Auster can do, like Marlow, is "engage in an act of imagination" (66), a reconstruction that may have little if anything to do with truth.

For Auster writing an account of his father's empty life is neither cathartic nor therapeutic: "There has been a wound, and I realize now that it is very deep. Instead of healing me as I thought it would, the act of writing has kept the wound open. . . . Instead of burying my father for me, these words have kept him alive, perhaps more so than ever. . . . [I]f I am to understand anything, I must penetrate this image of darkness. . . . I must enter the absolute darkness of earth" (32–33).

In the first part of Auster's text, "Portrait of an Invisible Man," the father is a "mere tourist of his own life" (9), someone without affect or appetites, a secretive man unable to look at himself and frightened lest anyone else look at him. Early on we learn he has recently died, but because the older man seems to Auster never to have lived, the son feels compelled to search for whatever meager traces the father has left behind. Auster cannot rely on memory since there is nothing substantial to remember about this unmemorable man. As a result the son searches the elder man's effects, conducting an investigation he hopes will convey something of his ephemeral being; but tangible, physical evidence of the father is either absent or insignificant, the few remaining objects mere ghosts of an illegible past. The father's possessions—canceled checks, old birthday cards, a monogrammed toothbrush—are as blank and indecipherable as the man himself:

> What is one to think, for example, of a closetful of clothes waiting silently to be worn again by a man who will not be coming back to open the door? Or the stray packets of condoms strewn among brimming drawers of underwear and socks? Or an electric razor sitting in the bathroom, still clogged with the whisker dust of the last shave? Or a dozen empty tubes of hair coloring hidden away in a leather traveling case? (10)

Auster initially attempts to reconstruct the father in his own imagination, but he worries that in attempting to depict a man who can hardly be remembered he may have generated a fantasy creation. Alarmed at the possibility there is no demonstrable person to discover, Auster turns to things that carry marks of the father he cannot otherwise represent. Auster's "research" into his father's life involves his seeking in material objects the evidence he thinks will reveal the "true" father otherwise inaccessible. To borrow a term from the British psychotherapist Adam Phillips, Auster hopes through his investigation into his father's meager physical traces to "translate a person," "translate" because he cannot reach the "original" who has sought to conceal himself (125). It is not clear that he is defeated due to the mundanity of the effects or because external objects cannot sufficiently express the person identified with them. He doubts that any "translation" from object to being is possible or, to put it another way, that he can get to substance through metonymy.

Auster regards himself as an archeologist examining his dead father's effects as if they were "the cooking utensils of some vanished civilization" (10–11), but they yield nothing to his curiosity. As he notes mordantly, "Even the facts do not always tell the truth" (20). A photo album labeled "This is Our Life: The Austers" contains blank pages. Auster handles a cache of photographs like holy relics, hoping for valuable information, but the man in the images seems scarcely present, so detached and remote is he. And always "the world of facts, the realm of brute particulars," such as a ring removed by the funeral director from his dead father's hand, says nothing beyond its mere materiality (65). Auster seeks to go beyond the inert thingness, but he is baffled by his inability to translate the surface into any coherent depth because the man himself appears to have been only surface. After his father's death, the few objects Auster has inherited seem disconnected from their owner. In his father's house he opens a trunk belonging to his grandmother, hoping for evidentiary treasures. It's as if he were opening a coffin, but the grave robber finds nothing inside, the emptiness merely another black hole of Auster family life.

Nevertheless the posthumous existence of each object gives it a curious iconic power, as if it becomes a story trying to get told. Auster examines evidence like a detective attempting to compose disparate facts and images into a coherent narrative. But there is no coherence, merely an accumulation of fragments: "The size of his hands. Their calluses. Eating the skin off the top of hot chocolate. Tea with lemon" (29). Such inchoate memories are like the items discovered at the father's death: neither fully "retrievable" nor wholly buried. Because Auster fails to achieve a definitive image of the father he will make him up in conjunction with meager memory fragments and the detritus of material remains.

Auster desperately wants to find in the circumstantial evidence some usable truth about his father that his insufficient memory of the older man cannot bring forth. But when, for example, he finds the photo album empty and realizes he cannot rely on that external "evidence" to restore an identity, he must create a story of his father. In the chapter on Auster from *Light Writing and Life Writing: Photography in Autobiography,* Timothy Dow Adams makes the discerning point that Auster "uses the photos he includes not to reinforce memory but to invent memory" (39). Several highly ambiguous photographs Auster includes in the text fail to provide anything by way of clear referentiality, and such "evidence" can hinder the autobiographer's task as much as it abets it. One goal of autobiography may be accuracy, but a text relying on certain kinds of potentially misleading evidence is no more "accurate" than the memory for which the evidence is a stimulus or a substitute. It is this melancholy perception on Auster's part that leads to the necessity of invention.

One of the ostensible pieces of evidence concerning his father's character is a photograph portraying the older man seated at a table. It is a trick photo: there are five images of the same person viewed from five different angles, each taken at a different place around the table. Each person seems to stare at the others, but in fact every gaze is indirect, for each of the Auster-images avoids eye contact with the four other faces. The effect is that of a séance, as if his father were attempting to bring himself back from the dead, precisely what the son attempts narratively but with no greater success. The photograph is identical to one made in 1917 by Marcel Duchamp, where five images of himself at roughly the same age as Auster senior also sit silently around a table, a pipe in each mouth guaranteeing the silence Auster claims characterizes his father's multiportrait.

What strikes me about these self-portraits is that the more the self is replicated the less individual it becomes; multiplication is a form of annihilation, an erasure of any distinctiveness the self might have achieved. This phenomenon is like Auster's project itself: the more he tries to write about the father the less he understands and the more the father recedes from his gaze. No matter how Auster turns the portrait, no matter how many facets and angles he examines, the father's image yields nothing by way of information. The photo becomes an emblem of autobiographical frustration, if not futility, false plenitude as difficult to grasp as the emptiness that it both resembles and mocks. One might assume that the inclusion of a self-portrait in an autobiography—even though not of the author—would help define that person, but the father's multifaceted image has the opposite effect: not of clarification but of obfuscation. The "utter stillness" (31) of the father's pose(s) mimics the "silence" of the son's representation; there is simply nothing to say. The father, who hoarded language lest it give him away, has made it impossible for the son to find *his* language to get to the heart of his father. The father is literally indescribable.

A second photograph included in the text shows another rupture in the family, this time not the rendering but the *rending* of an image. Auster finds a photo of a family group that includes his then one-year-old father, but his grandfather is missing from the portrait. Auster realizes the photo was torn and crudely mended and that his grandfather had literally been cut out of it, just as Auster *père* is necessarily cut out of *his* son's narrative portrait. Several years after the photograph was taken, Auster's grandfather was murdered by his wife, Auster's grandmother, over an alleged affair with another woman; the grandfather had been eliminated representationally as well, like a purged figure airbrushed out of a Soviet photo. We also learn that Auster's father never told him of the murder, but reported three different false versions of his death.

Whenever Auster comes up against a hiatus in truth about the family his own sense of identity becomes fragile. When he discovers the truth about his grandfather's death he cannot write; merely scrutinizing the photograph with the missing man causes him to shake with fear. The family history will not remain merely anecdotal or remote in time but is like "a cave drawing discovered on the inner walls of my own skull" (37). It's hard to know what is more disturbing to Auster, the disappearance and inaccessibility of the past or its return from the repressed realm of secrets he cannot control.

Auster remarks that his grandfather's fingertips remain in the photograph, visible on the head of one of his sons, "as if he were trying to crawl back into the picture from some hole deep in time, as if he had been exiled to another dimension" (34). Auster's project is partly to bring both father and grandfather out of a dark hole of silence and obscurity; and subsequently to bring himself out of the isolating solitude—and his very own invisibility—that the confining room in which he writes the text seems to confer on him.

As Auster confronts the difficulty of writing about family secrets, he senses a parallel difficulty in writing about himself. He asks a troubling question: What if he were, so to speak, infected by a family DNA and even less substantial than his father, inhabiting an even greater void? He must keep on writing lest by his silence he will disappear, as his father and grandfather have threatened to do, forever. Here is the crux of the autobiographical problem for Auster: He wishes to write about his father to uncover truths about himself because he believes that he may have inherited his father's disposition. Filiation cannot be denied. Since neither memory nor evidence can suffice, all he can do is invent. It may be fortuitous that Auster cannot get at the "authentic" father, for now he turns to *himself,* especially to the *idea* of fatherhood.

The title of the second part, "The Book of Memory," is somewhat misleading, implying that Auster has recovered the memory of his father. But the "memory" in the title is not really of his father nor even of Auster's own past; the word refers to the use others have made of *their* memories. Auster identifies with others who have engaged in similar attempts to rescue their pasts, and only when he identifies with those others and their stories can he move out of the isolation that has characterized his father and may also characterize him, especially in the solitary room in lower Manhattan that symbolizes Auster's lonely writing existence. Being part of others and their memories, having a strong sense of their physical presence, and especially feeling a bond with his own son that his father never felt with him, are ways by which he can begin to cultivate "memory":

> What he experienced...as he sat alone in his room on Varick Street was this: the sudden knowledge that came over him that even alone, in the deepest solitude of his room, that he was not alone, or, more precisely, that the moment he began to try to speak of that solitude, he had become more than just himself. Memory, therefore, not simply as the resurrection of one's private past, but an immersion in the past of others. (139)

He learns to read across time, as if experience were a palimpsest. He recounts looking at an old man and trying to imagine what he was like as a child, and at a child and imagining what he might be like as an old person. He reads stories from his childhood in terms of his current obsession, for example regarding *Pinocchio* as the narrative of a fanciful rescue of the father. In a parallel way Auster imagines his own son saving him in some future accounting. In the recitation of such stories and the perception of their patterns as congruent with those from his own life (what Auster refers to as "rhyming" events), a retrieval and understanding of the past takes place. "The Book of Memory" urges—though with more hopefulness than firm conviction—that our connection to others enables us to escape from the solitude to which our absence of significant memory confines us.

"Portrait of an Invisible Man" is written in the first person; "The Book of Memory" in the third. In an interview Auster claims that in the second section he paradoxically had to "objectify" himself to explore his subjectivity. Composed almost two years after the initial section, "The Book of Memory" continues the project begun earlier; namely, to perceive how "one might begin to speak about another person, and whether or not it is even possible"

(*The Art of Hunger* 312, 266). Auster wonders whether one can speak of, let alone know, another, especially one given to secrets. He has an even greater difficulty when applying the same question to himself.

Even as he describes his daily life trying to write in a dingy Manhattan loft, recently divorced and solitary, refusing to see other people, he gradually begins to view himself as part of a larger community. His life writing eventually becomes a kind of collaborative effort and makes him regard the book as a "collective work" (*The Art of Hunger* 309). Feeling empty, he fills the void with countless references to others—painters, writers, friends. Such an impulse doubtless springs from his terror of a vacancy in the self, a terror originating from his futile attempt to write the father's biography and his suspicion he may be equally insubstantial. Though Auster has expressed dismay at critics' characterization of his novels as detective fiction, he has also lauded the detective as an honorable seeker after truth who begins his work with the premise "somebody's missing."

When as primary a figure as the father continues to be so radically missing, it makes sense that Auster creates a closeness to imagined other fathers, filling up his empty relational life with secret filial relations of his own.

"The Book of Memory" comprises thirteen separate "books of memory," each one a variation on the motif of a loss of self and an attempt at recovery. The thematic glue of these set pieces is Auster's fear of fading away. As Auster (called *A*) sits in his room writing the book we are reading, "It is as if he were being forced to watch his own disappearance, as if, by crossing the threshold of this room, he were...taking up residence inside a black hole." The less he feels he is inhabiting his own body, is "not really here, but not anywhere else either," the more he "must dig...deeply into himself"; yet "the more he digs, the less there will be to go on digging into" (77–79). The first hint of escape from this series of spiraling negations emerges from a decision to render his life as a set of glosses upon it via other literary texts, many of which are preoccupied with fathers. Obsessed by the Jonah story and its modern analogue in *Pinocchio,* A imagines that he is both the boy who has rescued his own secretive father from oblivion, as Pinocchio rescued Geppetto, as well as a vulnerable father who will eventually be saved by *his* son Daniel, still a young child. A interprets the *Pinocchio* story as a boy becoming a man in the act of rescuing; so we assume Auster has achieved manhood in the act of narratively reclaiming his father from oblivion, a symbolic reconciliation based on understanding, if not precisely empathy. Father and son become one another, and in a similar act of mirroring A discovers in *his* son's life something of his own restored past. The imaginative act of merging with Daniel occurs throughout the text, each time producing a sensation "as if he were going forward and backward, into the future and into the past" (81–82). Auster's work is filled with discussions of artists such as Rembrandt painting a son, and poets such as Stéphane Mallarmé writing verse about a son. A's identification with these fathers and sons keeps him from despair. As he peoples his room with other figures who represent a search for identity within a confined space (Vermeer's women, Vincent Van Gogh, Anne Frank), he identifies with them and discovers a comforting familiarity in the process, what he calls "an immersion in the past of others" (139), whether characters from history, literature, or the visual arts.

A is haunted by repetition, especially by his notion that everything happens twice, a déjà vu regarded historically. For this reason he, like Michael Skakun in *On Burning Ground,* is fascinated by palimpsests, those manuscript texts where an ancient writing bleeds through a more recent one, much as a face from the past makes its presence felt in a more contemporary one. Where is that father, if not in himself and in his own son? What he calls "nostalgia for the present" (76) is his belief that the present has no significance without its recapitulative function, the gathering of past experience as it is reinscribed in the present. As these dualities permeate the text, Auster gradually recognizes something about his father worth saving, even understanding why in the first place he might have been an unobtrusive, secretive man.

For Auster "The function of [a] story [is] to make a man see the thing before his eyes by holding up another thing to view" (151). And so Auster "sees" his missing father by imagining what fatherhood might be, especially his own, which involves his reminding his son of the experiences the little boy will inevitably forget. Auster will speak across time to Daniel in a way his father failed to speak to *him.* If the father is to "speak" across time, Auster must imagine it, and more sympathetically than he had first thought possible. In a Beckettian meditation about his bedtime storytelling to Daniel, who drifts off and does not hear his father's voice, A notes "the voice . . . goes on. And even as the boy closes his eyes and goes to sleep, his father's voice goes on speaking in the dark" (154). Just as his text attempts to bring his father back into "being," Auster nurtures the image of his own son, completing the family narrative, uncovering all their secrets, shared and not shared.

John D. Barbour, in his chapter "Judging and Not Judging Parents" from John Eakin's edited volume *The Ethics of Life Writing,* perceives Auster coming to a new appreciation of his father by defining solitary life in a way that fosters creativity. Whereas "Auster initially makes a very negative assessment of his father's character," emphasizing the older man's "emotional disconnection" and his own resentment for never having received love from him, upon reflection Auster understands how "family trauma influenced his father's incapacity for intimacy" by armoring him to cope with terrible loss. Then, in the second part of the book, Auster reveals a growing sympathy with the father when he reinterprets solitude not as loveless distance and "soul-destroying isolation" but as a positive factor that nourishes imagination. In this way he identifies with his father and reestablishes a posthumous bond with him, seeing how the father's temperament was shaped by forces beyond his control and how his detachment may be redefined as playing a salutary role in Auster's literary development (75–77). Barbour asserts that Auster ultimately has "a far more nuanced and complex judgment on his father than the book's initial condemnation" (79), the more generous understanding permitting him to regard the father as worth rescuing from oblivion.

Barbour's position seems right to me. I would add only that Auster struggles not to place too much blame on his father, as if reluctant to accuse Samuel Auster for any deficiencies he acknowledges in his own character. Auster's memoir is finally about inheritance, and the temptation must have been great to hold the father accountable in the worst way, emphasizing only disappointment, grief, and writerly impotence. But while I suspect a word like *redemption* might not be accurate or appropriate to describe the impulse behind Auster's memoir, he certainly perceives in all the family resemblances an explanation for his own writing, one that gains from the connection and acknowledges it with understanding, even something like gratitude.

The next paternal figure I treat harbored a secret for over a half-century, a secret that led to a numbing if not to an absence of feeling that opened a gulf between him and his daughter. When she discovers his life-altering secret she sets about to learn the basis for it and eventually to reclaim a connection to him. Louise Steinman's narrative of her revelation and of the project she undertook to repair a relation that had been diminished by a furtive history attempts to turn lingering sorrow into redemption. Here, as in Auster's story, self and subject of inquiry share an imagined history, and again we see how probing secrecy brings both a painful reliving of the past and long-awaited relief. Such narratives are at once acts of felt indiscretion and necessary repairs of relational rupture.

The Letters and the Flag: Recuperating a Lost Father

As we have seen, several writers in this study appear genuinely uncertain whether they are justified in revealing the secrets of a parent, both concerned about the ethical problems of lifting the veil on the actions of their parents and fearful that in so doing they will inevitably distort the truth. In her memoir, *The Souvenir: A Daughter Discovers Her Father's War* (2001), Louise Steinman, my next subject, seems less prone to such internal conflict, largely because she understands that her investigations might bring her closer to the father from whom she felt estranged, a man whose emotions were sealed off by his traumatizing experience in World War II. Nevertheless she broods about how her dead father would react to her project, worrying that an interrogation of the past risks violating even his posthumous privacy.

As she gradually unravels that past, Steinman encounters a father more like the one she *wished* she had known, more deeply emotional, complex, interesting, and passionate than the quiet, subdued man who had so often appeared remote, impersonal, and with little or no inner life. "Until I discovered my father's letters, I hadn't realized that the war had stolen him away before I was born" (86). Steinman's discoveries ultimately bring her closer to her dead father, though her method, as she fully realizes, would have been difficult for Norman Steinman to accept. He might well have experienced his daughter's exploration of his past as a disturbance of the equanimity and silence he had worked so hard to maintain. But her work continually validates the importance of her quest, mitigating any uncertainty let alone guilt she might have experienced along the way.

Soon after Louise Steinman's parents died she came upon a rusted metal ammunition box from World War II in the storage locker of their condominium. Inside were 474 letters her father had written to his young bride from the Pacific theater and a small Japanese flag with Japanese characters inked upon it, "and speckled among them, faint drops of red-brown. Could they be blood?" (27). Steinman eventually learned that the flag was a good luck banner bestowed by his family on a Japanese soldier going off to fight. In one of his letters to his wife, Steinman's father writes that he had in his possession a Japanese flag and was planning to send it to her. Later he speaks of his continuous remorse, embarrassment, and guilt for snagging a souvenir from the war and sending the flag home as booty. He never tells how he procured it: He neither implies that he took the flag from a dead enemy combatant nor that he had killed the soldier, though Steinman darkly speculates about the possession: "I wondered if there might be another explanation why he had such a difficult time forgiving himself for sending the flag home" (72). The flag was put away, locked and forgotten, for almost a half-century until his daughter discovered it along with the letters. Steinman eventually traced the soldier's family to rural Japan and journeyed to their village to return the flag to several elderly, surviving relatives.

"When I occasionally plucked [a letter] out to read, it always had the same effect, detonating a land mine of longing for my father," Steinman writes

(27). Her account narrates how reading through the mass of letters allowed her to grow closer to the man whose stoic and somewhat melancholic life as she remembers it—a life that apparently sought to repress the horrors of battle he experienced—stands in contrast to the figure in the letters, who appears funny, ironic, fearful though courageous in battle, and exuberantly in love with his new bride. As Steinman construes her father, the war had robbed him of all fire; in the process of reading and transcribing the letters she gradually understands "who he was before the war changed him" (33). Only after assembling a new image of her father does she turn her attention to the flag, the souvenir and talisman that binds her to him and that stands as the centerpiece of the book and of her quest.

When she returns the flag to the Japanese family, its circulation across the Pacific becomes emblematic less of her father's war than of the daughter's way of regarding that war in human terms, thereby undermining the father's demonization of Japan that rages through many of his letters. The flag urges Steinman to level the differences between the two soldiers, just as her return to Japan allows her to share a common, "transfamilial" history with the Japanese relatives of the dead soldier (227). The word *souvenir* from the book's title derives from the Latin "to come up again"; appropriately the flag provokes an entire imagined history of the Japanese soldier and her father that has come to her mind, arisen almost unbidden. The book is a record of her reflection and rumination on the letters, as well as a series of fictional dramatizations (Steinman has long been a performance and theater artist), since the epistolary evidence cannot fully answer the questions it raises in Steinman's mind. Returning the flag allows her to fantasize a number of confrontations that open up interpretive possibilities of both her father's past and her relation to him, as well as her father's relation to the Japanese soldier. The very inaccessibility of his secret life drives her need to forge an imaginary account; if a documentary, historical version of his past is unavailable, especially given the subjective nature of the epistolary evidence, she will recreate that past with fictionalized narratives. She even fantasizes an encounter with her father before she was born. The flag has indeed "come up again," risen from its hiding place, a secret sign of shame that turns into a force of connection with her father and allows her to share a relation with the Japanese soldier, a relation that her father presumably never had. More important, the flag closes the gap between her and the man she never really knew, permitting her to join with him in a new way.

The letters and the flag—the latter which Steinman describes as "an incontrovertible fact" (151)—do the work that autobiographical memory often cannot perform and are themselves the subject matter of her life writing.

Steinman not only uncovers the lost father; she gains a new identity through the process of investigation, becoming her father's representative as both the bearer of the flag and as a spokesperson for a larger truth than he was able to comprehend. The book is at once her father's story and her own: a narrative of her father's experiences via the letters, and her own as a kind of emissary for him. She seeks on his behalf a reconciliation with the family of the dead Japanese soldier, and for herself a reconciliation with the man whose withdrawal and suppressed behavior were abiding perplexities in the family.

Much of the drama of the book involves the act of discovery. But unlike conventional detective works where the discovery is usually the penultimate action, here it generates the narrative. She describes in detail how she came upon the box of letters, pried it upon, and unwrapped the mysterious silk flag and the "yellowing airmail envelopes" from 1943–1945. The letters "lay in their inelegant sarcophagus" (27) as if her father and the Japanese soldier symbolically rested together in a common coffin. The box contains stories, and it will be Steinman's task not only to make sense of them but to create her own as a way to understand and perhaps to complete her father's history. Opening the box becomes a countergesture to what she believes her father had done with his life: locked inside himself sorrows he was unwilling to visit. When she returns the flag to the relatives of Yoshio Shimizu, the dead Japanese soldier, his elderly sister opens the box as she too gains her revelation—the astonishing returned gift and the completion of interrupted history.

The epigraph to *The Souvenir* is from Bao Ninh's *The Sorrow of War*: "[War is] a missing, a pain which could send one soaring back into the past." Steinman's text is a return to a past, before her birth, facilitated by letters which were numbered, dated, and bundled almost as if for her eventual inspection. Typically in the works in this study the child begins his or her quest by asking the simplest and most difficult of questions: "What was X like before…?" Steinman's search runs up against her father's inability to be in his past, as if the traumatizing experiences had put too great a space between Norman Steinman's prewar self and the pharmacist seeking a conventional, quiet, and normal life. He felt he had survived because he carried into war an old Russian adage of *"nichevo"*—a term he thought signaled indifference or a "what-the-hell attitude." But the word literally means "nothing," and Steinman implicitly recognizes that term represents the emptiness her father (dis-)embodied upon his return.

After his death but not long before she discovers the treasure trove, Steinman has a haunting Hamlet-like dream in which her father accuses her of ignoring him. The dream suggests she has willed him into urging her to pursue a past about which she knew little or nothing. The dream appears to defuse any guilt she may have felt on opening a potential Pandora's box of secrets, a voyeur of past secrets she has always sought to bring to light and now has license to do.

As she begins her pursuit, Steinman becomes not merely a reader and interpreter of letters, but a researcher whose project involves her in a scholarly study of World War II, interviews with veterans of the Pacific war, reading about the psychological effects of killing in wartime, racist attitudes on both sides in the Pacific war, and travel to battle sites in the Philippines where her father fought. At the same time she is compelled to balance historical research with made-up stories, believing that this composite narrative strategy will account for her father's postwar changes.

Because Steinman insists on learning about and humanizing "the enemy" that her father, given the racism of the war period, had dehumanized, she imaginatively re-creates the dead Japanese soldier in a gesture that she hopes will bring peace to the former combatants; in the process she inserts herself into the narrative as both commentator and creator. In a telling scene, she goes to a writer's colony to transcribe the letters, and in the course of an afternoon's walk stumbles on a World War II bunker; when she makes her way down the steps into a dark claustrophobic underworld, she thinks of her father in fearful Asian jungles. Such moments of identification eventually lead her to imagine she is with her father when, on her trip to the Philippines, she spends difficult days climbing over the same terrain in northern Luzon where he fought against Japanese troops and procured the flag. She hears his voice in her head: "Why in God's name have you come to this place?" (192) She cannot explain, but it's clear she is there to answer the questions about the war and his feelings toward it that she was forbidden to ask as a child. The letters, which offer up intimacies regarding his inner life, "his appetites, longings, fears" as well as a "passionate, unguarded, emotional, poetic" side, express what his daughter had missed and longed for (47).

The central pattern of her book establishes a parallel between the humanity of her father's "enemy" and the newly discovered humanity of her father. When she visits the Yasukuni Shrine in Tokyo, created to honor those who died to defend the emperor, and the adjacent war museum, Steinman is appalled by the exhibits that ignore the context of the Japanese militarism in World War II, honor as gods Tojo and others executed as war criminals, deny Japan's aggression, and are silent about the Nanking Massacre, Bataan Death March, and Korean comfort women. She is drawn not to the exhibits displaying warrior values but to those "that contained the humble personal effects of the war dead. Here was the human face of war: notebooks, binoculars, a small rocking horse, a harmonica, reading glasses, a torn photo of a child...a poem written in human blood on a rice paper scroll...from a soldier who committed ritual suicide" (129–130). Analogously the letters from her father reveal an intimate, personal, familiar quality long absent.

A major portion of Steinman's book tracks the complex process of locating the family of the dead Japanese soldier. She has to jump through bureaucratic hoops, and Japanese government officials render her desire to return the flag extremely difficult, though her "obsession" eventually encourages others' "detective work" (99, 98) to assist her project. The climax of the work is the description of the informal ceremony when Steinman presents the flag to her Japanese hosts in the small village from which Yoshio Shimizu left for war. His aged sister's opening the box and drawing out the flag echoes and mirrors the scene where Steinman herself had discovered the ritual object in the ammo box. To her relief the flag is "now in their possession—home where it belonged" (157). In a parallel way she has returned her father to his own earlier self, and though he might have been bewildered, even distressed at what he doubtless would have regarded as the project's misplaced idealism, she fantasizes his pleasure at her newfound closeness and understanding. Her gesture of reconciliation plays out both historically and familially. "Together...we are creating a new transfamilial history.... Through a traumatic encounter on a battlefield, our families—Steinman and Shimizu—share a story. Each family will continue to tell it in their own way" (227).

Given his expressed contempt for the Japanese, her father might have disdained Steinman's efforts at reconciliation with his enemy, though she insists that the families now "shared a common history" (154), especially since her action shows how both sides suffered. Steinman's adventure begins when, instead of regarding the owner of the flag as anonymous and ghostly, she is able to affix to the flag a name, a person, a family, and a history, in a fashion analogous to how she now perceives greater depths in the once shadowy paternal figure.

In granting Yoshio Shimizu a unique identity, her memoir functions like Clint Eastwood's film *Letters from Iwo Jima,* where the point of view compels even American audiences' sympathy to the anguish of the Japanese soldiers. In this regard, Steinman's work participates in a cultural moment when such reconciliations seem right and timely, her own corresponding to the larger historical *rapprochement*. Familial bonds here cannot be disengaged from transnational ones. Steinman interviews Japanese veterans, many of whom report they too could never speak about the war; she mentions a collection of Japanese war letters whose editor, like Steinman, says she had never heard *her* father talk of his war experiences, an even more common trait in the Japanese than in her father's contemporaries. Steinman draws telling parallels between the two cultures, helping to set her father's long-harbored secrets in a larger historical context.

It's important to see that Steinman is neither affirming nor condemning her father, but trying to understand him. It is too late for a mutual reconciliation; she is surely not granting him forgiveness for whatever deprivation she experienced in her childhood. She believes forgiveness in her own case is irrelevant, and forgiveness for anything he may have done to the dead soldier is surely not hers to bestow. Rather she makes a good-faith effort to comprehend the influences on him and how he changed under extreme circumstances, demonstrating not merely empathy for his trauma but a sympathetic imagination as she visualizes several hypothetical encounters.

Steinman expresses a desire to eradicate secrets, especially those of silence. Granted the issues are immensely different, nevertheless the official Japanese policy of obfuscation about the past parallels her father's reluctance to speak about *his* own past; and Steinman, in a way that attempts to respect yet to uncover that past, declares herself as one who cannot live in the unknown. If her father protected his core identity by guarding against others "coming too near, learning too much, observing too closely" (Bok, *Secrets,* 13), Steinman probes that identity to lend him a greater fullness and to make sense of her own perplexed childhood. Just as she does not regard her father's silence as deceptive or concealing shameful practices, so her decision not to protect his posthumous privacy is undertaken with no desire to solve an enigma for the sheer pleasure of the solving, let alone to question his integrity. Not revenge but self-understanding and the rehabilitation of the father and of their relation drive this narrative.

Her father's silence about the provenance of the flag suggests his reluctance to remember wartime violence, let alone to tell its stories. But Steinman is a surrogate memorialist. She asserts that her father "wanted to never forget and he needed to never remember" (171). Such ambiguity is typical of these autobiographical texts: The parent's memory is vivid but repressed, and the child's imperative is to uncover what could not be expressed in order to acknowledge the sources of puzzlement and pain and to establish the child's abilities as storyteller. As a result of the flag's return to its home, the Shimizu family begins to tell its own stories—of the young boy whose siblings, now in their eighties, remember and memorialize him. Storytelling in her memoir is a way to bear witness to mutual suffering and grief and a gateway to forgiveness and reunion. Steinman takes on the very burden of ancestor-honoring she perceives in the Japanese families whose history she now shares.

Storytelling becomes her way of exposing secrets; in this case speculating how the flag came into her father's hands. There are fairly mundane versions of how it could have happened: Steinman imagines her father retrieving a flag left behind on the battlefield or glimpsing it inside the helmet of a dead soldier. But she fantasizes a more astonishing scenario, one she imagines perhaps to overcome her fear he had killed the soldier and taken the flag as booty. The imagined scenario conveys her role as maker of the narrative. It is an admittedly fantastic vision, but makes perfect sense thematically. She learns from a letter that her Jewish father was excused from battle to celebrate Passover. But Steinman takes over the story, and breathes an imaginary life into it. She proposes that on his way to the base for the Seder her father left his jeep to urinate by the road. From the bushes a ragged soldier emerges: Yoshio Shimizu. He is flushed out, seized, bound, and taken to the base by her father and a fellow soldier. While the Seder is in progress, her father arrives with the dazed prisoner who is seated at the table, given food and wine, and treated as the honored stranger, which the Seder commands celebrating Jews to do. At the conclusion of the supper, as Shimizu is led away, in gratitude he gives Norman Steinman his flag.

Steinman has taken control of the narrative (her invented story is introduced with such phrases as "I mentally prepared a table," "I constructed," "What if it happened, say, like this…?"), but her narration complements, not supplants, her father's story (75). His letters and her imagination work together, not unlike mother's and daughter's complementary talk stories in Maxine Hong Kingston's *Woman Warrior.* Steinman has told me that she sometimes refers to the book as "a posthumous collaboration with my father," adding, "that's when I feel the narrative is most successful" (e-mail correspondence, July 2007). And so, in Steinman's mind, father and daughter achieve reconciliation. Reconciliation is one of the thematic centers of the Seder, which involves welcoming a stranger who is taken in as a guest. Understanding the Egyptian suffering consequent upon the Jews achieving freedom is crucial, since the celebration of freedom must be tempered by the necessity to remember the other's affliction (in this equation the Americans are the Jews, the Japanese the Egyptians). Steinman's richly conceived imagination resists unilateral perspectives, and in rewriting the story of her father's wartime Seder she enacts its spirit and amplifies his understanding.

Steinman revises her father's past to meet her own needs in the present—imaginatively "editing" him to affirm a lost relation or, more accurately, a relation she never had. Autobiography for Steinman is a rewriting of the past from a deeply felt revisionist perspective. Because memory alone constitutes an unsatisfactory sense of who her father has been, she reconstructs his identity through both the new evidence and a redemptive fiction.

I want to conclude this section by discussing a lovely scene in Japan that becomes emblematic of Steinman's entire project. After the return of the flag she is taken to Lake Hyoko, seasonal home to five-foot-tall whooper swans which, early in the twentieth century, stopped coming due to hunting and pollution of the environment. By midcentury they began suddenly to return, and were protected by a dedicated and revered citizen called the Swan Uncle, whom Steinman met. Like the migrating swans, Steinman returns in winter (three years later) to the lake region. One of the Shimizu family, unaware of Steinman's intention to revisit, dreams of her, much as her father appeared in his daughter's dream just before the momentous discovery. At the lake Steinman watches as the graceful birds arc overhead, and in a reverie imagines the boy and youth whose flag has been so crucial to her revision of her father's image and to the narrative. In an invented scene Steinman portrays the youth anxious to fight for Japan, inspired as she envisions it by his sighting a squadron of Youth Air Soldiers flying over and tipping their wings to the village. Yoshio Shimizu went to war and died before the swans came back to Lake Hyoko, and in Steinman's fancied scenario the planes clearly stand in for them.

This paradigmatic scene corresponds to her imagining her father's war, but this time she no longer requires his letters to spur her vision, only her own creative power. The book ends not with her father but with her invention of the young Japanese boy, as if that imaginative act stakes her claim to right and to write the story of her father's war. The vision that allows her to fantasize others' lives enacts the multiple returns narrated in the memoir: Steinman and her father to one another, Yoshio Shimizu (through the flag that embodies him) to his home, and the swans to Lake Hyoko, and herself to a previously unknown family. And in sending Yoshio Shimizu off again, she seems to be giving him a chance of returning alive, an alternate scenario. The book begins: "In January 1944 when my father crossed the Pacific for the first time, he did not know where he was going" (1). That destination was a secret as, eventually, was his war and the origins of his damaged self. Steinman did not, for the longest time, know where she was going either, but at the conclusion she comes "home" to the most unlikely of places and in the most unpredictable of ways.

In the next section we will see once again how paternal absence has profoundly affected the writer, both in her growing up and in her painful effort as an adult to account for her father's nonpresence in her life. The emptiness—a kind of paternal blank space—produced a vacuum in the father's daughter, which she initially filled in ways that misshaped her. But for Anna Cypra Oliver, just as for Louise Steinman, autobiography becomes an act of justifiable self-renewal.

Speaking Him into the World:
A Daughter Reenters Her Father's History

Perhaps the most dramatic absence of a parent occurs in Anna Cypra Oliver's narrative *Assembling My Father: A Daughter's Detective Story* (2004). When she was five and he thirty-five, her father, Lewis Weinberger, for many years divorced from her mother, shot himself in a desolate cabin in rural New Mexico. Years later, in her early thirties, married and living in Minnesota, Oliver felt a sudden, overwhelming desire to learn not just the reasons for her father's suicide but his life story: his family, his work, the cause of her parents' estrangement. But most of all, realizing that his identity had been kept hidden from her, she sought to discover her connection to the man who had become a tabooed secret, a figure barely mentioned by her mother and someone Oliver had been told was utterly irrelevant to her life.

Oliver's parents were both Jews from New York. Her maternal grandparents were intellectuals, left-wing activists, and bohemians; her paternal grandparents comparatively conventional business people. Her father was trained as an architect, and after graduating from college and marrying he moved with his bride Terry to Florida, where Weinberger helped design houses for his father's real estate business. It became apparent to Terry that she was more adventurous than her husband, and though they eventually lived in a cabin in New Mexico and immersed themselves in the late 1960s counterculture, her restlessness continued; after the birth of their two children they agreed to separate. Terry and the children joined a commune near Taos and after a year in Colorado returned to New Mexico. Meanwhile she had a long relationship with an abusive man, and a second marriage to a violent, authoritarian alcoholic. During this time Terry turned to Christian fundamentalism, repudiating her parents, raising Anna and Anna's older brother Peter in a Pentecostal church, and censoring any film, book, and idea outside the orthodoxy of their sect. After Weinberger's suicide she refused to speak his name, repressing any mention and virtually all memory of him. It is this absence—definitive and absolute—that drives his daughter to reconstitute him.

Before his suicide Weinberger had become deeply involved with drugs, first using, then smuggling, narcotics from Mexico. As his life began to disintegrate, he feared he had wasted his talent, ignored his children, and discarded photos from his past as if he were destroying "evidence...that any of us ever knew each other" (301). He seldom saw his children, preferring to live a virtually isolated life. He grew fearful the FBI was on his trail and became increasingly lonely, paranoid, and depressed. His journals from this time portray someone unsure of his identity, and the entries leading to his suicide become increasingly fragmentary and incoherent. Since her father's life and death were almost total secrets to Anna, all this, of course, was unknown to her until she began to reconstruct his story.

Perhaps because a number of friends who had known Lewis Weinberger kept telling his daughter how much she looked like him, Oliver continually employs physical, even visceral metaphors to suggest the palpable urgency of the task of restoration she sets herself: "And so, skin pasted to muscle wrapped around bone, joint slipped into joint, I reconstruct him" (n.p.). Each verb—*pasted, wrapped,* and *slipped*—suggests a strategy for writing his story, a way to attach newly discovered images and facts about her deceased father to her own dormant but slowly awakening traits that reflect the father in her. As she discovers truths about him she never knew, especially his intellectual curiosity, openness to new ideas, and creative talent as architect and artist, she "wraps" the account of her own budding desires for expansiveness to a narrative of how she learns about and has inherited those qualities. And as we will see, she "slips" into his identity, "pastes" herself onto the father she gradually brings out of obscurity. "I would feel the thrill of a [physical] connection that was explicitly, exclusively, between him and me. The way I cocked my eyebrow..."(9). "My father...suddenly 'bodies up' on me" (65). When many years after his death she procures a chest her father made, "I think...of artifacts, the evidence of hands on wood. My father is in the perfectly fitted lid of the box he made for his camera....He is in the chest....He is in the sound of his name spoken out loud" (57). Oliver strives to represent her father in the face of the erasure her mother had tried for years to achieve. Given Terry's refusal to transmit to her daughter anything connected to the father, the acts of researching and "assembling" an absence and an enigma, and of "[speaking] my father into the world" (13), make for a complex and difficult undertaking. Such speaking, both to expose her father's secret life and to define her connection to him in genetic terms—bodily and intellectual—constitutes the burden of her memoir.

Early in the narrative Oliver quotes a Robert Frost poem, "The Sound of Trees," which she interprets as the poet's striking a difficult balance between a desire to stay at home and a longing to abandon the familiar. Oliver's decision to take up the investigation of her father's troubled history involves her in a typically Frostian paradox: launching herself out into the world will take Oliver home—back to her geographical origins and increasingly back to the missing father. The act of entering her own past is a transgression against her mother's strictures of silence and erasure that allows her to trace qualities she comes to embody and which were her father's own fiercest traits: intellectuality, rationality, and a passion for art and aesthetics. As she slowly distances herself from her restricted childhood, she yearns to return to the man whose death ultimately led to her narrowed life. He had been a dark secret at her heart, and her yearning to branch out had been a secret even from herself. To change she must return to a past she scarcely knew and "reenter memory at the place where my mother veered off" (56).

Oliver's transformation from staunch fundamentalist to secular skeptic occurs when she experiences a conflict between her earlier freewheeling hippie life and the restraints of her severe Christianity. During the transition, she becomes curious about her father in part because curiosity itself was forbidden but also, though she cannot know it at the time, because his inquiring personality comes to symbolize for her the world of books, mind, and imagination she had been taught to disdain. In addition she grows interested in learning about and reconnecting to her Jewish identity and family.

Not surprisingly, the trope that appears in several other memoirs of secret fathers comes up here. When Terry decides not to tell her inquiring daughter any more of the past, especially not of Oliver's father, she invokes the familiar story of Noah's son Ham gazing illicitly on the nakedness of his father, cursed by both Noah and by God (66–67). The lesson is clear, but of course it has the opposite effect: the more she feels her father as a void in her life the more fierce is her desire to gaze on him, as if the recovery—through whatever means available—will restore a part of her past. The urgency overcomes any guilt implied by the biblical allusion. Oliver's is no idle or salacious curiosity; in re-creating her father she tries to compensate for all she has missed and to repossess the man whose death betrayed her childhood love for him. Her act may feel somewhat illicit to her, but she will not let that disrupt her investigation. Though she does not fully deny a residual bitterness toward her father and displays a frequent self-consciousness about her self-appointed task, she seems to believe her father would have approved her uncovering his secret life, and this belief serves both to justify her search and help her achieve a posthumous closeness.

Assembling My Father oscillates between the story of her ongoing search, the more distant past of her childhood, her parents' marriage and family history, and her own troubled first marriage. The text alternates between the discoveries she makes and the process of that discovering. The story of the story is never just a series of engaging anecdotes but a narrative that seeks to justify her endeavor, since she sets herself the task to achieve and validate a new identity, one predicated on that of her father, especially on their mutual commitment to inquiry and questioning. The narrative weave shows how her current life is ineluctably conjoined with her father's, a truth she discovers by degrees as she constructs the portrait in all its complexity.

The thought of what has been missing bedevils Oliver at every turn. "I think of myself, growing up with a hole in the center of my being. For most of my life, I experienced my father as a void" (335). When she returns to her father's college, she photographs vacant classrooms in an attempt to "portray absence" (150). When she looks at photographs of the Florida house her parents lived in, she is struck by the absence of people from the rooms and feels rage for his disappearance: "For the first time, this under-the-skin truth registers in my mind: My father abandoned me. My father left me behind" (203). The problem of portraying absence is fundamental to Oliver's text.

As she delves into the secrecy, the problems she encounters are how to gain access to evidence, how to be sure of its accuracy, and how to evaluate its relevance to her. We watch her struggling with the uncertainty of what she discovers, as the authority and conclusive belief system of her upbringing gives way and solid faith dissolves into uncertainty. I am speaking not only of the numerous, often conflicting, hypotheses regarding his suicide but of Weinberger's entire life history as it comes to her incrementally and sometimes contradictorily. In contradistinction to her earlier belief in absolute and unyielding principle, she learns to accept unfamiliar ambiguity, perhaps even to revel in the opportunity it allows her to interpret for herself, especially given the many disparate readings of both his and her own motives.

Her narrative results from a determination to shape coherence out of fragments. At times the father is a puzzle defying intelligibility, but that realization only intensifies her effort. She deciphers taped interviews, tracks down relevant people, and structures otherwise rambling accounts; we sense her strain as she strives to "reassemble" her father and put "Humpty Dumpty back together again" (107).

How to go about understanding what often seems incomprehensible? First she seeks grounding in material reality. The memoir is punctuated by sections containing lists of her father's possessions, with such labels as "Remains: An Inventory of My Father," "Items Missing From the Inventory of My Father," and "Remains: An Updated Inventory of My Father." Common to memoirs of secret lives, Oliver procures a trunk of her father's artifacts, though for months she hesitates to take ownership, presumably for fear of what she will find (or what she will *not* find) and how it might change her life. "The photographs [in the trunk] were at once too much and too little to absorb. I went on with my life" (23). She cannot know at that moment that discovering unexpected truths, confronting and absorbing what she discovers, and assembling the findings into a narrative will *become* her life.

She initially believes that only tangible objects will "speak" the father to her, whereas stories and anecdotes gained through interviews appear too subjective. The trunk contains numerous items that she interprets in light of her own needs, such as family photographs, his journals, magazine articles about him, several of his books, letters, and a tape of his voice. The lists of his artifacts reappear in the text like a tape loop played over and over, and reveal how she will endow these metonymic signs of her father with significance.

Though Oliver puts little credence in a curious tale told to her by close friends of her father, who claim that on the evening Weinberger killed himself the latter's "fluttering heart" visited them hours before they learned of his death and that he appeared in their bedroom as if trying to come back from the dead, Oliver takes over the story and makes it her own. She assumes the role of appointed summoner of her father's spirit by facilitating his desire to return expressed in the tale.

While others remember Weinberger and contribute their memories to his daughter, having no memories of her own gives her carte blanche to re-create him from those shreds of recall. This is paradoxically both a limitation and a freedom, since her inability to rely on memory releases her from an obligation to accuracy, but it creates a different sort of problem: She feels at the mercy of others' memories, and the "father" she reconstructs ultimately depends on *their* images and *their* words. "My 'you' is nothing but a plagiarism. That's all you are. A ripped-off citation. A soup of quotations." At the same time "You resemble whomever I say you resemble" (134). Though she feels uncomfortably beholden to others, she nevertheless seeks out those who had known him, hungry for information even if the father who emerges is a pastiche of imagination, rumor, suspicion, and others' memories that may be more self-interested than accurate.

Oliver reminds us that when we try to solve a secret identity from our familial past, especially when the missing figure is "beyond verification," we are compelled to "make him up." "Outside my head my father no longer exists" (212). But rather than being a liability, this necessity provides an opportunity for the imagination to work and to give her the father she needs, even the past she requires. And so she emphasizes the autobiographical trope of performance, making explicit the self-conscious act of creating a story and a new identity.

During the course of her investigation she reestablishes a connection with her father's sister, who in turn puts her in contact with several of her father's high school friends who remained in touch with him nearly until his death. They supply her with stories about Weinberger that arouse her interest in his life, so different from the one she experienced as a child and young woman. A long e-mail exchange ensues with one of them, Stephan Klein, and though she's grateful to him for taking the time to unearth facts and convey them to her, she fears he has inadvertently appropriated her father, preventing him from belonging only to her. She knows she's being overzealous in her desire to have her father all to herself, as if, given his long absence from her life, only total and exclusive possession could fill the gaping void. The more she learns from Klein the more palpable and poignant is her father's absence. We sense her ambivalence about the search, though any reluctance she shows is very different from her mother's, and centers on her realization he is no longer "out there in the actual world to find... [but] is here, in the center of me" (109).

As the search continues, Klein's reports take on a greater importance, and his stories of her father's life prompt Anna to further research, including trips to venues of his past: college at Rensselaer Polytechnic Institute, a home he helped design in Florida, and the New Mexico house where he died. Klein's correspondence with her, initially focusing on the investigation, eventually becomes more personal, and while he begins as a conduit for the father's identity, he comes to represent qualities her father embodied and which she has missed in the course of her life. Like her father Klein grew up in Queens, is Jewish, an architect, and is passionately engaged in the world. As the search continued, she and Klein were each about to leave an unhappy marriage, and in 2003, after increasingly frequent and intimate conversations, they decided to marry. Oliver acknowledges her awareness of the Oedipal implications of the relationship, but is careful to assert Klein's difference from Weinberger and his uniqueness. Still, I want to point out the obvious irony of her radical reappropriation of her own family history. When she quotes from Auden's poem about Yeats, "The words of a dead man/ Are modified in the guts of the living," we can read those lines as ironically applying not only to her incorporation of others' *words* about Weinberger into her portrait of him, but to the curious sense in which her new marriage allies her to her father's surrogate. It is no surprise that she reports of her first meeting with Klein a feeling that "I am meeting my father, if only by proxy, from the grave" (72). Reencountering and then reconstituting the past is a more dangerous and complex project than she could have imagined.

One way she justifies her increasing feelings of love for Klein in defiance of tendentious Freudian objections is to recall Roland Barthes's claim that symbols are always empty signifiers, never fixed or codified but free for interpretation. Klein can stand for a "father figure" or for a person in his own right who fills a gap in her psyche and experience. Their e-mail correspondence, in its play with ideas, substitutes for the restricted orthodoxy of her childhood and adolescence, a time for her when symbols had absolute and inviolable meaning.

Referring to Dashiell Hammett's Continental Op, Klein speaks of the detective's inevitable fiction-making activity; this is precisely Oliver's project and the source of the work's subtitle, *A Daughter's Detective Story.* The more secretive the father's life appears to have been, especially in his later years, the more she needs to create (or re-create) him in her mind. Though she occasionally claims to be working with concrete materials ("I'm building my father...one scrap of evidence at a time" [153]), her own subjectivity is the primary stuff of restoration.

The personal nature of her approach is marked by the frequency with which she addresses her father directly, even entering into imaginary dialogue with him—questioning, berating, praising, explaining. In one of these appeals she asks him questions about his artistic point of view and pleads with him to inspire her, so the "you in me [might] come forward and speak" (209). Such moments imply an impulse to merge with him, so impassioned is the need to get him back. It is no mystery why she often in the text addresses him in the second person; to call him "you" is to invoke him and implore him to come forth, as if the rhetoric itself had a restorative function.

She had once thought of becoming an architect in order to gain access to her father's mind, and in the course of her quest architecture becomes the metaphor for her act of reconstruction. Houses figure prominently in the work. When she expresses to Klein her fascination with the Florida home where she lived with her parents as an infant, he suggests that she think of the house as an "environmental autobiography" and allow her father to serve as her guide to the various rooms, revealing all that was previously hidden. But the ghostly father will not cooperate in this scheme; she tries to summon him into her imaginary scenario but, typically, he remains absent, and Oliver is forced to become her own guide, once again taking his place in the narrative and doing the work herself. We will see how the suicide house becomes a sacred site, as she again attempts to conjure forth her father in "a site of memory where no memory exists" (233).

She refers to Gaston Bachelard, the French phenomenologist, who invokes Jung's analogy of the historical layers of a building to the structure of human consciousness. Oliver (195) quotes Bachelard from *The Poetics of Space,* who declares, "Our soul is an abode." Oliver is drawn to such analogy-making: she attempts to re-create Weinberger's life, as the title has it "assembling my father" as if she were constructing a building, creating an image composed of "one pebble I can mortar to another, and say 'There'" (152). She seems to be in loving competition with her father, and it is no exaggeration to argue that while Weinberger failed as an architect and left his ambition unfulfilled, his daughter replaces him in the act of assembling a past and constructing the edifice of his identity. She is quite explicit about this: "I am trying to build a house, if only of language and memory, in which my father can live in peace" (338). Oliver discovered how her father's professional life began to fall apart in Florida when he gradually surrendered his passion and artistic vision, designing row houses for subdivisions; I suspect she regards her memorial project and the literary structure she designs as restoring both the integrity he had abandoned and the coherent self he had fragmented.

By the end of her search she is inundated with information: artifacts sent by friends and family, journals, photographs, home movies, taped recordings of his voice, and letters, to mention only a selection of relevant items. Add the countless stories, often contradictory, and she has a daunting task. Much of this material presents contradictory views of her father, and to Oliver's credit she never rationalizes the plethora of images into a single unitary whole; this is why the text is a collage of styles and perspectives, incorporating drawings, architectural plans, photographs, newspaper clippings, and journal entries, and veering between straightforward narratives of her past, ruminations on her father's past as she imagines it, even telephone conversations and reconstructed dialogues with witnesses of Weinberger's life. The fragmentary narration corresponds to the unresolved image of her father, who alternately appears dazzlingly intelligent, ambitious, charming, sweet, but also depressed, paranoid, delusional, and drug-addled—a narcotics-trafficker, a sell-out and self-admitted failure, and, of course, in the most ultimate way self-destructive. In his journals, which in later years have the incoherence of a man in the midst of a crackup, he refers to his "multi-layered reality." And his daughter concurs: "My father is like a man patched together from . . . spare body parts" (304). Like the friend's image of him as a fluttering heart, Weinberger flits in and out of definitiveness; he "danc[es] away from me . . . He shifts, he moves, he feints" (303). Anna knows that any truth is hers alone, and yet she relishes the contradictions, happy to escape a strict system of closed ideas and doctrines.

She is often tempted to abandon the search, not because she worries it is an unethical intrusion into a private realm (it is her mother, not she, who invokes the "Noah" story of illicit looking), nor because the task is too cumbersome, but because, as details pile up, she fears the search will go on forever, an obsession that has already taken over her life. Still, despite not being prepared for the shocking details of the denouement, she presses on. The search winds down to a place and a scene: the suicide room, a report from a friend who came to the father's house after the shooting and cleaned up the mess, and a specific tree under which the father's ashes were scattered. It will take the vividness of others' memories of the endgame to release her from a fantasy that by the force of her will she can magically hold him back from death, a fantasy that suggests how great an emptiness he has rent in his daughter's life and how desperate she is to engage in an act of more than literary restoration.

Here then is the crux of the problem for Oliver's reclamation: because the quest and the story drive toward the culminating event of the suicide, she knows she is inexorably moving to a confrontation with the darkest and most terrible of deeds. It is the one fact of her father's life she has known all along, and the event into which everything she discovers necessarily funnels. The suicide in all its particulars traumatizes Oliver in the learning and in the narrating, and she instinctively recoils from it, as if there were something unseemly in her uncovering and transcribing the details, her prying into what she perceives as a private and shameful act. Yet she simply cannot resist a *frisson* of the illicit. I am not attributing a voyeuristic impulse to the culmination of her search, but we sense something like that incitement as she completes a story her mother has resisted transmitting. Her narrative functions as an act of subversion *and* of renewed closeness.

Her attempt to discover truths, however tentative, becomes part of her own self-making, and this is ultimately the goal of the project. Here too there is resentment (for having been molded into rigidity) and reconciliation (as she acknowledges that her own desire to transform her life is not dissimilar to her mother's impulse). This complication doubtless allows her to regard herself as fully her parents' child. But most of all her curiosity about the secrets of the past aligns her with the father, especially in their passion for complex ways of seeing the world. On a similar note, we might conjecture that Oliver comes to love her father, despite his abandonment of her, precisely because he is already inside her, or at least she imagines having absorbed his sensibility. This is why Oliver's text could just as well be entitled *Assembling My Self.* One of the surprising revelations of the work is that the resurrection of and renewed love for the father turns out to be ineluctably conjoined with, not indistinguishable from, self-love. As Adam Phillips has said, "People are loved . . . because they are not other, that is, outside and alien" (*Intimacies,* 101).

In so many of these stories of deprivation and damaged selves, the children urgently seek to rewrite history. But it is never clear whether they actually think that by unveiling all the secrets and establishing the motives for the parental absence they will realize or even approach that goal. Perhaps this is why we occasionally sense as much unresolved melancholia as worked-through mourning.

In the next work, a remarkable film by Nathaniel Kahn, the questing son attempts not only to gain information about his famous father, the great American architect Louis Kahn, who was continually missing from his childhood, but also to reestablish a connection with him thirty years after his death. Nathaniel Kahn is bitter about his loss and the fact that his father maintained three families with children in each of them, but seems willing to justify the absence in the name of the architect's ferocious creativity that necessitated distancing himself from conventional familial responsibilities. In the film we hear a refrain, really a *cri de coeur,* uttered by the son to his long-deceased father: "What *were* you thinking, Lou?" We can take that interrogation as both a straightforward question about intent (would Kahn leave his wife to take up residence with Nathaniel's mother?), and a lamentation characteristic to all the broken relations of child and parent. Indeed, we must not overlook such ongoing sorrow and regret even as these writers attempt to understand, rationalize, and even validate the parental behavior.

A Father Gone Missing: Documenting a Broken Bond

All of the works in this study, with one exception, are literary texts. In this chapter I turn to a documentary film, *My Architect* (2003), written, narrated on- and off camera, and directed by Nathaniel Kahn, the illegitimate son of the subject of the film. Louis Kahn designed such important buildings as the Jonas Salk Institute in La Jolla, the Phillips Exeter Academy Library in Exeter, New Hampshire, the Kimbell Art Museum in Fort Worth, the Yale Center for British Art in New Haven, and the National Assembly Building in Dhaka, Bangladesh. Married for over forty years, Kahn had a daughter with his wife Esther, and a second family with Anne Tyng, a young architect in his office, that produced a second daughter; when that relationship ended he began another with Harriet Pattison, a landscape architect, and that relation produced Nathaniel, born when Kahn was sixty-one. Wife and both mistresses lived in Philadelphia, a scant few miles from one another; eventually all of them knew about the others. Nathaniel was eleven when his father died in 1974, stricken by a heart attack in New York's Penn Station. He had just returned from Dhaka, where he was designing the National Assembly Building. His body lay in a morgue, unidentified and unclaimed for three days. Almost thirty years after that death, Nathaniel decided to learn more about the mysterious father whom he had seen only occasionally, and whose periodic disappearances, public denial of his son, and inability to say why he was so marginal in the boy's life had never ceased to torment Nathaniel.

Kahn would occasionally show up for dinner at the home of Nathaniel and his mother, but would always leave the same evening, having delighted Nathaniel and then frustrated him by the shortness and infrequency of his visits. His mother would drive Kahn to downtown Philadelphia, "he'd walk down the block and disappear into his house—his wife's house." Nathaniel's mother was convinced that Kahn would soon leave his wife to marry her, that in fact he was planning to do so when he died. In the face of lingering uncertainties about who his father really was his son sets out to capture the enigma on film.

The documentary revolves in part among Nathaniel's interviews, including those with several famous architects—Frank Gehry, I. M. Pei, and Philip Johnson; with men who worked with Kahn on his buildings; with critics who discuss his life and architectural principles; with people involved in his professional life, including a project manager at the Salk Institute, his secretary, and the former head of the Philadelphia City Planning Commission who successfully opposed Kahn's utopian plan for rebuilding that city's downtown; with Nathaniel's half-sisters; with Kahn's first mistress; and finally with Nathaniel's mother. (Kahn's wife died before the film was shot; we see her only in a tape of an interview conducted by an architectural scholar.) In addition to the interviews, there are conversations with the taxi drivers who took Kahn to his assignations and with Bangladeshi workers who remember him fondly.

There is stunning photography of Kahn's buildings, as well as a good deal of archival footage; we frequently see Kahn strolling the streets of Philadelphia, working in his simple office, giving a Master class, and inspecting building sites under construction. There are stills of Kahn's own boyhood and young manhood, others with him and Nathaniel as a child together. The film does not progress chronologically, but is structured around Nathaniel's journey through Kahn's life, as he searches for answers to the question "Who was Louis Kahn?" Nathaniel is driven to his inquiry largely because he cannot make sense of the man who played so minimal a role in his life and yet so powerfully left his mark on him.

The film veers between Nathaniel's dismay, even resentment, that Kahn could not devote himself more fully to him and his mother, and an understanding that, as another architect claims, creative men like Kahn give their love less to their families than to their work. The film is sandwiched between two scenes that express Nathaniel's emotional polarities. The first shows him looking in *The New York Times* for his father's thirty-year-old obituary, written by the architectural critic of *The New Yorker,* Paul Goldberger. Nathaniel scrolls through a microfiche machine, searching across the past and hoping that the history reported in the paper will enlighten him. But it delivers only frustration, culminating in the revelation of his own absence from the obituary: Kahn's listed survivors include his wife and daughter by his marriage, but not the other two children. Nathaniel's name has effectively been expunged from the record. The film will attempt to explain and to correct that erasure, and the continual presence of Nathaniel himself, interviewing, walking through Kahn's buildings, and revealing himself to those who knew his father, asserts an identity that, if Kahn did not always and explicitly deny, was unknown to the world as that of his offspring. One of Kahn's clients who knew of Nathaniel's existence informs him in the film that he was asked never to reveal that Kahn had a son. The film that aims to be a portrait of Kahn is at the same time Nathaniel's autobiography, the purpose of which is to announce, validate, and legitimize his identity.

The film's title, *My Architect,* stakes a claim that Kahn was Nathaniel's maker, the architect of his being as much as of the great buildings; at the same time Nathaniel's use of "my" reverses the power relation as he appropriates his father and takes possession *of him.* In the film Kahn becomes the son's creation, the filmmaker declaring his right to authorize this familial relationship and to examine if not to challenge his father's role in it.

As Nathaniel scrolls across the pages of the *Times* we notice his own face reflected on the screen of the machine. Nathaniel's image looks out at us as if to forge a relation with the viewer, both of us investigators of the mystery. As he stares at the newsprint, surveying the incomplete facts, we gaze back at him, scrutinizing the scrutinizer. Nathaniel becomes a spectral presence superimposed on his father's obituary notice. Ironically he regards his father in similar terms: In a print interview Nathaniel says about his film: "We use [my father] a lot like a ghost. He's someone who appears and then is gone. So for quite a while you see little glimpses of him, which was always the way I saw him. In a way, the film was like conjuring him, bringing him back from the dead for two hours" (Pederson, n.p.). Here we have a trope common to these texts— the rescuer who resurrects the father, returning the Lazarus-like figure not just from the dead but also from a palpable, perceived indifference to the child. In the microfiche scene two ghostly figures confront each other across time.

The other scene bracketing the film occurs at the conclusion and functions to redeem Kahn in his son's eyes. Nathaniel is taken across a river in Bangladesh, heading toward the cluster of structures designed by Kahn that houses that nation's government buildings—a massive series of powerful cubes and cylinders that gleam across the water. Having been recently told by an architect in India that Kahn "has not come back as yet but he's there, watching, blessing," Nathaniel imagines his father will be at those buildings in spirit: "If he was anywhere, he'd be here." He feels as he often did as a child, hoping that his father, who was forever leaving soon after his arrival, might reappear; indeed after his father's death young Nathaniel looked for him in crowds, thinking the older man might turn up one day on Philadelphia's streets. In effect Kahn *does* reappear in Dhaka, for the climax of the father's architectural career coincides in the film with the culmination of the son's quest.

FIGURE 1.   Boy gazing at Louis Kahn's capital building, Dhaka, Bangladesh. From *My Architect: A Son's Journey.* A film by Nathaniel Kahn. Copyright © 2003 Louis Kahn Project, Inc. Copyright 2004 New Yorker Films Artwork.

As the camera trains on the monumental Bangladesh capitol buildings, we perceive a little boy standing on a stone walk and staring across the tidal pool at the voluminous mass, seemingly entranced as if he were gazing at "a giant castle across the water." In one of the extra features on the DVD we learn he is a local child who comes everyday to look yearningly at the building. Hypnotized by the structure, he seems to stand in for Nathaniel himself, as if Nathaniel were learning and recreating his father through his own intent gaze upon the work.

Nathaniel's crossing of the waters conveys an almost mythic sense of things, in both the son's journey to discover his father and in the Indian architect's declaration that Bangladeshis regard Kahn as Moses, bringing them into a promised land of democracy with his monumental building. The motif that connects various episodes as well as son with father is the persistent image of water. Kahn crosses the ocean as a small child when in 1906 his family escapes from the Czar Nicholas II's pogroms; the relation of several of Kahn's buildings to water is vital, especially the Salk Institute with the Pacific just beyond and the Bangladeshi National Assembly Building, which seems to float on its tidal pool; Kahn's first structure is a bathhouse; and a boat designed as a floating concert stage figures importantly in Kahn's career and in the son's film. We see Nathaniel rowing across Penobscot Bay to his mother's house in Maine, taking a boat down the Buriganga River on his way to Dhaka, and gazing at a child who in turn gazes across the tidal pool at the Bangladeshi capitol buildings. These scenes point to the motif of a journey in which Nathaniel crosses bodies of water in his quest for the father, seeking to uncover his secrets, to repair the rupture in their relation, and to join with him. The Mosaic reference suggests a mission that involves traversing treacherous waters to the promised land of revelation and reconciliation.

But rather than mythifying his father, Nathaniel's last words in the film assert that in the son's eyes Kahn has become real and understandable, not inexplicable or larger than life. The son acknowledges the man for his gifts of architecture to the world, perceiving a new humanization despite, or even paradoxically because of, Kahn's single-minded devotion. He may not have designed his personal life as carefully as he did his buildings, but Nathaniel appears to accept him, as he perceives for their value the buildings he has long regarded as rivals, competitors for his father's attention and time.

We might even imagine the Bangladeshi boy longing to touch the facade as young Nathaniel used to touch his father's scarred face that, when Kahn was three, had been badly burned by a fire. The project manager of the Salk Institute conjectures that Kahn insisted the surfaces of his buildings be scarred or pitted, as if, in revealing the imperfect nature of the material, he were exposing in a public work an aspect of his private self, that private self which, in terms of his family life, had to remain furtive. Nathaniel ultimately and somewhat begrudgingly acknowledges that Kahn's secret life of multiple families is not simply a clandestine endeavor but an expansion and enlargement of the man, analogous to Kahn's insatiability expressed in the desire to design and construct monumental structures of enormous weight and primitive power. It is as if something in the man would not allow him to be limited and narrowed in any way.

But as is so often the case with these narratives of disappointed children, Nathaniel makes an important compensatory gesture to regain a sense of self, though one less independent of his father than allied with him. In an earlier scene corresponding to the one of the Bangladeshi boy who gazes silently and reverently at the capitol, when we first see the Salk Institute a digitalized image of a child runs through the vast plaza, as if Nathaniel were inserting himself into the structure and his father's creative life. Immediately after, we see Nathaniel himself at age forty, rollerblading alone through the empty space of the plaza, weaving across it as if he were dancing in joyous affirmation of his father's accomplishment and declaring a connection with him. As he skates he seems to take possession of the building, sharing it with his father. There's a freedom and grace in his movements, an artfulness which, in combination with the art of the film he has made, asks to be seen as worthy of his father. But there

FIGURE 2.   Nathaniel Kahn skating on the plaza of Louis Kahn's Salk Institute, La Jolla, California. From *My Architect: A Son's Journey.* A film by Nathaniel Kahn. Copyright © 2003 Louis Kahn Project, Inc. Copyright © 2004 New Yorker Films Artwork.

is another way to interpret this scene: Nathaniel also appears to skate free from his father's control, as if he has become his own person, absent the crushing memory of his father's weighty absence. Such moments constitute an attempt to overcome his initial disillusionment and pain.

Given the personal nature of the film, it was inevitable that it would draw complaints of self-indulgence. Among the critiques in numerous reviews is that Nathaniel inserts himself too publicly into what ought to be a private story shared only with a therapist; that the son's personal grievance exceeds what ought to be an exclusively aesthetic focus on the glorious buildings; and that Nathaniel's emphasis on his personal journey distracts from the more important story of Louis Kahn's life and career. It is true that the film is as much autobiographical as biographical; but these twin generic emphases are inextricably bound together, for Nathaniel cannot know who he is without discovering who the father was. He tracks the private life of the architect and shows how it has influenced his concept of architecture; by the same token the narrator's own personal history is always at the center of his judgments. There is a parallel movement in the film, for as Nathaniel exposes his father's secret to colleagues, clients, and others who knew him, he correspondingly places himself into the story his father told that excluded him. As an instance, when Nathaniel films the Kahn-designed musical barge, part of which opens to form a stage for performances, he discovers that the owner of the boat and its orchestra conductor is the man who had been enjoined to silence about Nathaniel so many years earlier. Here one of the father's creations is integrally connected to the son's enforced anonymity.

As if to assert that he too is capable of art, Nathaniel self-consciously informs us of the process of his filmmaking—the way he arranged those interviews, what he thinks of the subjects, and the difficulties he has carrying out his project. Such moments in the film correspond to a common trope in autobiography, where the writer speaks of the reason why the book needed to be written or of the process of the composition. What Jim Lane, in *The Autobiographical Documentary in America,* calls "the cinematic apparatus" is often in plain sight. The reflexive or self-referential materials—elements of which comprise what hostile critics designated as the narrator/director's egotism—accentuate the autobiographical aspect of the documentary and suggest that Louis Kahn as subject cannot be separated from the filmmaker and his ongoing search to establish an identity. Contrary to any "egotism," Nathaniel's uncertainties about his enterprise and his findings are always evident. He is not an authoritative narrator shaping a definitive view of his father but one plagued by doubts and tentativeness, as unclear about his own subjectivity as he is about Louis Kahn's motives.

The critics' resistance to the film's autobiographical subjectivity probably derives from common assumptions that documentaries ought to focus on public history, that even when revealing the private life of public figures a film's narrator ought not to be as self-interested in the exposure as Nathaniel obviously is. But Lane argues about recent documentaries: "By repositioning the filmmaker at the foreground of the film, the new autobiographical documentary disrupt[s] the detached, objective ideal of direct cinema, which excluded the presence of the filmmaker" (12). He refers to a tension between the "documentary impulse" to record a world "out there" and an "autobiographical impulse" to record a world "in here." *My Architect* deliberately refuses to be in the same category as the "American Masters" television series, a relatively "objective" documentary genre shown on Public Broadcasting stations in America, and one which, had he authored such a work, would have felt to Nathaniel like a made-for-TV film that anyone could do. In addition, critics who claim that Nathaniel has violated documentary conventions do not realize that the film insists on the inability of the central figure to be fully and accurately represented, and that this inability, born from the subject's need to maintain a secret life regarding both behavior and motivation, is part of the frustration that was the motive for Nathaniel's film in the first place. *My Architect* veers between what can be referenced and what can only be imagined, and so it combines traditional documentary with subjective autobiography.

We might ask "Why has Nathaniel shot a film rather than written a memoir?" One obvious answer is that he cannot remember very much, or rather there is not that much *to* remember, and so, in the absence of memory, the only way to represent Kahn is through a visual collage of his work and the effect it has had on Nathaniel's conception of the father as well as on his own self-conception. But it is important to understand that the footage of the buildings does not exist simply to celebrate a style or to represent a set of masterful objects, or even to validate Kahn's historical importance. Rather their inclusion is related to the problem of Kahn's absence from Nathaniel's family and the way the son gradually accepts that the architect's emotional life was embedded in those structures and thus substituted for family.

The film's autobiographical narrator provides a filter through which we view Kahn, not only as a result of Nathaniel's live presence but also more subtly through his arrangement and structuring of the materials. I am thinking here of the archival footage of Kahn, so placed as to make Nathaniel a voyeur of his father's movements. Nathaniel constantly watches his father, more aware of Kahn than the latter had been of Nathaniel. We see Kahn walking on city streets or entering and disappearing into buildings, a *flâneur* more given to roaming than to a settled domesticity; this movement back and forth, in and out of buildings, corresponds to Kahn's elusive movement in and out of Nathaniel's life. It confirms the judgment of the Israeli architect Moshe Safdie, who sees Kahn as a "nomad at heart," a never-settled wanderer; and it seems to validate the characterization of Kahn by his secretary that he was always "missing in action." Moving in and out is a motif of the film. Nathaniel imitates Kahn's movements from the archival footage, for just as he imagines Kahn constantly walking through those structures, Nathaniel enters into the buildings to join himself to his father. The peripatetic movement is the cinematic representation of the fluidity and mystery of the subject and of the son's detective work.

The film interviews affirm how powerful a presence Kahn remains for many people, or, as Nathaniel puts it, how he continues to be "a kind of ghost…weaving in and out of these people's lives." Since Nathaniel may not achieve all the facts and truth he seeks, to some extent Kahn remains an inexplicable mystery. (It is appropriate that the enigma of his final intentions regarding his marriage is never solved, an enigma symbolized by his crossing out his address from his passport just before his death and a mark of his resistance to a fully accountable private identity.) Nevertheless Nathaniel ends by knowing more about his father through his undertaking than he could from mere memory. The lack of filial memory or of material evidence vexes Nathaniel and is only partly compensated for by his interviewing. But though that activity may not always elicit sufficient information from others, it seems to suffice; as interviewer Nathaniel compels others to do the remembering and to express a usable emotion for him.

In thinking about Kahn's absence from his life, Nathaniel ruefully remarks that at the time of the architect's death there was no physical evidence in their house suggesting he had ever been there, not even one of Kahn's characteristic bow ties hanging in the closet. As we have so often seen, in the absence of memory physical evidence often constitutes a fundamental referential fact on which the autobiographer depends. But there is not much for Nathaniel to go on except what he manages to unearth with research (whether the archival film footage or the persons from his father's past); however, even that "evidence" is often unclear and unreliable. So when he interviews a man who claims to have seen Kahn in his dying moments in the men's room at Penn Station, the man's memory is understandably fuzzy and of little help to Nathaniel. What would this story really tell us, anyway? Nathaniel meets this man in front of the "Information" booth at Union Station in Los Angeles, but the "information" is notoriously uninformative.

But if he cannot look to iconic objects, or even language, to help forge a bond between father and son, what will work? I want to claim for Nathaniel, and perhaps for texts (or films) that serve like his as recuperative operations, the simple yet powerful element of desire. There is something like wish fulfillment at work here, the need if not precisely to redeem the father then to regard his actions as comprehensible and less abusive than Nathaniel previously believed. A powerful impulse to assert the legitimacy of his son-ship (I mean this in psychological more than legalistic terms) drives the film, and as it unfolds the initial bitterness gradually melts away.

Nathaniel seizes every opportunity he can to reveal the fact of his relation to Kahn. Some might think that in "outing" the secret that Kahn strove so decorously to maintain Nathaniel has violated his father's wishes We do not have to go so far as Janet Malcolm, who once announced, "We do not 'own' the facts of our lives at all. This ownership passes out of our hands at birth, at the moment we are first observed" ("The Silent Woman," 86). But it seems right to say that Nathaniel's identity depends on the public as well as his private recognition of filiation, that the exposure of his father's history cannot be disassociated from the impulse to share in the father's private life, and that this latter desire is an achieved act of love. Explaining his long-lasting sense of diminished identity, Nathaniel earns the right to make a full disclosure. There is no glee in revealing his father's resistance to the truth, only pleasure in the expression and representation of a newly created bond, even if posthumous, between father and son.

CHAPTER 4

Becoming One's Parent

One of the most intriguing statements about secret lives is made by the narrator of Anton Chekhov's well-known story, "The Lady with a Dog." He speaks of a character who lives two lives, the first of them "open to view by—and known to—the people concerned." This life is public and overt, comprised of banalities and stereotyped ideas, some true some untrue, but a life much like that of others. The second life "proceeded in secret," and this hidden yet more genuine and profound life is, ironically, the more sincere one: "everything which made up the [authentic] core of his life...took place in complete secrecy, whereas everything false about him, the façade behind which he hid to conceal the truth...all that was in the open" (19).

I mention this paradoxical distinction because the writers of the texts discussed in this chapter tend to find their parents' secret lives more engaging and compelling than an ordinary and less problematical life would have been, however frustrating, even anguishing it was for the children when they were young. As for sincerity, here is where the greatest incongruity occurs because in several cases the secretive fathers seem most "true" and "real" to their children when they are most concealed and resistant to social convention and the demands of "normal" life.

The works in this chapter also stress a father-child resemblance despite an initial assumption that the two could not have been more dissimilar. The urge to see oneself as not so different from the parent becomes implicitly a strategy to recover a lost closeness. It also allows the adult child to connect to a figure who might otherwise appear too formidable, threatening, or alien. Though there may be a kind of thrill in outing a parent, there is a different pleasure in discovering an unexpected likeness, one that explains what was previously mysterious, and that may affirm a surprising *entente cordiale*. These works resist what an exposure of parental secrecy often asserts; namely, a triumph in uncovering the elder's subterfuge or a desire for revenge.

J. R. Ackerley's *My Father and Myself* narrates the author's delight in perceiving and revealing the ways he is like his father, each of them having led a covert, even clandestine existence. Ackerley, who was gay at a time when English laws practically demanded that one conceal a demonized and illegal sexuality, makes tentative stabs at openness about the fact. But he is most ready to speak about his gayness as he gathers circumstantial though never definitive evidence of his father's similar sexual orientation. While the framing of this hypothesis does not occupy the same space that revelations of his father's secret second family do, the bond of the son with his father coalesces around that putatively shared experience. As such, the tentative assumption of their similarity subverts the old image of the father as a threatening, hypermasculine figure whose disapproval of his son's weakness ends only with the father's death. Geoffrey Wolff's *The Duke of Deception* is an account of his complex attitude toward his father: both admiration and vilification. The father's compulsive falsifications for a while got him jobs he hardly deserved, and his conning others had a breathtaking recklessness that arouses Geoffrey's horror as well as awe. But the heart of the work lies in the son's admission that he has learned his father's wiles and for a while imitates, sometimes deliberately, sometimes inadvertently, the older man's virtuosity. Feeling bound to his father qualifies if not prevents judgment. Modeling his life temporarily on his father's suggests the seductive power of dissimulation, even when the son suffers from his father's bravado.

Clark Blaise, whose French-Canadian father had a criminal past and constantly abandoned his family, veers between discomfort and acceptance in acknowledging their similarities despite the disturbing secrets the older man maintained and the grief he caused his family. While less delighted than Ackerley by his discoveries, and less ready than Wolff to forgive his father, certainly less eager to admire the father's daring inventiveness, Blaise resists insisting on the evident differences between a respected arts administrator and novelist on one hand and an addictive lawbreaker on the other. Not unlike Wolff, Blaise the fiction writer understands how he may have inherited or at least absorbed his father's ability to make up stories. Each one is a master of deceptions, whether on paper or in life. Just as his father's skill inhered in his ability to cross between truth and fiction, so the novelist in Blaise understands his ability as a version of that skill. Gradually—perhaps as he writes his memoir—he comes to see that claiming an identity definitively separate from his father's would be both a falsification and an evasion. In *Fun Home: A Family Tragicomic,* the only graphic memoir I treat, Alison Bechdel explains as best she can her father's closeted life and possible suicide. Bechdel came out as a lesbian at the same time she learned of her father's gay life. In her remarkable work that blends skillful draftsmanship with a highly literate and literary text, she acknowledges both father and daughter as "inverts," borrowing Proust's term for lesbians and for men who have a woman trapped within them. Bechdel calls the father and herself "entwined," sometimes in regards to their cover-ups (though by the time she begins writing she is very much "out"), sometimes for her imitation of his deceptions and dissimulations, at other times for their mutual uncertainty about what is genuine and what is counterfeit. Despite the distance from her father she often seeks, and the occasional hostility she demonstrates in the face of his attempts to normalize her even while refusing to be open about *his own* homosexuality, Bechdel's work is both critique and homage. For all her attempts to probe his secret life, she will not deny their consanguinity of indirection and artifice.

The narrator of Chekhov's story concludes that because individual existence is based on mystery, we tend to "make such a neurotic fuss about having [our] privacy respected" (19). The narrating children in the works of this chapter worry they might be infringing on their father's privacy, but because they reveal secrets of their own, usually tied in some way to those of the parent, they appear free of any violation, certainly of voyeurism. Finding parallels in the behavior of child and parent seems to relieve the writer of self-consciousness about the investigation let alone guilt over allegations of questionable or transgressive ethics.

The Limits of Privacy: Decorum and Exposure at the Ackerleys

J. R. Ackerley, the mid-twentieth-century British author and for many years the editor of a weekly magazine published by the British Broadcasting Corporation (BBC), *The Listener,* feels no guilt, self-recrimination, or even hesitation about investigating and exposing his father's secrets, assured of his entitlement and need to scrutinize his father to make sense of both the latter's past and his own identity. Ackerley begins his project convinced of an ingrained distinction between the two men, but in the process of writing he learns of a surprising yet curiously gratifying connection between them.

Shortly after his father's death when the son was in his mid-thirties, Ackerley learns that the older man had a second family, what the father called his "secret orchard" (195), and his son sets out to learn all he can about that complicated situation. He has no hesitation searching his father's life, in part because the discovery is prompted by posthumous letters his father wrote to him so that the revelation is proffered rather than extracted, but mostly because, even as he writes about his father's life he is so forthcoming about his own, never adopting a tone of moral superiority.

The frontispiece of *My Father and Myself* (1968), published the year after its author's death, shows an adolescent Ackerley and his father together, the hand of the boyishly handsome son resting lightly on the shoulders of a weighty Victorian paterfamilias with "his large top-heavy figure, his Elder Statesman look...eternal cigar, his paunch, his moustache" (193). In this photograph the two men form a touching bond, and in many respects they are joined far more closely than one might imagine, though they could not have been more unlike in external terms: the father a twice-married, philandering, gregarious businessman, a fruit merchant known as the "Banana King" of London; the son a poet, solitary figure, and a shy homosexual. The son's desire to learn and understand his father's past emerges not from any wish to defame him nor to invade his posthumous privacy, but to gain a closeness denied in life. That separation was partly a function of the father's reticence about his son's sexual preferences, which he dimly suspected and mused about but had no inclination either to confirm or discuss any more than he wanted to tell his son of his own affairs. Ackerley and his father reached a pact of silence about their lives: "if there were opportunities for a quiet conversation with me he did not take or make them; he asked no questions, invited no confidence—and offered none; if I had my secret life, he had his" (150). Ackerley trusts that writing about Roger Ackerley's covert life after the latter's death will allow him to enter into the father's world and make him transparent to the son, however late it may be for direct explanation.

Throughout his life with his father Ackerley acutely felt significant gaps in his knowledge of the older man, an emptiness that produced, on seeing a photograph of his father and three friends when they were in their twenties, a desire "to peep and eavesdrop . . . [to] discover their secrets, if any" (29). The hope for transparency is a belated one, but it nevertheless speaks to a desire not to be isolated and solitary. Sissela Bok, in *Secrets,* her study of concealment and revelation, notes convincingly in terms relevant to Ackerley: "[A]midst the vastness of all that we are conscious of not knowing, or of trying to ascertain, we experience as secret the spaces from which we feel shut out" (10). It doesn't seem to matter whether we have good evidence of deliberate and specific concealment; if we feel excluded we are likely to attribute furtiveness of behavior and motive to persons inhabiting those exclusionary spaces. Given Ackerley's statements that "I was fond of him…but I was not quite at ease with him," and "our relationship was never to be…close and confidential" (75), it is clear he writes not only to avoid continuing exclusion from intimacy, even a posthumous one, but as well to crack the secrecy he attributes to his father's life. His surprising and daring move is to counteract their separateness by narrating a pattern that, despite all their obvious distinctions, makes them appear more alike than either had imagined.

We also might think that when Ackerley reveals a cluster of paternal secrets—his parents' furtive marriage that took place when the son was already twenty-three, the father's many sexual conquests, his dying from the syphilis he didn't know he had, and the father's keeping Ackerley's mother in the dark about his second family of three offspring—he does so to gain an advantage lacking in his earlier life. But Ackerley structures his autobiography around a series of strikingly intimate revelations *of his own* that almost outflank anything he uncovers and divulges about his father.

Ackerley sets out the history of his own sexuality. He risks alienating his reader even as he attempts to ingratiate himself with his audience by the honest and daring revelation of truths shocking for an Englishman in the 1960s, when homosexuality was still controversial and potentially dangerous to divulge. He gives us a litany of highly personal matters: other boys attempting to seduce him at school; his masturbating some of those boys; his having slept with hundreds of young men; the details of his revulsion toward oral sex; his attitudes toward venereal disease in his lovers; his premature ejaculations; and, in a note placed in an appendix, his passion for his beloved Alsatian bitch Tulip, including some provocative sexual gestures toward the dog that replace any further human sexuality. If he has concealed his sexual life from his father, he will be frank with us, as if to confirm his greater integrity and to show that although his life had once been as furtive as his father's, he will now redress that in the act of writing. If he felt shut out from his father and resisted acknowledging his own private life on the grounds that the older man did not wish to know or that disclosure would destroy whatever respect existed between them, Ackerley will at least take *us* into his confidence. His willingness to speak his own secrets seems to confer the right to explore and unmask his father's. In addition his openness becomes a defense against any accusation he has unfairly violated his father's privacy and dignity.

Ackerley wrestles with the propriety of revealing his own darkest truths. Should he proceed? "Curiosity about myself has carried me somewhat further than I meant to go." He appears to be speaking both about himself and his father, or rather about self-disclosure and the exposure of paternal secrets. "[H]owever honestly we may wish to examine ourselves we can do no more than scratch the surface. The golliwog that lies within and bobs up to dishonour us in our unguarded moments is too clever to be caught when we want him" (140). The "golliwog" represents both the private and difficult-to-speak facts of a life and the imp of the perverse that demands those facts be made public. Ackerley feels justified in disclosing his father's life because he has been forthcoming about his own, even though we cannot be sure what may have been held back in either case. In his eyes, self-confession enables and justifies exposure of the father. When Ackerley announces that "I was generally regarded as an open, truthful man, not secretive as my father turned out to be" (145), he signals that his openness is the very attribute that grants him a license to investigate he could not have had otherwise.

The question that lingers in this text of exposure and self-exposure is not so much whether Ackerley's motives are, to use old-fashioned terms, decent and honorable, or even psychologically transparent, but just how much *is* he willing to tell us. Much of the book is devoted to overcoming his instinctual reticence about himself, one not different from his father's, however forthcoming he appears to be. But it is questionable whether the mutual transparency Ackerley claims to seek is ultimately an illusory goal. As he notes ruefully, "To understand and explain oneself, which I am trying to do, is very difficult" (121). Ackerley recognizes that once you embark on a mission to turn up secrets, either others' or your own, there is no end to others' suspicion, let alone clues to yet further concealments and evasions; you inevitably maintain secrets unconsciously forgotten or repressed, secrets you are unwilling to divulge or unable to recover.

Ackerley lives in a family of secrets: Many of his parents' friends were stunned to learn that the couple was not married, and when they eventually learned of the marriage that occurred over twenty years after Ackerley's birth, they were even more shocked. Ackerley himself does not discover these facts, nor his father's previous marriage, let alone his father's secret family, until many years later. But these discoveries are not the cause of grief; rather he claims to be delighted, for the evasions lend his parents a romantic air more in keeping with his own outsider status.

As Ackerley moves toward the revelations that virtually serve as the raison d'être for his project, he unfolds several curious stories that become transitions to the discussion of and speculations about his father's sexual life. The first one concerns the time when his father, who is dying, reveals with considerable pleasure to his son that he has had a wet dream. The other episode comes after a final paralytic stroke when he asks his son to help him urinate by inserting his penis in a bottle. "I had handled a good many "tools" in my life," Ackerley archly notes, "but with this dread gun that had shot me into the world I may have been awkward and clumsy; at any rate he pushed my hand away and finished the job himself" (152). How should we understand the paternal revelation and this intimate little filial drama? Perhaps as instances of voyeurism and disturbing invasions of the older man's privacy, but also as gestures of identification and moments of closeness with the father. There is something, especially in the second story, akin to the famous narrative in Philip Roth's *Patrimony* where Roth reveals to the reader how his father "beshat" himself, after having promised his father that no one else would know, not even Roth's wife. No promises are made with the Ackerley's, but the tension between what Nancy Miller calls "bequest and betrayal" is evident. The desire to be like his father emerges via his desire to know the father's secret life. Patrimony indeed. And once again he has the urge to "peep and eavesdrop," to "discover . . . secrets." The son's sleuthing in the family serves both to ratify his identity and to affirm a filial closeness despite earlier tensions.

While Ackerley is wrestling with his father's posthumous wishes regarding a financial settlement with the mother of his other family, the father's business partner mentions that the father's desk is now Ackerley's property, but advises him to burn it. Ackerley concurs, but says "I regard [the decision to destroy the desk] now with such astonishment and horror that I can scarcely believe I ever agreed to such an act" (158). The desk might have contained private papers "unfit for filial eyes to see" (159), and Ackerley may have been uncharacteristically reluctant to explore secrets, especially about the second family, that his father had not wished to share with him during his life. But I suspect Ackerley's reluctance has less to do with respect than with a fear that further revelations could obligate him toward his half-siblings or force him to regard them, the father's mistress, and even the father himself in ways Ackerley did not wish to contemplate.

The burned desk and its putative contents corresponds to what we often have in such histories: the empty box with its documents. Given that such "evidence" is usually problematic and ambiguous, it represents the tension in Ackerley's text between the satisfaction of gaining clear, substantial proof of a life and, in its absence, of indulging in speculation and suspicion. Fantasy may turn out to be a more profound or at least a more solipsistic pleasure than even the attainment of definitive grounds for belief. There's enough doubt and uncertainty about the details of the father's history to seduce the son into endless curiosity; because he knows relatively little about him he creates a portrait based almost as much on imagination as on slender threads of newly discovered fact. The word "conjecture" rings through the account; Ackerley's pleasure in speculation ties him closely to his father, for each man wonders about the other's life, the father's "as shady as my own" (165).

Ackerley had long maintained an image of the older man as a respectable, dutiful, dull, Victorian father. Yet as he probes the past he unearths an evasion more profound than any he has suspected, one that shatters the image of paternal propriety that even the discovery of the "secret garden" could not completely destroy. In the course of reconstructing his father's life, he tracks down enough circumstantial evidence to surmise that his father may have had a secret gay life. Ackerley's running to ground his father's concealed homosexuality is a finding more conjectural than definitive, but naturally it links the father's sexuality to Ackerley's own, helping to overcome the ostensible differences that played such havoc with the son's early life. The disclosure promises to undermine if not reverse the earlier power struggle between secretive parent and divulging son.

There's a suggestion the father had a prolonged affair with one of his good friends; when Ackerley interviews several men who were in or close to his father's circle, he doesn't get the desired proof, but neither does he get outright denial. Ackerley delights in the possibility his father may have been like him: "Hoping...to drag him captive into the homosexual fold, I pursued my historical researches" (201). He examines records of his father's British Army cavalry regiment known as the Royal Horse Guard, and interviews associates from that unit still alive. He knows from personal experience that a pub his father frequented was and continues to be a famous place for picking up gay cavalrymen. But though he seeks certainty, he is more likely to run against evasions and amnesia. As the past comes fitfully to light, hedged around with uncertainly, Ackerley allows his penchant for speculation to run free: "Was not a man who was capable of so much, capable of almost anything?" (198). The Father's putative secret sexuality yet again arouses Ackerley's impulse to conjecture: "What fun it would be if I could add the charge of homosexuality to my father's other sexual vagaries! What irony if it could be proved that he had led...the very kind of life that I was leading!" (199). As he assembles his father's life from the slender available evidence he increasingly wishes his father were like him; what might seem like narcissism ("Be like me!") is really an attempt to create an affiliation missing in their relation. Ackerley's exposure of his father parallels his own self-exposure, so while the unmasking conceivably raises an ethical objection, his acknowledgment of the possible likeness of father and son subdues any guilt he might have felt.

He summons correspondence and photographs as evidence; his father's desk has long since turned to ashes. As he writes he continues to regret his compliance with the father's partner, and so years later when he has an opportunity to rummage through his *mother's* belongings, he seizes it, hoping for useful information about her marital life. But in her "personal luggage" he discovers a heap of ephemera, dejecta, and the banal flotsam of a dismal life; his list of found items reads like a parody of useless evidence: "old receipts and circulars . . . Christmas cards, bits of Christmas crackers . . . cooking recipes, household lists and memoranda, old theatre programmes, visiting cards, blank pieces of paper." Cardboard boxes, drawers, and "old cosmetic and power containers" are filled with "buttons, hairpins, desiccated suppositories, decayed . . . cigarettes, old and used sanitary towels . . . stumps of pencils" and other useless items pointing to nothing in particular. A rotten black bag belonging to his mother contains piles of papers and a note in her hand: "Private. Burn without reading" (206–208). He reads anyway, but his hopes are dashed: The bag contains only wastepaper, the documents more obfuscating than revelatory. Of course the greater the enigma the greater Ackerley's speculation, and the more he is inclined to fictionalize his parents, his only recourse in the face of evidentiary failure. And so, studying a photograph of his father in a Horse Guards' uniform—similar to those worn by men with whom Ackerley himself has slept—he tries to imagine picking up his father. He can't quite do it though there's a strange sense that he'd rather fantasize such an encounter than undermine his suspicion of their similarity.

Ackerley takes a bemused pleasure in attempting to establish his resemblance to his father. But though he finds a certain delight, even joy, in contemplating their likeness, he knows his baffled detective work may end up as only so much fabrication. The paradox of *My Father and Myself* is that the more Ackerley probes reality, the more he turns away from definitive truth to something beyond what can be provable. Still he will not allow doubt to stand in the way of surmise or hunch. For all his investigative energy he spurns anything that stands in the way of what he seeks.

Ultimately nothing will come of nothing. But Ackerley's final words pay homage to *Hamlet,* not to *Lear:* "Some facts have been established, much else may well be fiction, the rest is silence" (208). Yet for Ackerley the rest is never silence; he goes on imagining to the very end, however unverifiable his suppositions. His father may be nothing like the demanding ghost, and Ackerley nothing like the ironic Dane, but indefatigable preoccupation with the father joins the Shakespearean hero and the autobiographical inquirer. Hamlet may break free of the ghost, but Ackerley is left to the very end attempting to puzzle out the enigma. No matter that he won't know everything; the father remains a mystery and the questioner realizes that detection ultimately reaches its limits.

In his posthumous letter to Ackerley informing him about the second family and asking him to carry out certain financial transactions on his behalf, his father hopes people "will generally be kind to my memory" (208). But that "memory" (what others remember of him) depends in part on what his son, like Hamlet hearing the ghostly father's "Remember me," recalls and records. Paradoxically the injunction to remember cannot enjoin his son to the kindness Ackerley's father hoped for; the result is an exposé that qualifies the sanctified image the father hoped to retain.

Oliver S. Buckton, writing about the "secret selves" in Victorian same-sex confessional autobiographies, suggests that many of those works were "undertaken as a response to charges of secrecy, duplicity, or corruption or initiated in an attempt to disburden the author of secrets by means of a purifying confessional act" (*Secret Selves,* 6). While Ackerley's father did not write such an autobiography, and Ackerley's own work is as much biography as autobiography, *My Father and Myself* functions to "disburden" both of them, and the outing of the father is something like the older man's catharsis by proxy. To disburden another person may seem gratuitous if not vindictive, since no apparent charges had been rendered against the father necessitating a confessional response, and even had he felt uneasy he never expressed it as such. Still, the work of double-confession, as it were, suggests a bond rather than a violation. The son challenges the father's concealment, but, at least in the son's eyes, the revelation and even the ensuing narrative bring them closer.

In the face of the secrets that characterize the father, Ackerley continually attempts to identify with him; the copulative "and" in the book's title encourages that conjoining. Ackerley and his father are, as Philip Roth says about his father and himself, "intermeshed . . . and interchangeable" (*Patrimony,* 225). At times Ackerley seeks to distance himself, but more often he seeks to merge with his father, whether from guilt or because he wishes to discover a transgenerational continuity.

There's an important sentence in the final paragraph: "Of my father, my mother, myself, I know in the end practically nothing" (208). We can understand his ignorance of his parents, but why of himself as well? I would venture that Ackerley's lack of *self*-knowledge derives from his not having a clear sense of the older man, as if ignorance of the other leads to ignorance of the self. He cannot tell the other's secret story without its being enmeshed in his own. His story will always be part of his father's story, and without that recognition Ackerley will not have a story he can call his own. Combining their stories so integrally in the book, whether we regard the inclusion as exploitation, violation, or a deeply empathic gesture, inevitably helps to reestablish a lost connection.

Geoffrey Wolff's *The Duke of Deception,* arguably the best-known work in this study and the next book I will treat, is another example of a vexed son struggling to achieve a bond with his father despite a lifetime of tension and occasionally outright hostility toward him. But in his double-confessional text, in which he unveils a concatenation of family secrets including his own as well as his father's, Wolff, the older of two sons (his younger brother is the well-known fiction writer Tobias Wolff), takes an almost mordant pleasure in unmasking the older man, alternately appalled by and begrudgingly admiring of his father's daring deceptions. Once again the rueful task of exposure and disclosure of a secret life serves less to separate than to ally father and son, though such affiliation scarcely comes easily to Wolff. What in Ackerley is a delightful surprise of resemblance, in Wolff is a doleful accommodation.

"Lies Like Contagious Diseases": The Secrets of the Duke and His Son

The Duke of Deception: Memories of My Father (1979) is Geoffrey Wolff's litany of his father Arthur's subterfuges, hoaxes, and high-wire feats of fraud, most of which were known all along by the son even though as a young boy he did not understand their meaning and implication. While Wolff's father was obsessively bent on a life of secrets and lies, he concealed little from his son, who was acquainted with the paternal evasions and illusions, and—at least for a long while—seemed more impressed by the father's virtuosity than upset by his fabrications.

Arthur Wolff—"Duke"—was a self-educated man who prized himself on his ability to con others into believing that among his many accomplishments he had attended a stellar lineup of schools and universities and had credentials as an aeronautical engineer. Faking résumés and fabricating experience, he was continually fired from and rehired into jobs in the air industry. Perpetually struggling economically, he exercised charm and impressively devious strategies to convince people to lend him money or to sell goods to him on nonexistent credit, accumulating the increasingly expensive material trappings of an aristocratic dandy, which in turn he used to convince others of his merit. For many years he was beloved by his older son, to whom he served as mentor and guide; but on numerous occasions he bewildered his wife and children by constantly moving the family to stay a step ahead of hounding creditors, until, after years on the run, heavily drinking and out of luck, he landed in prison. By this time Geoffrey, in his twenties, had become profoundly disillusioned by his father and had only sporadic contact with him until the older man's death a decade or so later. Some years later, with the aid of his mother, who was long estranged and divorced from her husband, Wolff turned to memoir.

Rather than a work of detection, *The Duke of Deception* sets up as both a complex indictment and a grudging admiration of a clever but exasperating man, as well as a confession of the son's own (mis-) behavior that uncannily mirrored that of his father. What begins in retrospect as an aggressive attack on the father's life of falsifications becomes, by the end, a surprising tribute, not merely *in spite* of the Duke's machinations but also *because of* them. The text veers between admiration and disgust: admiration for his father's ability to live just as he wanted without caring for the consequences, disgust for the jeopardy in which he placed others, even those close to him; admiration for his father's extreme self-confidence, disgust for his indifference to his gross distortions and falsifications. The praise may stem from Wolff's need to justify his own youth, one modeled on his father's life. He is inescapably his father's son, and Arthur Wolff's furtive life was, for a time, his own as well. Wolff makes us understand the seductive charm of secret lives, especially when they embody a driving force of invention, will, and self-making; and though some of that persuasive power results from Wolff's impressionable adolescence and early manhood, some of it lingers even as he writes the book in his early forties. It may be that secrets are inevitably attractive to writers, especially novelists (as we shall see with Clark Blaise), as if authorial fiction-making shared something with the con artist's fantasizing.

A brief prefatory chapter and an equally brief concluding one are book-ends establishing Wolff's conflicted attitude toward his father, not merely balancing opposed feelings of savage indignation and bemused admiration, but keeping the reader off balance as well. The opening signals a shock: Wolff describes the occasion when he learned of his father's death, replying instantly and unguardedly, "Thank God" (5). The memoir is his attempt to explain this filial irreverence and to unravel the secret lying behind his uninhibited outburst.

The conclusion, coming as it does after 265 pages enumerating his father's panoply of false selves, strikes a very different note. It describes a character-istic scene following parental death where a surviving child takes inventory of feelings and challenges himself not to fall into self-deluding attitudes. Wolff describes being "delivered from" his father on hearing the news of the death, freed from having to confront further secrets, lies, and evasions and from being subjected to if not victimized by the older man's irresponsibilities (273). In addition he feels the shame of his father's squalid end (he was found in a fetid room filled with fake driver's licenses, fake identification papers, and unpaid bills, lying naked among empty liquor bottles and barbiturate pillboxes). But at the same time Wolff is "ashamed of [his] shame," and uneasy at being in his father-in-law's house when he learns the news, lest he collaborate with his in-laws' harsh judgment of his father. More significantly, he is embarrassed that he had not made his father welcome in his own house during the past ten years. And so Wolff begins to wrestle with the process of judgment: on one hand his severe criticism of the father whose fraud had so disturbed the son, and on the other a counterfeeling that his father's secret life was what bound them together, and that repudiation of the father is tanta-mount to self-repudiation. Without denying his father's "mendacity," Wolff refuses in the end to surrender to others' caustic evaluation of his father or merely to celebrate an emancipation from "chaos and destructions" (274).

The book ends with Wolff describing how he fell into exhausted sleep in the arms of one of his two young sons, and this tenderness merges into an unexpected feeling of sympathy toward his father, causing him and us to reassess everything Wolff had previously staked out as critical judgment. His acknowledgment that he still loves the father, a feeling long-since denied during the time when he felt betrayed by the older man's relentless chicanery, is the secret he has kept from himself. The memoir, then, is the unfolding of an elaborate process of reevaluation, a criss-crossing of emotional con-tradictions. As Wolff puts the issue when arguing for a clarity that may be counterinstinctual: "A writer's root charge is to distinguish what you really felt in the moment from the false sentiment of what you now believe you should have felt" (*Best American Essays,* xxxiii).

Early in the text Wolff tells us that though his father was a self-made man—*self-making* defined as an ability to appear all things to all people—he was never a "fictioneer" in the sense of someone who would seek to nar-rate his own chameleon identity. As a man who once had a ring made bearing an engraved motto in Latin "Leave no trace behind," Duke was not likely to compose autobiography any more than he was to maintain careful records and offer truthful evidence of his life. Because a con man like his father would naturally resist autobiography, fearful to commit himself to a traceable docu-ment, Wolff dedicates himself to write the account in his father's stead. "I was trained as his instrument of perpetuation, put here to put him into the record" (10). In effect he claims his father sought to be represented by the one who knew him best, and we can appreciate, even relish the irony: The man who had a secret identity wanted his son to reveal the artfulness of his evasions. The book grows out of an implicit obligation as well as a desire to set the record straight, and that record is always inflected by Wolff's ambivalence. The loving exasperation Wolff expresses toward his father depends on openness between the two of them, an openness that makes a dramatic contrast with the secrets each has kept from the world—the son until his mid-twenties when he drifted apart from his father, the father to his dying day.

Arthur Wolff taught his son how to function in the world, especially how to live with style and flair, what choices to make (whether the "right" friend or the "correct" brand of shirt), and what to do to be admired. For the father possessions were never just "things" nor even mere objects of value, but metonyms for his identity. Like several other fathers in this study, he is a virtual reincarnation of Gatsby ("it was his notion to disassemble his history, begin at zero, and re-create himself" [9]); at one point the father addresses his son as "old sport," Gatsby's favorite expression. To reinvent himself he makes up a long list of imaginary school attendance (Deerfield, Groton, St. Paul's, Penn, Yale, the Sorbonne), a fake degree (bachelor of science), unwarranted job skills (aeronautical engineering), a phony accent (naturally British), bogus war experience (as a fighter pilot), and a borrowed religion (he denies the Judaism in which he was raised and claims to be Anglican, fearing Judaism will be a drag on his plans for social and professional advancement). While Wolff is far less interested than Mary Gordon in the origin of a self-hating Jewish father's habits of dissimulation, he alerts us to his stern physician grandfather's ever-increasing demands that *his* son perform beyond all measure ("How hard it must have been to grow up under the measuring gaze of that father! From the beginning my father heard talk about the best of this, the best of that"). Unable easily to please *his* father, Arthur Wolff "became a student of evasion" (24). Attempting to satisfy the ever-more-demanding father produces a range of scams from boyhood pranks to serious crime. In every case the resulting self-aggrandizement and transformation are more important than the material gain. Acquiring a sports car on false credit, Arthur Wolff is more pleased to pass for a rich man than to have the car itself.

One of the surprises in Wolff's memoir is that he celebrates a certain integrity in his father even as the latter deceives and practices on others. Though the older man dissembles and falsifies, Wolff insists on the paradox of his father as an "honest," "truthful" man. "[M]y father…taught me that we should distinguish in this life between what we feel and what we feel we should feel. That if we can distinguish between these things we may have access to some truths about ourselves" (34). His father apparently means that obeying orthodox morality is simply dull compliance and surrender of autonomy, while authenticity resides in "what we feel" regardless of its consequences. Ironically, the father encourages directness and truth over pretense in his son, ignoring the applicability of the idea to himself. Listen to this farrago of exhortations: "Choose friends with care, don't boast or lie. Study hard, listen, be polite, don't neglect the fingernails. Be brave. Dress with care but without ostentation" (168). Whether he refuses or is unable to see the Polonius-like banality, if not hypocrisy, of his position is never clear. What convinces "Duke" of the legitimacy of this viewpoint, one that momentarily seduces Geoffrey, is his reluctance to lie to his son and his resistance to conventional roles.

Much of the memoir is a story of the Wolff family's comings and goings as the father acquires and loses jobs. Constantly fleeing from repossessors, creditors, and fed-up employers, the family leaves a trail of addresses in California, Alabama, Tennessee, Texas, Georgia, New York, Connecticut, Massachusetts, Florida, and Washington State, with the father taking positions in England, Peru, and Turkey. In the United States he is hired and fired by Sikorsky, Northrop, Lockheed, North American Aviation, Bell Aircraft, and Boeing. Amazingly the industry as a whole does not blackball him. After each lost job he procures another thanks to a résumé written on "creamy, thirty-pound stock, hundred percent cotton" from Cartier and bound in Mark Cross leather (173), each résumé increasingly padded and more improbable, including such hyperbole as a list of seven fluently spoken, written, and read languages—including Turkish, Persian, and, "in one of those bravura gestures he could never resist, Burmese"; an advanced degree from "La Université de Sorbonne, Ecole Aeronautique"; a list of fictitious publications; and a citation of nonexistent responsibilities and accomplishments including such vagaries as a claim to have "integrated a survey of entire aviation industry for War Department" (128–129). The more Wolff accentuates his father's breathtaking bravado including his application for a position as an investment consultant in which he gives as a character reference the very man who that day had fired him (John McCone, Director of the CIA), the more we see how his defiant self-confidence is the basis for Wolff's near-mythologizing and suspension of moral judgment.

Like so many of the fathers in these stories whose identities intrigue, baffle, and frustrate their children, Arthur Wolff seems to be simultaneously a plenitude and an absence, a man who is both everywhere and nowhere, anything he claims to be and yet nothing at all. His astonishing virtuosity in accumulating, so to speak, a curricular vitae of identities differentiates him from such fathers as Louise Steinman's and Paul Auster's, both of whom seem to be empty rather than inflated ciphers. Still, his indefinability leaves everyone wondering: "Who was he? Where had he come from? Here was a man in close proximity to atomic bombers who seemed to have been dropped into this country, a few years before a world war, from nowhere" (150). When Wolff's mother, dubious about her husband's claim to a Yale education, asks her mother-in-law if it is true, the latter replies: "'What did he tell you, dear?' 'That he went to Yale.' 'Then I imagine he must have gone to Yale'" (66). The refusal of definitive truth is inherent in the family program: How can anyone who comes into the orbit of "Duke" Wolff know anything? The man of multiple aliases and plagiarized identities can never make an unqualified assertion, so virtually everything his son says about him, even events he witnessed and experiences he shared, necessarily have something of the speculative and conjectural. The consistently ambivalent tone of the work suggests not so much a refusal as an inability to come to clear conclusions about his father, the man of opacity and emptiness forever resisting definition.

The father's attempts to justify his actions are no less fraudulent than the actions themselves. There is a spiraling effect, a *mise-en-abyme* in which the warrant for behavior can hardly be distinguished from the behavior itself, each act producing its own rationalization, which in turn becomes another self-ratifying act. When Wolff describes a series of actions that lead down a rabbit's hole of self-replicating justifications, he is struck by the father's heroic but fatal self-confidence. "He was slippery: he used the telephone company to persuade the telephone company he should be allowed a sixth month of nonpayment without suffering disconnection, because he needed to call people long distance to borrow money from them to pay his telephone bills" (223). It is not only that he maintains a life of secrets; he enjoys the play of outrage that seduces others to go along with him because his claims seem too extravagant not to be authentic. Who else would tell his psychoanalyst that he was most recently a psychoanalyst? The protean shape-changing even entangles the father–son identities. Inverting the classic scenario where a son charges his bill to a parent's account, the father runs up a huge expense at a Princeton clothing store and charges it to his undergraduate son. When Wolff received the statement he first thought it was a case of mistaken identity, and though it was not literally so, the father's identity is in effect *always* mistaken, a product of obfuscation in which nothing resides at the heart of an emptiness. He steals his son's identity just as on another occasion he steals his son's stories and passes them off as his own: "My father had become so careless in his fictions, so indifferent to them, that he forgot their provenance" (220). Dukean narratives are fallacious and malleable, invented and manipulated at will.

The conflict between father and son is particularly intense because for many years they were like each other. Much of the drama of the text comes from Wolff's account, in the context of growing hostility and disillusionment, of his imitation of his father: the quest for glamour, the powerful and oppositional will, the adventurism, the lies, and the overall cunning. It's important to understand that, in a narrative about their common traits of secrecy and imposture, when Wolff declares "my mind...was never empty of my father" he is speaking not only of his childhood and adolescence, when the instinct for imitation was strongest, but of his entire life up to the writing of the memoir (256). The father fills a space in that mind; the less Wolff admires him the more he becomes like him, his every effort to distance himself countered by a correspondingly powerful reaction pulling him back. Long after he has essentially broken with his father he remains obsessed with him. The power of the past cannot easily be set aside, and though Wolff rejects his father, even his defiance of authority is paradoxically a trait learned from the older man.

When a dean at Princeton, confronting Wolff's student problems including exorbitant bills, drunkenness, and mediocre grades, asks him to explain his behavior, Wolff expresses a kind of gravitational pull to his father: "I explained about predetermination, being a father's son" (209). That may sound like a weak excuse, but it's an apt description of an aspect of Wolff's childhood. Until he fully escapes from his father's influence (if in fact he ever does), his own identity remains provisional. There are amusing versions of this impersonation, as when each one wrecks his sports car within three weeks of the other. Or when Wolff plays the same pranks in prep school his father had played decades earlier in his. Or when, in a striking approximation of his father's sartorial council, Wolff advises his younger brother on proper clothing to wear. But there are more troubling patterns of resemblance. He lies to neighbors about his father's whereabouts and work; lies to a girl that his mother has died to win sympathy and sexual favors; lies to another girl about his playing on the Eastern tennis circuit and having nonexistent invitations to coming-out parties. His own postgraduate job résumé is as fraudulent as his father's. He forges Ted Williams's signature on a baseball; steals and shoplifts; drinks as heavily as his father; leaves restaurants without paying; tries to buy a boat on a credit account he does not possess; and at stores runs up massive bills he cannot and will not pay. He pals with boys who "figure the angles," dreams of living by his wits, and even imagines a life of crime with Duke—a kind of father-and-son Bonnie and Clyde.

Though Wolff feels linked to his father however much he may wish to break loose, and though he wants to define himself as unencumbered by the traits to which he long adhered ("I wanted not to be like him, to let him sink alone" [221]), the desired freedom from judgment is analogous to his father's unwillingness to take responsibility for his deceptive behavior.

As Wolff strives to assess his father with complexity and integrity, he struggles toward self-definition. His difficulty in both regards is a function of the orbit of secrecy and concealment into which he has been drawn. Even when his father advocates a policy of honesty for young Geoffrey, the son is unable to call it hypocrisy, even to assert its incongruity, despite being fully aware of his father's machinations. Fear of his father's power? Realization that because these words apply equally to himself he cannot risk sanctimoniousness? Awareness that the father meant well and cared? Wolff won't say too much, but even as he bluntly states "[my father] was a lie, through and through," and again "There was nothing to him but lies," he adds "I had this from him always: compassion, care, generosity, endurance" (184, 192).

In a work describing so much fabrication, the question how Wolff has discovered the fraudulence is important. His father occasionally told him stories about himself, but given that so many of those stories were either false or *about* falsity, what could the son trust? Wolff is sparing in the details of how he eventually learned about the pretense and the lies beyond what he knew as a boy and young man; he does not describe the process by which he gained knowledge, though he garners some from interviews with his mother and some from archival material, including his father's school files, letters from his father's educators as well as from his own teachers and prep school headmasters, records of unpaid debts, his father's employment records and assessments of his work, and the unreliable résumés in which he specialized.

But this "evidence" is as provisional as Duke's identity, and given a person of his shadowy personality and dealings ("shadowy" in the sense of both the disreputable and the indefinite), we are left with the image of a ghostly after-presence, an incomprehensible and undecipherable trace no matter how astute the son's memory nor how much "research" he conducts. Wolff may attempt to see the father anew, but he can never see him with absolute conviction that he "has" him just right. How could he? The title of the memoir, "The Duke of Deception," has an ongoing, present force: Arthur Wolff was a man of deception and secrets, and his influence is *still* a deception, preventing his son and us from discerning exactly who he was. He is always both intrigue and exasperation.

Despite Wolff's desire to separate himself from the father, he comes to admire if not quite to respect the latter's devious nature and deceptive practices. The next writer, Clark Blaise, also veers between discomfort and resignation in reconciling himself to disconcerting similarities to his father, but Blaise construes the resemblance as less a matter of occasional imitation than of inheritance, a family likeness and legacy he will neither discredit nor deny. Blaise claims that he possessed all the traits his father had, and only a combination of accidents and will have kept him from becoming just like the older man. In reading how Blaise investigates a life not his own but close enough to his so that it *might* have been, it becomes apparent that the more distant and ghostlike the father's existence the more Blaise seeks to insert himself into the interstices of that other life.

Imagining Himself in the Paternal Matrix

Throughout his autobiography Clark Blaise explains what has motivated him to learn about his father, the French-Canadian Leo Roméo Blais who became the Franco-American Lee Blaise. The older man was a duplicitous chameleon of multiple identities—furniture salesman, liquor-runner, hustler, con man, wife-beater, occasional criminal with a police record, and a man often on the run and estranged from the family he periodically abandoned, reentered, and left again. In *I Had a Father: A Post-Modern Autobiography* (1993) the son undertakes a quest to comprehend the father who kept disappearing from his life, a necessary project because, as he puts it in an article written for *The New York Times Magazine,* "The face I sense looking out on the world is his...he is inside me, we are becoming one" ("A Middle-Aged Orphan," 64). If he is turning into his father and the father is unknown, the project of finding and bringing back the other man is a matter of utmost urgency.

Blaise is the former director of the International Writing Program at the University of Iowa, a fiction writer, and coauthor with his wife, the novelist Bharati Mukherjee, of a memoir about Calcutta. He often admired his father, a tough character and amateur boxer who reminds him of Humphrey Bogart or Jean-Paul Belmondo, though for a long while he remains anguished by his father's refusal to have been truthful or responsible to his family. And because the father's evasions torment Blaise, he is not at ease until he learns who the furtive figure really was and why he had been so elusive. *I Had a Father* is the record of a son's search to discover and identify the man concealed beneath a lifetime of secrecy. To this end, investigation and evidence gathering are central. Because recall alone fails to re-create the father, as he writes this memory-less memoir Blaise is compelled to rely on research and imagination. Only then can he begin to understand the father and his own past, "watching myself and my prior selves being born" (ix).

Blaise visits the Quebec region where his father was born, examining employment files, divorce papers, parish and police records, and other official traces of his sketchy presence. Every document becomes a mini-autobiography of the older man, a trail his father has left but which deliberately or inadvertently throws the hunter off the scent. From his diggings in Quebec Blaise compiles a list of addresses and possible former acquaintances of his father, but no reliable history—data without a story, information without a narrative.

His research yields suspect parish entries and "fragile" birth and death records. Even New Hampshire police files, which he hopes will clarify, authenticate, or refute his father's pervasive "fictions," have been destroyed (10). Blaise scrutinizes any evidence he finds: talcum powder on the bathroom floor, a tumbler of Scotch—"a kind of archeological record, a small-scale human history" (4). When, deeper in his research, he turns to police records, ledger books from Lac-Mégantic in southeastern Quebec province, birth and death certificates, and histories of French-Canadians, he is never sure he has captured the man. What remains is a series of hypotheses, stories that cannot be verified, memories that are hazy and incomplete, sensory impressions as evanescent as wisps of smoke or stale odors. He concludes that his father's evasiveness and desire to uproot the family (they moved over thirty times) or to uproot himself *from* the family prohibits any investigation from adequately pinning him down. The man who was a rum-runner during Prohibition, who was always fleeing from creditors, police, and women, cannot be defined. "What made Léo Blais run?" asks the son, in puzzled frustration.

The more he speculates about the older man, the more he exposes him as a liar, one who fabricated, among other things, a Paris birth, an Ivy League education, and a huge family he claims to have supported. How can the researching son hope to get at the truth of a man whose identity consisted in self-invention, whom Blaise calls a Gatsby? He catalogs his father's fabrications, including "his heroic, highly secret service in the French Underground, his medical training at Harvard" (154), both nonexistent.

It's not surprising that after Blaise declares, "I have to retrieve every scrap, inhale every whiff, subpoena every document related to him, pester the town clerks, hire a private investigator" he adds "Then I can invent him" (15). Missing, unavailable, or misleading, evidence of the father or its absence frustrates Blaise and ultimately leads to his necessarily imaginative reconstruction of the man. A postmodern pastiche, Blaise's life writing consists of a collection of fragments, and while his task is to assemble them into a composite whole, he will not force matters, allowing the father's scrap heap of a life to stand for his inconclusiveness. For all the search for documentation, the account ironically echoes with tentativeness, doubt, and irresolution. Blaise conjectures like mad about his father's impulses, especially when evidence is erased. He desires to create a comprehensive image of his father, but the text implicitly questions whether, in representing the older man by attempting to unify piecemeal and contradictory bits of evidence, the autobiographer has done anything other than undertake an act of invention.

As he examines baffling records and maps that trace an endless succession of their moves through towns in Canada and the United States where they barely settled before moving on, Blaise increasingly realizes that nothing about him was specifiable or clear. He was a man of "fictions," and when Blaise poses questions to the father in his mind, everything spoken by the internalized father's voice unravels as another possible falsification.

Even the history of the family's geography seems to be a kind of fiction, as if the locales themselves had little permanent reality for the boy, so frequently did they appear and disappear from his life. Florida, New Hampshire, Missouri, Winnipeg, Montreal, Toronto, Atlanta, and Cincinnati are just a few of the places where he lived. Blaise experiences himself as a "native of nowhere...because I have come from just about everywhere" (106), one whose "future is noplace" (38). He defines himself as a border person, one who denies fixity and lives as a shape-changer. This disturbing fluidity forces Blaise to search out whatever parental records might counteract his felt sense of formlessness, but once again every attempt to establish and assert a clear sense of self collapses in the face of putative evidence about the father that turns out to be suspect and makes Blaise fear he has inherited a similar evasiveness. Each record, each parish entry from Lac-Mégantic, and each family story is as unreliable and ephemeral as the towns from Blaise's childhood that pass by in a kaleidoscopic blur.

Gradually Blaise begins to imagine that he himself is equally incomplete and not unlike his father. The inconclusive research and the writing of autobiography allow him to probe the ways his father not only *shaped* him but also *resembled* him. For all Blaise's lifelong reluctance to acknowledge any similarity to the man who, in every conceivable way, seems unlike the novelist and man of letters his son became, the memoir shows Blaise gradually admitting a startling similarity to the older man. "I have aged into my father's likeness, into his patterns,...after a lifetime of denial, of defining myself against his example" (16). It is a common enough recognition—the shared family DNA of psychological structures, behavior, and outlook—and investigating the father teaches him that identity, perhaps especially that of the life writer, is provisional.

At times Blaise seeks to distance himself from the father, but at other times he seems to admire and crave intimacy with that larger-than-life personality. Of course he cannot edit out his persistent ambivalence: "I'd been composing my father...squeezing all the love and dread that was in me" (166). The autobiography correspondingly veers between these poles, unwilling to settle on either ground. But ultimately Blaise sets aside any bitterness about the father's neglect of his family and investigates their unexpected likenesses. When he characterizes his growing into his father's image much the way a photographic negative imperceptibly develops into a clear print, he is aware of the pun implicit in the metaphor: "I walk around, a late-developing negative" (16). The long-felt "negative" fear of a perceived resemblance gradually develops into a surprisingly positive acceptance, even a begrudging approval of the older man. The text winds to an acceptance that appears to astonish even its author.

Though the obvious goal of evidence-gathering is to render an "authentic" image of the man whose identity was defined by his *in*-authenticity, for Blaise it is equally important to understand himself through that evidence. As a talent scout of international writing Blaise himself continually crossed frontiers, fearing that in so doing he was gradually morphing into his wayward father. Blaise perceives wandering and border-crossing as family traits: if the father continually picked up women and changed families, Blaise picks up hometowns and changes countries, having moved twenty-six times in twenty-nine years. Blaise narrates how he covered the world "selling" the Iowa program to emerging writers from all over; like his father, Blaise was endlessly on the road, each of them, as he wittily says, traveling salesmen. He perceives the ephemeral and transitory aspects of his life, his love of the temporary, as not unlike his father's tendency to go "through marriages like a diplomat changing posts, each marriage a fully absorbing experience with languages, scenes, friends, and stepchildren" (112). Blaise wonders if he, no less than his father, is "a construct of pieces adding up to a self." He insists on his own "sense of incompleteness" (45, ix). Father and son are both fragmented, voyagers fated to the homelessness and disorientation that results from their fascination with crossing borders, whether national and ethnic in the son's case, or of propriety, responsibility, and legality in the father's. The only cure for a life he calls incoherent and "pointless" is "one long search for meaning," which he hopes to achieve in the act of life writing (109).

We need to take Blaise at his word when he says "That's what I had tried to do in moving my family to Montreal at the age of 26: wipe out my early history, be reborn" (27). When Blaise declares "I have made myself a native of twenty different towns and spent a life in reconstructive, autobiographic surgery," he suggests his need to put himself back together, and at the same time implies he may never achieve a definitive fix on himself—he's spent a lifetime in that surgery, and it is an ongoing, unending process of repair (113).

The past tense of the memoir's title might imply that the child once *had* a father, but when he left the family permanently the son was robbed of a paternal figure. Or, by the same token, when the father died (Blaise was thirty-eight) the son lost a powerful force in his life. But the work insists that despite appearances the father has been there all along, the older man's "vestigial structures" firmly embedded in the son. Blaise can perceive himself only "in the paternal matrix" (201). The title declares in effect "I still have a father and, despite his death, I always will." It is through loss that Blaise can understand and argue for the continuity and intertwined nature of the generations; but perhaps just as important, his father's habits of being are part of the son's identity no matter how hard he might be tempted to deny them.

The text seems like an interview with the dead, as Blaise stresses that his father's voice emanates from beyond the grave. But though Blaise conducts a kind of séance, interrogating and prodding the father to speech and folding Leo Blais's character into his own, the taciturn, circumspect, and secretive man is no more accessible to the writer's *memory* than he was in the son's *life*. Novelist that he is, Blaise must invent the father almost as if he were a literary character. Perhaps the most profound aspect of identity joining father and son is their ability to make up stories. Here too a potentially negative trait of Blaise senior becomes, in the son's interpretation, the source of and inspiration for the son's own creativity. Though he attacks his father's tendency to lie and to create an imaginary self for his own aggrandizing ends, Blaise like Geoffrey Wolff nevertheless admires the skill involved in that practice. As a salesman the father knew how to sell a bill of goods; instead of holding him up to moralizing judgment or ridicule, Blaise insists that that habit defines his father as a fabulist whose fiction-making anticipated and perhaps even inspired Blaise's own. "Like most people, he lied for advantage, and to avoid accountability. But he also fabricated a life" (111). It is that very talent Blaise claims to have inherited, and in finding common ground between them he not only acknowledges his father as a progenitor of Blaise's own fictionalizing but attributes his ability to see his father fully and imaginatively to their common trait: "I'd been composing my father" (166), which is to say he has been creating (a version of) his father to suit his own literary and psychological purposes. Because they are experts in fabricating stories, both about the self and about others, he can say "Once again, I am my father's son, only a more scrupulous liar" (201).

But Lee Blaise, as he came to call himself, lived largely to make himself look good in others' eyes, whereas the son must invent his father because the records he pursues and his memory are unreliable. Defining himself as a maker of fictions, "a more scrupulous liar" than his father and one whose faith in language enables him to reinvent the world at will, Blaise is able to "imagine" his otherwise inaccessible father.

What launches Blaise's project is a traditional prompting for autobiography: the recognition in late middle age of mortality. "It's in the air these days, middle-aged children calling their parents back … as the whiff of mortality reminds us we're far, far closer to death than to childhood.... We'd rather have them round in all their meddlesome, infuriating ways then let them go. We'd be better sons now, we'd understand their panic just a little better. We'd understand because slowly, unavoidably, we're becoming them" (184). It is tempting to see an autobiographical trope in this configuration: the genre representing the child gradually arriving at the age of an elderly or deceased parent. But Blaise is not after simple matters of the life cycle. What once might have seemed a troubling and easily denied recognition now becomes a central theme of the memoir. The resemblances between father and son are neither incidental nor biological; Blaise searches out every imaginable and unimaginable parallel to undermine what he believes is an inadequate myth of the filial replacement of the father. He wants his father back, despite the difficulty of their relationship. His autobiography centers on an alternative myth of union.

Should we see in Blaise's portrait of his father either a violation of the older man's right to privacy or an exploitation of his character in the son's effort to establish his own sense of self? Blaise seems aware of the problem when he suggests that learning about his father's concealed life is a form of forbidden knowledge, an Adamic sin that might, even though the father is dead, impugn the quest and the revelations with the taint of illegitimacy. On the contrary, his account of the father's life is respectful, both in its attempt to understand the older man's character and in its conclusions about the causes of his own behavior. Though Blaise does not withhold criticism, his willingness to perceive their identities as merged diffuses what might otherwise be condescension or attack. The exploration of the father's life is never placed at the service of self-justification.

John Barbour, in his essay "Judging and Not Judging Parents," discusses autobiographers who judge and those who withhold judgment in writing about their parents. Barbour applauds writers who recognize "the difficulty of determining a parent's responsibility" (91) by attributing that parent's behavior to complex historical and psychological influences, and who forgive behavior they previously condemned when they understand the difficult process of the parent's identity formation. I am not investigating here the origins of the character of Blaise's father in terms either of ethnic issues or of family dynamics. That is another story. I simply wish to note that by advocating a nuanced moral evaluation Barbour perceives life writing as "the best vehicle in our culture for sustained, probing, and public examination of the process of moral judgment" (97).

I agree with this perception and would add that Blaise's use of imagination—his ability to conjecture who his father was and how he himself inherits a family likeness, albeit in ways he only recently comes to understand—allows

Blaise to regard the father with empathy. I hesitate to say "with forgiveness" because that might imply a condescension alien to his task and sensibility. Certainly Blaise does not write to exercise power over the father, nor does he assert an autonomous self wholly apart from the father's character. Paul John Eakin speaks of "an unresolved tension between relational and autonomous modes of identity" (*How Our Lives Become Stories,* 180): the recognition that in writing the life of another person one inevitably bestows on that person an identity that is a function of the writer's own needs. It might seem as if Blaise writes his father's story to reverse the control the father once had over the child, but the text preserves the father's dignity, restoring to him a value that Lee Blaise himself came to doubt, and affirming the son's need to comprehend as much as to condemn, to affiliate as much as to deviate.

So far in this chapter all the children who find their lives uncannily similar to their fathers' are sons. In the final work embodying this theme, a daughter discovers traits linking her to her father, though in her narration there is an inversion of genders—he the more feminine, she the more masculine. Alison Bechdel, a lesbian graphic novelist and autobiographer, represents herself and her father, a gay teacher and mortician, as a criss-crossing chiasmus. Slowly unraveling *his* secret life, she acknowledges *her own,* though he maintains a furtive existence up to the moment of his death, only hinting at aspects of it to her, whereas she fully acknowledges her sexual identity. Still, no matter how much she laments she cannot emotionally break from her father nor condemn his closeted life. In her graphic memoir Bechdel enmeshes her identity with her father's even as she attempts to free herself from the inhibitions and secrets that narrowed his life.

Shared Secrets in the Fun House

Alison Bechdel's graphic autobiography *Fun Home: A Family Tragicomic* (2006) is a portrait of her father and herself, both of whose truth telling is frequently in doubt, each of them given to evasion and disguise. Bechdel's life writing and life drawing focus on the discovery and revelation of family secrets in which each one has participated, as well as their nature and possible cause. In charting the family deceptions, which linger through many pages of exploration and puzzlement, she draws her father and herself together in unexpected ways; that they share a bond yet do not comfortably share it with one another makes their relationship troubling and problematic.

At issue here is the father's gayness, and her own. Bechdel's father was a small-town Pennsylvania high school English teacher and the director of a funeral home, a business he had inherited from his father. The "fun home" of the title is the rambling, labyrinthine Victorian house the father—a meticulous restorer preoccupied with a love of artifice and intricate detail—spent his free time remodeling and curating like a museum. In the process he treats his family as an adornment of the house for his aesthetic pleasure. Giving his energy to the task of restoration and the arrangement of elegant details, from flock wallpaper to gilded moldings to velvet draperies, he neglects the family, treating them like furniture and the furniture like people. The house is his obsession and his sublimation, and in his daughter's eyes a sign of his closeted homosexuality. That house is at once the environment in which he acts out his questionable identity and a metaphor for that identity. She speaks of the house as a "simulacrum" produced with his "legerdemain" (17, 5), and as she gets older she realizes that his pose as ostensibly straight is no less fraudulent than the faux gothic of the house.

Bechdel even calls the ornate embellishments of the home's décor "lies," as if the physical spaces her father has created and inhabits are cover-ups, masks hiding his fear of openness. With characteristic visual emphasis, immediately after drawing a panel depicting her cleaning the crystal pendants of a sconce she shows her father applying a "bronzing stick" to his face, another gesture of artifice and camouflage (16). Seeking to make his external world perfect obscures her father's confusion about his identity and contributes to his daughter's own uncertainty about how to represent him: as a conscious liar or someone whose secrets signify a lack of self-knowledge.

The house is a maze of concealments: mirrors, multiple doors, and passageways seemingly designed to bewilder visitors; by the same token it is a sign of his own facade, such as his attempt to appear the family man and "ideal husband," a reference to the play by Oscar Wilde, the master of indirection and one of his heroes. How could he both be an "ideal husband" and have sex with teenage boys? his daughter asks. By assuming dualistic roles and identities—devoted husband and pederast—he creates confusion in the family and appears to his daughter more illusion than reality.

She suspects her father of being gay, but is convinced only when her mother provides the proof. Bechdel learns her father had spent a lot of time with teenage boys in town and had probably had an affair with several of them, including her own adolescent baby-sitter. Ironically, her mother reveals the truth about her husband in response to Bechdel's acknowledgment of her lesbianism, effectively upstaging her daughter's confession. Mere months after this double revelation Bechdel's father is killed, hit by a truck while walking on a country road; she fears his death may have been no accident but a deliberate act of suicide resulting from the shame that his secret was no longer private. Bechdel wrestles with guilt, suspecting he felt particular shame because the secret was out to his daughter, thus wondering if she may have indirectly caused his death. Her consternation occupies a substantial portion of the work.

Trying to gain insight into her remote, dispassionate, and evasive father, Bechdel raises a host of questions about his behavior and motives. But hers is not mere garden-variety curiosity about a parent. She not only gathers and questions "evidence" wherever she finds it—in his letters to her and to her mother, photographs, and the diaries she kept throughout her childhood and adolescence—she also wonders how much she has inherited from her father and how much she resembles him. Nor is her work a casual study of parental influence. Bechdel surmises that categorizing her father as someone just like her is "a way of keeping him to myself—a sort of inverted Oedipal complex" (230). Their stories are linked via their secrets and their complex roles within the family.

Fictions of all kinds predominate in both their lives. A major connection between father and daughter is an obsession with shaping themselves through texts. Unlike what one might anticipate from a graphic narrative, *Fun Home* is filled with literary references; many of the links between father and daughter were forged from her reading of his favorite books, which he shares with her even when she is a young girl. His library is the center of the house, the room on which his artifice is most fully exercised and where much of his identity is established and confirmed, usually in imitation of characters from his reading. By the same token many models for *her* behavior are located in the same texts. These literary works often provide clues to relations in the family and to her bond with her father, as well as to her psychological development. The comic book genre may symbolize childhood, but the literary texts in which father and daughter immersed themselves suggest that she grew up under the sign of her father's instruction, perhaps even his manipulation.

Bechdel tells us about, draws, and gives brief but cogent analyses of many of the books that structured her life and in turn structure her narrative: Kenneth Clark's *The Nude* (there are panels of Bechdel naked with her female partner), *Anna Karenina* (she wonders if she like Anna is destroying her own life), *The Great Gatsby* (she sees her father and herself both trying to remake themselves), *Portrait of the Artist as a Young Man* (her father too is an "artificer"), *The Taming of the Shrew* (her parents met when acting in the play, a model for their problematic liaison), Edward Albee's *The American Dream* (a scenario for her parents' marital nightmare), E. M. Forster's *Maurice* (an expression of her father's closeted experience), Colette's *Earthly Paradise* (a franker admission of sexuality), Kate Millett's *Flying* (a manifesto of sexual freedom), *Ulysses* (especially relevant for Bloom as a "spiritual father" to her father's adolescent students and lovers), *The Odyssey* (the mother reminds Bechdel of a lonely wife while her absent husband cruises for boys), *Remembrance of Things Past* (like the father's mask, heterosexual Marcel covers for homosexual Proust), and a large stack of classic lesbian titles such as Radclyffe Hall's *Well of Loneliness* and Anaïs Nin's *Delta*.

In addition to giving the graphic form an unexpected gravitas, these references become codes for complex attitudes about her family and herself. They are inspirations if not guides for behavior and for ways of being in the world without which she is often confused, though doubtless many of the modernist works only reinforce her lack of certainty. In addition they signal a central theme of the narrative: her father's inability to understand the distinction between reality and fiction. He has chosen to live his life emulating the characters of his favorite novels (Gatsby, Bloom, and Proust's Baron Charlus), establishing his life via their fictional identities. In effect he becomes a character acting many parts. As a result "facts" are always in question, and the real and the make-believe meld into one another. His desire to live in and through his reading corresponds, in Bechdel's view, to his inability more generally to tell the truth; he harbors secrets not just because he is closeted or has deceived himself about his sexual ambivalence but because he hardly understands himself or his motives, beliefs, and relationships. At one point Bechdel claims her parents are most real to her in fictional terms. She means by this that both parents were given to play-acting, her father regarding himself in his library as a nineteenth-century aristocrat, her mother performing roles in local theater productions and, in her daughter's view, a character in a Jamesian novel: the naïve American woman who made a disastrous choice in marriage and had been "ground in the very mill of the conventional," to quote James on *Portrait of a Lady*'s Isabel Archer.

Bechdel speculates that given what she believes was her father's unexpressed guilt regarding his gayness, his death on the country road may have been a suicide; it was "his consummate artifice, his masterstroke." "It was suspicious. Perhaps even counterfeit" (27, 57). What could this mean? Perhaps his death prevented him from having to confront publicly the reasons why his wife, only two weeks earlier, had asked for a divorce. Would his wife's declared rationale expose his false front and his sexuality? Or perhaps he had imitated several suicides whom he had buried in his occupation as undertaker. Bechdel shows him applying cosmetics to several cadavers: Is his own death a similarly artificial act? Later she speaks of gay men she sees in Greenwich Village displaying "cosmeticized masculinity" (190); her father's concealed sexuality is no less an artifice. He had been reading Camus' early novel *A Happy Death* when he died: more impersonation? Bechdel complains her father was basically absent from her childhood and surmises his death was a performance magnifying the disappearing act that characterized his behavior all along. She even imagines that his death, at the same age of forty-four as that of his beloved Scott Fitzgerald, could be "a deranged tribute" to the author (86). At every step of the way we encounter mimicry, obfuscation, and sham.

Most of Bechdel's discoveries are made after her father dies. She becomes a collector of evidence—letters, books, journals, photographs, maps—that constitutes her archive and substitutes for memory, which she knows is unreliable. This collection is analogous to her father's "museum," the house itself. Though such "evidence" represents a documentary impulse there is so much literariness and fiction-making in the memoir that it keeps the reader off balance: what is real and what is a simulacrum of truth? Can she really know what she claims about her past, and is anything from that past certain beyond a shadow of doubt?

Bechdel's hypotheses also suggest the ironic pleasure she takes in speculation. Significantly the most common word in her text is *perhaps.* In the absence of clarity her guesses about her father are the only ways she can represent him. Bruce Bechdel hides what his daughter calls his "erotic truth," but she, no less than he, scarcely knows what that truth is, and for a long while that includes her own sexual identity. When she says her father has led a life "of the imaginary," (65) she might just as well be speaking of her own practice of imagining—another link between them. In a work that keeps raising the issue of just how self-consciously aware father and daughter were about their sexuality, Bechdel wants their "entwined stories" to yield up some version she can affirm, however indefinite it may be. "Entwined" is a phrase from the work's final panel, which shows the child Alison, probably four or five, leaping off a diving board of a swimming pool into her father's arms, plunging toward the water like Icarus, whose myth of destruction she invokes throughout the work. She has called her father both Icarus the suicidal plunger and Daedalus, the artificer. Now she joins with him, like Icarus having hurled herself into the air only to be caught by him "in the tricky reverse narration" that drives their stories (232). As author of the work she too is the artificer, but one destined never to be sure what is artificial, what is authentic. The force of that final image, where she renders herself as a little girl, shows how affiliation with her father was once possible although, in the intervening years, his secret has created an unbridgeable distance between them. Nevertheless, despite obvious differences between them, their stories are familially "entwined" in that they are both outsiders, though he remains closeted and problematic to the end, while ultimately she rejoices in her lesbianism. (For many years Bechdel has published the celebrated lesbian-feminist comic strip "Dykes to Watch Out For.") Bechdel's acknowledgment is central to her self-portrayal; though I've been speaking of her sexuality as "a secret," it's fairer to say it is a slowly developing truth, initially unknown to or unperceived by her, that gradually emerges during adolescence and young womanhood.

But Bechdel, no less than her father, is attracted to make-believe, which complicates a work devoted to exposing secrets. Her father, in a photograph his daughter discovers after his death, had dressed in a woman's bathing suit either as a fraternity prank or as an experiment trying out his "other" side; for her part Bechdel as a teenager occasionally dressed up in men's clothes. (A significant difference between father and daughter is that he stashes the incriminating picture in a box while she draws her transvestism for all to see.) Illusions appear at every turn: she tries to put on a show of grief at his funeral, but doesn't really feel it, and wishes "they made smelling salts to induce grief-stricken swoons, rather than snap you out of them" (52). There's a chilling panel depicting her at her father's gravesite, lying on the ground beside the tombstone, one leg thrown casually over the other, as if she were unable to summon any sorrow for his death. Her more public mourning is merely a show of grief; nothing about that death, its fact or its cause, seems to her genuine. Her father's deception appears to have induced her own.

Bechdel is so used to living in a world of fabrications, she cannot be sure of anything she herself feels. Absorbed by the problematic nature of her own observations and insights, she finds it difficult to expose others' secrets when the certainty of her own truth is unclear. Her diaries that become the source for much of the memoir and substitute for the role of memory are the locus of these ambiguities. The phrase "I think" occurs in them frequently, and, as she rereads pages expressing uncertain feelings, she states outright "It was a sort of epistemological crisis. How did I know that the things I was writing were absolutely, objectively true?" (141) The diaries are a set of codes, and in them she refuses to be overt and direct about herself, much as her father has been about himself. For example, she uses the term "Ning" to represent the experiences of both menstruation and masturbation, pleased with the word's "indecipherability" (170). Her diaries are filled with unreliable stories, falsehoods, and cover-ups at every stage of her development. When she describes the disclosure to her mother of her first period, she draws the diary with a blank page, calling it "the implicit lie" (186). We're never told what exactly was concealed in that emptiness. Nevertheless she draws several items on her desk next to the diary, all suggesting an ongoing preoccupation with falsification: a sketch of Richard Nixon, arms raised in

FIGURE 3. Excerpted from *Fun Home: A Family Tragicomic* by Alison Bechdel (p. 186 bottom). Copyright © 2006 by Alison Bechdel. Reprinted by permission of Houghton Mifflin Harcourt Publishing Company. All rights reserved.

the "V for victory" sign (the events described in the diary occur during the Watergate cover-up); a program from her mother's production of Wilde's *The Importance of Being Earnest,* a play explicitly about deceptions and implicitly about gender concealments; and a copy of *GQ,* a favorite magazine of her father, which functions as a coded reference for the hypermasculinity that conceals his sexual ambivalence. Convinced anything she might have said was a lie, unable to match language to experience, she regards her upbringing as a training ground for contending with the chimeras and illusions of the household. *Fun Home* is the work of a would-be truth-teller, but those "truths" remain ambiguous and questionable.

Even when she is the detective on the track of a missing person, father and daughter continue to be allied. Citing Proust on the "invert" (his term for one "whose gender expression is at odds with his or her sex" [97]), Bechdel states that she and her father were inversions of one another within the family; because he had feminized himself she would take on the opposite identity and try out a masculine role. "I was...Butch to his Nelly" (15). Such confusion of identities at once differentiates them and identifies her with him. In a poignant drawing of the desolate road where her father was killed, two captions announce: "And in a way, you could say that my father's end was my beginning," and "more precisely, that the end of his lie coincided with the beginning of my truth" (117).

Ever the investigator she attempts to understand her father as well as herself but runs up against his stonewalling. The most painful episode in the work appears when, as a college student, she goes to the movies with him and tries in vain to speak of her own sexuality; he indirectly and shamefacedly hints at his inclination for boys, but no real sharing comes of this, only awkward stammering and silences. The two pages addressing this broken encounter contain the most number of panels per page, twelve on each, depicting the sequential, moment-by-moment frustration of nonconnection, mutually embarrassed sputterings and incomplete sentences that substitute for dialogue. Once again, at this critical juncture, she perceives him as a fictional character. "It was not the sobbing, joyous reunion of Odysseus and Telemachus. It was more like fatherless Stephen and sonless Bloom.... But which of us was the Father?" (221). Though Bechdel's revelation of her sexual identity never suggests any sense of superiority to her father's, it validates her right to expose him—or at least to imagine and express *his* sexual truth, the love whose name he dared not speak. And the greater his emotional distance from his family the closer hers will be, as she places herself fully within the family circle. The work's subtitle, "*A Family Tragicomic,*" refers to the tragedy of her father's death and his marriage, and the comedy of her fulfilled coming out, sexually and as investigator/author.

What about the *comic* in the "tragicomic?" Bechdel's graphic illustrations are as central to her story as the text. The literary references often function as an elevated supplement to her drawings of everyday experience, as when captions concerning Proust's love of young men accompany the illustration of the teenage boy who became a baby-sitter for the family and eventually her father's lover. The captions do not dictate how we should interpret the illustration, but their juxtaposition provides richer understandings of the image. Bechdel's memoir juxtaposes archival photos with drawings that reproduce them with great accuracy, thereby thematizing the central issue of the work: What is real, what is made up? *Fun Home* may be a comic book, but as Bechdel notes in a 2006 interview, while it is "drawn in my regular cartoony style ... the photos are drawn very realistically. It's a way to keep reminding readers, these are real people." The photos "anchor the story in real life" (Chute, 1006). The drawings of the chapter heads are made from photographs taken from family albums; in other instances Bechdel has drawn or traced images from William Morris wallpaper patterns in the family home, from childhood diary entries, and from her father's handwritten letters. Reproducing her father's writing makes her feel like a "forger," a suggestive word since forgery or fraudulent imitation is a recurrent theme in the work.

The middle of *Fun Home* reveals a "centerfold," a two-page drawing of a photograph of the babysitter "Roy" in his underwear, stretched out on a bed, languorous, postcoital. Bechdel found the photograph in a box of family pictures shortly after her father's death; on the edge of the photo her father had blotted out the year but not the month of the printing date, evidence, she believes, that he wished to be "simultaneously hidden and revealed" (100). This illustration functions as a clue to his desire and as an emblem of her investigation, the twin poles of the work. In the interview Bechdel speaks about this drawing and the photograph on which she based it:

> It was a stunning glimpse into my father's hidden life, this life that was apparently running parallel to our regular everyday existence. And it was particularly compelling to me at the time because I was just coming out myself. I felt this sort of posthumous bond with my father, like I shared this thing with him, like we were comrades. I didn't start working on the book then, but over the years that picture persisted in my memory. It's literally the core of the book. (1006)

She goes on to describe her "detective work" in sleuthing for his police record when he was accused of providing beer to underage boys in his town (though she suspects his interest did not stop at beer) and of her "archiving impulse" to examine family photo albums and the letters her mother handed over to her. Nevertheless, if Bechdel thinks such items will yield definitive truth, the drawing of Roy's photograph suggests that no evidence she probes can ever be conclusive. Though her drawing of archival materials such as photographs, maps, letters, or discovered iconic objects—all of which show up in *Fun Home*—might appear to be irrefutable proof of one kind of secret or another, they are not. Who can tell the real story of Roy's photograph? There might be Roy's version, the father's, or the mother's. Even Bechdel's version is provisional, and she seems content to leave it—as she leaves many of her stories—unresolved. She also knows *her* story cannot be separable from *others'* stories, let alone granted authority. Perhaps uncertainty and ambiguity give her a more liberalizing kind of truth. This is why, I believe, she discovers herself in her father and has him imply that his story, however inexplicable, cannot be fully divorced from her own.

Concealment defines Bechdel's way of positioning herself within the family and explains how she often saw herself. But the publication of *Fun Home* asserts her dawning and open commitment to art. When she represents how she received the news by telephone from her mother that her

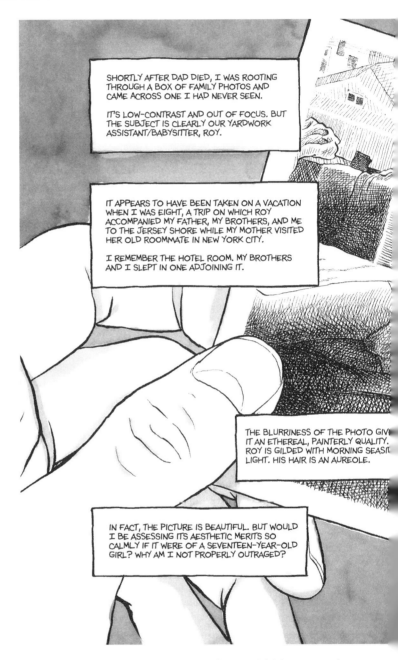

FIGURE 4. Excerpted from *Fun Home: A Family Tragicomic* by Alison Bechdel (pp. 100–101). Copyright © 2006 by Alison Bechdel. Reprinted by permission of Houghton Mifflin Harcourt Publishing Company. All rights reserved.

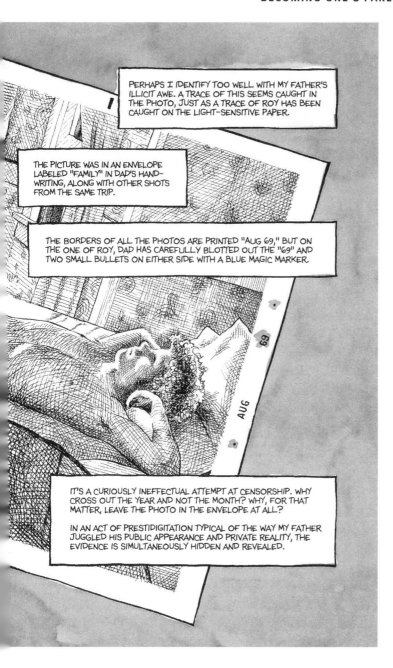

PERHAPS I IDENTIFY TOO WELL WITH MY FATHER'S ILLICIT AWE. A TRACE OF THIS SEEMS CAUGHT IN THE PHOTO, JUST AS A TRACE OF ROY HAS BEEN CAUGHT ON THE LIGHT-SENSITIVE PAPER.

THE PICTURE WAS IN AN ENVELOPE LABELED "FAMILY" IN DAD'S HAND-WRITING, ALONG WITH OTHER SHOTS FROM THE SAME TRIP.

THE BORDERS OF ALL THE PHOTOS ARE PRINTED "AUG 69," BUT ON THE ONE OF ROY, DAD HAS CAREFULLY BLOTTED OUT THE "69" AND TWO SMALL BULLETS ON EITHER SIDE WITH A BLUE MAGIC MARKER.

IT'S A CURIOUSLY INEFFECTUAL ATTEMPT AT CENSORSHIP. WHY CROSS OUT THE YEAR AND NOT THE MONTH? WHY, FOR THAT MATTER, LEAVE THE PHOTO IN THE ENVELOPE AT ALL?

IN AN ACT OF PRESTIDIGITATION TYPICAL OF THE WAY MY FATHER JUGGLED HIS PUBLIC APPEARANCE AND PRIVATE REALITY, THE EVIDENCE IS SIMULTANEOUSLY HIDDEN AND REVEALED.

father was gay and likely had an affair with Roy the babysitter, Bechdel draws herself on the floor, and we look down on her from an overhead perspective. Although this view tends to diminish her and make her appear defenseless, the mother's news overshadowing, even erasing, her own coming out, the drawing nevertheless portrays material evidence of her future profession as artist: a sketchbook lies next to her. The illustration suggests she ultimately will resist erasure and turn vulnerability into an asset, as she becomes the far-seeing creator or "artificer" of her life, a term I use deliberately to echo the one she invoked about her father in the first chapter head drawing. Julia Watson calls attention to *Fun Home* as both a coming-out story and a coming-of-age story (34). Bechdel's career as artist is implied in this description of the work.

In assessing Bechdel's attitude toward the family secret that she uncovers as a detective and assesses as an engaged party, it's important to see that even though she makes a distinction between her father's repressed and closeted gayness and her own openness, between her father's covert relationships and her own admission of her emergent lesbian sexuality, she never attacks his repression nor his defenses. Nor does she write her story as a traditional one of rebellion against a conventional parent. How could she, even if we grant that in this case paternal counterfeiting and repression effectively substitute for the social conventions she might have scorned? Her sense of herself as confident lesbian and skilled artist coincides with her decision to link herself with her father, growing into confidence and artistic mastery as she draws and narrates the discoveries of both their sexual identities. Using Proust's word *inversion* joins father and daughter no less than the drawing of him in a woman's bathing suit parallels one of herself in "butch" dress. As she examines and interprets the photographs she discovers in a box after his death, she realizes there is more identification than separateness. The dual instances of same-sex desire, the parallel cross-dressing, the criss-crossing and analogous inversions all connect father and daughter.

Nevertheless the allegiance to her father she felt as a child partly conflicts with her need as a writer to expose whatever truth she can glean from the past. In the interview she claims that the memoir "is in many ways a huge violation of my family" (Chute, 1009). And yet the memoir is also an homage, and it appears she both usurps and honors her father. There's a drawing in which she shows her father taking a photograph of the family on the front steps. The caption reads: "He used his skillful artifice not to make things, but to make things appear to be what they were not. That is to say, impeccable" (16). Though these words may seem like a condemnation, Bechdel does portray the family as a unit, and the tone of the work is one of sadness more than alienation, sadness that he, unlike she, could never acknowledge publicly who he was privately, could never get beyond subterfuge and fakery. The drawn sketchbook, evidence of her eventual artistic career, is a sign of the new function that she will take on with all its ambiguities and with which she will produce the complex narrative of her dysfunctional family, which she is as much a part of as apart from.

CHAPTER 5

Breaking the Silence

I began this book with a reading of three works portraying the ways imperiled Jews disguised themselves to survive. Knowing full well who they were (if they hadn't known someone else would have told them in no uncertain terms), they elected to transform themselves for their very lives, and in one case, for life. This final chapter treats two contrastive yet comparable works in which the writers show how their fathers kept them from knowing the truth of their identities. In each case a daughter learns of an unexpected paternity. One discovers that her father is literally not whom she thought, and as a result is enjoined, or rather enjoins herself, to secrecy and silence; the other's discovery may not be so startling (her father is the man she has known all along as such), but that father is quite unlike the one whom she thought he was, and she neither accepts the identity previously thrust on her by his fraudulent one, nor will she be mute about her courageous exploration of the truth.

Essie Mae Washington-Williams, the black daughter of Senator Strom Thurmond, the white supremacist South Carolinian, in *Dear Senator* reveals how she learned about the paternity when she was a teenager but held her tongue for almost a half-century, suppressing her secret and repressing her identity out of an impulse to protect both Thurmond and herself. Whether her resistance to speak out counts as personal caution matching her father's political pragmatism or as a form of pathology is not my concern here.

What I'm interested in is the difficulty she suffered in the course of her long voicelessness, and the consequences for self-assertion and self-reclamation when she finally and publicly spoke the truth. Unlike with Mary Gordon and Louise Steinman, Washington-Williams knew the parental secret for decades, and kept it. Her identity is of course intimately linked to that secret, and she differs from the other children in this study in that she neither makes a belated discovery nor speaks openly about the acquisition of the forbidden knowledge for a long while after learning it.

Bliss Broyard simply assumed she and her father were white until, as he was dying, she learned he was a closeted light-skinned black man with Haitian Creole ancestry. Fascinated rather than upset, she researches her father's heritage and revises her self-understanding, in large part to get back to and reclaim connections to the family she believes was effectively stolen from her. Her bold act of self-redefinition is achieved despite how she imagines her father would have reacted to his daughter's unraveling the strands of the covert identity he had meticulously constructed. At the same time she celebrates a freedom of self-determination and an ability to re-create herself, an act paradoxically corresponding to his own achievement, however different the motives. So her work *One Drop: My Father's Hidden Life—A Story of Race and Family Secrets* is at once an attempt to separate herself from his shame and to rejoin him in the racial identity he had long since repudiated. She exposes the truth about her father's dissimulation, but in some ways she is less interested in him than in defining who she now sees herself to be. How she will characterize *herself* is at the heart of her project.

It seems appropriate to close the book on Broyard's note of triumph, though she hardly would call it that, being too modest and concerned less with personal aggrandizement than with exploring the mysteries of identity while acknowledging and assenting to the complexities of race. I use the word "triumph" to describe how she has broken free of the family secret—a secret that appeared to grant her a freedom her father never felt and a release from his self-consciousness, but one she comes to view as having constrained her identity. I think "triumph" is appropriate also in that she actively redefines herself in a way that once would have seemed unimaginable.

Nevertheless children who discover secrets withheld from them will not easily avoid a suspicion they have been betrayed or asked to live in a twilight world of half-truths that affect them in fundamental ways. If the fathers represented in these two works are analogous in some sense to mechanisms of institutional power that prescribe, instruct, regulate, and control behavior, all the while concealing motives and operating in secrecy, the question of the children's freely determining behavior or, just as important, their self-recognition becomes necessarily problematic. Of course uncovering the secrets is not what either of the authors in this chapter ultimately seeks; rather, it is to understand and perhaps to condone the impulse to the secrecy while not being determined by it. Still, like less triumphal figures such as Auster, Rips, Wolff, and Bechdel, not even Washington-Williams and Broyard dispel anxiety and uncertainty; even as they invent themselves anew they are preoccupied with the secretive parent, never fully emancipated from filial absorption. The drama inheres in their negotiation with the authority and power of the secrecy, even as they struggle against its domination.

Race, Secrecy, and Discovery: Black on White, White on Black

In this chapter I compare two autobiographies by women who discover, at different stages of their lives, that their race is not what they thought it was because in each case their father's identity was not what they thought *it* was. In each of these texts about racial secrecy, the writer tracks the process of exposing the cover-up and the duplicity. I will discuss the nature of the parental deception and the complex ways in which each daughter responded to her newly acquired knowledge and embarked on an act of self-revision; how each reconceived of her father in light of her new racial identity; how each defined herself as a part of American history previously unknown to her (in one instance living in the South and feeling like a spy in alien territory, in the other carrying out cultural and genealogical research about her roots); and how each woman shapes her story as a journey of exploration, confrontation, and accommodation.

The first case is that of Essie Mae Washington Williams, the daughter of Strom Thurmond and of a woman who was a maid in his South Carolina family home. Washington-Williams was a teenager when she learned that the woman who brought her up and whom she thought to be her mother was really her mother's sister and that her biological father was not her aunt's husband but rather the man who would serve for over fifty years in the U.S. Senate, the architect of legislation that consistently denied African-Americans basic civil rights. The second case is that of Bliss Broyard, the daughter of Anatole Broyard, for many years a writer, book critic, and editor at the *New York Times,* who never told his two children the truth of his black ancestry and who, as a descendent of a light-skinned Haitian Creole, passed as white, though many friends and colleagues, unlike his daughter, suspected he was not.

Because of her father's political career, Washington-Williams was forced to conceal her identity as his child. Her narrative emphasizes how she voluntarily repressed their secret and experienced the emotional costs, a silence she owed not only to a willingness to respect an implied "social contract" between her father and herself but to acquired traits of taciturnity and an instinct for privacy. It is also the story of her ambivalence toward Thurmond—on one hand pride in having an esteemed, powerful, and well-placed father, indebtedness for his financial generosity, and even affection if not love; on the other hand a lingering sense of having been betrayed for his refusal to acknowledge her publicly and a continual disillusionment at his unapologetic racism. Her text expresses that lifelong doubleness, and its title, *Dear Senator: A Memoir by the Daughter of Strom Thurmond* (2005), is an oxymoron of affection and formality. The work veers between her meetings with Thurmond, a number of which occur in the office of the president of the small Negro college where Thurmond sent her and which are hedged around with secrecy on both their parts; his refusal of intimacy (he treats her less as a daughter than as a charity case); and an inventory of southern mores and politics that put her constantly in a double bind, forcing her to regard her father as a distant "other," herself as "'back street' family" (192) as the southern expression had it. Washington-Williams never doubts that Thurmond loves her in his way, but she refers to it as "segregated love," the double entendre capturing both the wall between them and the Jim Crow laws and attitudes of the South. Feeling more like "an accident" (155) than a daughter, she can never be fully a part of his life, merely an object of toleration, someone he visits infrequently and always surreptitiously.

She also calls his feeling for her "an unspeakable love" (148), and an irony of the memoir is that for so long the unspeakableness is mutual—both of them protecting his career and public reputation, while she additionally defends herself against the unwelcome publicity sure to follow any revelation. The work examines what it means to carry an unspoken secret for so long, one that confuses her about the meaning of love, causes her to express ambivalence toward a man whose politics she seeks in vain to change as she summons the courage to suggest to him a different course, and threatens to undermine her later marriage to a man who urges her to speak out to embarrass and destroy the racist he loathes. Her father's dissimulation has provoked her own.

When she first learns her true paternity, initial bewilderment gives way to astonishment that she is part of "Southern aristocracy" (40), but this naïve reaction quickly yields to disillusionment as she discovers that the closest friend of Thurmond's father had organized lynch mobs. Her historical consciousness gradually raised, she begins to perceive Thurmond as part of a savage legacy, soon undergoing her lifelong vacillation between "great expectations" (93) and the realization he will never acknowledge her publicly as a daughter. She defines herself as a riddle, the mixed blood a marker of her confused state that causes her grief less because she cannot bear the racial hybridity—in fact it gives her a certain pleasure—than because her father invokes the "one drop of blood" iron law and barely conceals his conde- scension and belief in her inferiority. Her ambivalence is so powerful that at one point she regrets she had ever been made aware of her real parents; she is unequivocal in her doubleness: "I somehow couldn't dislike him the way I wanted to" (148).

The work is painful because throughout there is so much she wants to know but dares not ask. As a young child she is continually cautioned to keep her mouth shut, to make no inquiries; so when the man she believes to be her father leaves his wife, Essie knows she must not question why. When she learns her supposed mother is her aunt, inquiry is again taboo. Probing the origins of her own light skin is similarly forbidden, until as a teenager she is taken to meet her father. Enmeshed in a web of dissimula- tion, committed to silence, she tells no one other than her husband, not even her children. The "lifetime gag order" (160) may be culturally sanctioned, but it is, for a long time, self-imposed; never does Thurmond swear her to secrecy, she simply internalizes the prohibition and defines herself as "a state secret" (191). The only interrogation she permits herself is one she conducts internally: Is she too forgiving of her father? Does she have "filial blinders" (170) on, her historical awareness conflicting with a self-deceiving anticipa- tion of a closeness she intuits will never come?

Washington-Williams never suggests that she has been damaged by the repression, though when Thurmond dies at one hundred she senses how it has dominated her life and has become an almost instinctive reaction to events. The story ends with her finally revealing the secret to her daugh- ter, who urges her mother to challenge Thurmond's will (another excision of Washington-Williams from her father's life), to expose the lie, and to write the book. In time the Thurmond family reluctantly acknowledges the paternity, and the book ends with Washington-Williams refusing to call herself black or white, preferring to define herself not by race at all since the genetic mixture necessarily defends against a tendency to stereotype. Thus she appears to resolve the problematic question of selfhood by claiming that her identity can be a freedom, certainly a challenge, rather than a burden.

And yet something about her almost-too-easy embrace of black and white ("In my past lives, as defined by my genealogy, I was a slave and I was a mas- ter. . . . I was the glorious president of the South and I was a lowly maid in Edgefield") appears to evade the truth about the experience she has suffered

(223). She is so anxious not to hold a grudge, and so resistant to admitting the hatred she feels but muffles at every opportunity, one wonders if she forces herself to transcend the conflicting emotions by seeing herself as a symbol and signpost for biracialism, a kind of allegory of national multiplicity, rather than as a woman whose mixed heritage, given the social conditions at the time and the circumstances of her father's political role, threatened to damage if not disable her at every point in her adult life. Her adulation of Thurmond is understandable, but I am tempted to ask how her doubleness toward him gets internalized to produce exactly the same doubleness toward herself. We can be grateful that she has emerged relatively healthy after undergoing an ordeal in which the mixed-race legacy forced her into a repressed identity and an evasion, even a counterfeiting analogous to her father's own that, if not precisely hypocritical, does lend a tragic dimension to her life. On the other hand, what does it say that her lifelong secrecy was maintained out of loyalty to him and dread of his power, whatever the cost? Just how much self-hatred did her ambivalence produce? Washington-Williams's attitude toward her mixed race is tantamount to a compromise of identity. When you really do not know who you are—and she was puzzled to the core of her being—and when the "most important man in [her] life" (94) is responsible for that confusion, then the profession of secrecy is not merely a strategy or a defense but something close to self-laceration, if not pathology. Because of that I am somewhat suspicious about the ringing positive note of the finale, when she describes herself as "a simple person who loves America as the wonderful place that has allowed me to discover, and to be, exactly who I am" (223). But who exactly is that?

Were we to ask whether her outing of Strom Thurmond violates their "social contract" and his implicit expectations of concealment, we might answer it in historical and cultural terms, insofar as certain social issues no longer disturb us so much as they once did: illegitimacy, mixed-race children, and the disclosure or confession of such matters. More important, Washington-Williams's decision to speak out and to write about her history *is* an achievement and assertion of a confident selfhood, a self-invention if you will, and a desire to claim her place in a complex weave of history—familial and racial. But perhaps more crucially her work implicitly raises and confronts a different though not unrelated problem, one that arguably stands to finesse the ethical issue altogether. It is a problem that Bliss Broyard examines in more detail and with greater insight in *her* account: In what ways can or should identity be defined in racial terms at all?

Broyard's search for her father's origins, *One Drop: My Father's Hidden Life—A Story of Race and Family Secrets* (2007), begins this way: "Two months before my father died of prostate cancer, I learned about a secret, but I had always sensed that there was something about my family, or even many things, that I didn't know. As a child, when I was left alone in the house, I would search through my mother's file cabinets and my father's study for elaboration, clarification, some proof. . . . Of what? I couldn't exactly say" (3). Going from childhood snooper to adult inquirer, Broyard investigates and speculates about the history and motivations for her father's great secret that he was partially black, and her text tracks her decision to embrace her own mixed-race identity. Aware for some time her father harbored a secret, she assumed it had to do with a crime. Perhaps in the father's eyes it did—there is considerable evidence that he felt guilty for both abandoning his birth family and deceiving his children, continually resisting any revelation of his Creole ancestry. Washington-Williams's and Broyard's books appear to be written under the spell of the famous opening sentence of Maxine Hong Kingston's *The Woman Warrior*—"'You must not tell anyone,' my mother said, 'what I am about to tell you.'" Immediately after Anatole Broyard's death, his wife reveals the truth to her children, a confession that for years she had urged Broyard to make to them. The son's reaction is contemporarily casual ("That's all?"), while the daughter's sets up the terms of her future project: "The idea thrilled me, as though I'd been reading a fascinating history book and then discovered my own name in the index" (17).

One Drop is predicated on the daughter's curiosity when her father dies. Unable to ask him anything, she must delve, going to the available scraps of evidence—birth certificates, court records, biographical sketches—documents that can convey how a society determines the nature of race. Searching represents both a need to know and a desire to get back to the family that in some sense had been stolen from her; to reconstruct that family and to be with it in a fuller, more honest way. We might even say that her investigation is an act of mourning and that the text is a kind of elegy, as much for herself as for the extended family of which she had been deprived. The casualness of her brother's reaction on hearing the news may suggest that to him race is no big deal, but his father knew it was, and so does his sister. Bliss Broyard's quest to learn the truth grounds her identity very much in race, only her response is the opposite of her father's: a willingness to reaffirm what he spent a lifetime fleeing and denying.

The central issue in Broyard's search is her right to know about her identity and her conviction that she, as much as her furtive father, owns the rights to his story. Her narrative attempts to validate and authorize that possession, and her detective work in the realms of family and racial history entails a claim, even a prerogative or a kind of inherited entitlement, to do whatever is necessary to know and to interpret, even if it means she must "carefully strip away the father that I had known…like uncovering a pentimento" (318). Though her mother urged her husband to speak the truth to his children, he acknowledged only he was French, perhaps vaguely Portuguese, with a New Orleans ancestry. Broyard imagines her father's posthumous impatience with her investigation, especially his resentment at her unearthing and disclosing what he spent a lifetime concealing. Broyard learns a fundamental truth about her father's secrecy: It is not so much something impossible to know, but rather something impossible for him to have acknowledged.

Much of the burden of her text is to explain to the reader but particularly to herself why the secret lingered for so long, why indeed her father went to his death without confessing it to his children. She also fantasizes his seeking forgiveness for having presented a false front, for putting her now to such trouble, and especially for causing her to confront and perhaps accept the very blackness from which he was fleeing, thus exposing her to the prejudice he so feared. Her text traces an arc from initial anger at his betrayal of his family, his deception of her, and his violation of their heritage, to an act of empathy as she imagines that he bestows on her, consciously or not, the option of deciding just who to be. It is a legacy that is both predicament and self-determination, dilemma and freedom.

Anatole Broyard was Philip Roth's model for the protagonist of *The Human Stain,* an African-American who passes as a Jew. Like Coleman Silk in that novel, Broyard repudiated and ignored his birth family, especially a dark-skinned sister who might have threatened his ability to pass. While Broyard wrote often about black culture, jazz, and African-Cuban music and frequented nightclubs in Harlem, he feared being typed as a black writer, and in his work as a book reviewer for the *New York Times* he seldom discussed African-American novels. He deliberately married a Scandinavian woman so his children would look as white as possible, and he sought to recreate himself so as not to be trapped by his racial past. But as secrets piled on secrets, and he resisted confessing anything that might reveal his ancestral past and unravel his web of dissimulation, he must have felt like Macbeth fearing the impossibility of the dead remaining firmly buried in their place.

His daughter believes that the shifts in his behavior he required in order to pass, including changes in speech rhythms, evasions about family history, and indifference to racist slurs, guaranteed an inauthenticity that turned him into an "imposter." Ironically his daughter once took a personality test that caused the examiner to declare to her "[Y]ou're not living in a way that's true to who you are" (63). That accusation of fraud will come to haunt her, and I suspect that the memory of it years later impels her, in the face of her new discoveries, to avoid the resistances and self-deceptions that marked her father. Imagining his wish not to be trapped in a black identity that would confine his liberty and narrow his choices, her decision to rewrite his history and implicitly her own stems from a desire to act unflinchingly on matters of *her* racial definition and to reevaluate *her* identity and accept it fully, even eagerly. In the face of parental dissembling, her revisionary text expresses frustration at what she has been kept from and deprived of, as she seeks to embed her identity in a concrete history of New Orleans Creole culture, the very one her father denied and from which he escaped.

Broyard embarks on a long research project that combines archival history with visits to family members and to the Creole community of New Orleans, as well as to Broyard families in Los Angeles. On the scent of her father's trail of deceptions, she traces his family through genealogical and census records, city directories, marriage licenses, wills, obituaries, and interviews, and, perhaps most thoroughly, she immerses herself in New Orleans Creole history. She learns that her white great-great grandfather married a black woman descended from refugees from St. Domingue (modern Haiti); while her father passed as white, her ancestor passed as *black* because in New Orleans at the time interracial marriage was banned. Later, when the ban was rescinded, he changed his identification to "white," that of his children to "mulatto." Eventually Creoles were treated as "colored," and for several generations Jim Crow laws made them no different from blacks, many Creoles resigning themselves to the label "Negro" and taking on black lifestyles. It is from that label and ancestry that her father made his escape.

One Drop veers between Broyard's investigations and a rumination on her own racial position, the two aspects of the text suggesting how her identity is imbricated in her historical work. Her research involves her attending a "Creole Plantation Revelers" dance at Mardi Gras; here she confronts others' skepticism about, even contempt for, her quest, as well as her own confusion about her race and her project. Like so many autobiographers in this study, Broyard is at times uncertain whether the project is worth the disturbance to her equanimity and the threat to her filial respect. Her quest raises questions about her father's history as well as her own identity. Gradually we realize that the drama of the work pivots less on the revelation of her father's racial background, something known early on, than on the agonizing question of how she will define herself.

She displays a fine self-consciousness about how embracing a mixed-race identity might alienate those who never enjoyed her privileged upbringing in the white world, or who never had the luxury of choosing an identification without risking the consequences. Indeed her undertaking raises complex questions about racial identity: Is it a genetically determined essence, or is it a deliberately chosen construction, even a performance—a question brought to mind when she goes to the Mardi Gras ball dressed as she puts it in "plantation attire" (287). Though she hopes "to transform myself from the outside in" (292), she can only dress the part, fearing she will be regarded once again as an imposter, as when several black men she meets mock white youths for slumming and romantically playing at being African-American. It is one thing to be a *"passablanc,"* as her father was termed, quite another thing to *wish* to be a *"passanoir."* And yet she's determined neither to hide her African ancestry nor to harbor secrets, though what she precisely is never becomes clear. "I hated how uncertain I became when trying to locate myself on this racial landscape or even recognize its terrain. Torn between trying to pinpoint the boundaries between black and white and an urge to deny their existence at all, I was caught in a dialectical tug-of-war" (295). Her young adult existential question, "Who am I?" has turned into a social and genetic one: *"What* am I?" The answer to *that* question depends on what she discovers about her father, so linked are the two investigations. We might assume that she is in the process of becoming what she feels herself most to be, but how does she really know what that is? The quandary and the questions abide: If, for example, she accepts herself as *Creole,* could that be a way of not having to be African-American, a facile way out of her dilemma? And yet she refuses to flee from herself as her father did in an act of self-annihilation. The only way out of the problem is to plunge ever more deeply into the secret.

Washington-Williams suffers in a different way from Broyard. Strom Thurmond's daughter knows who she is, but laments how she has been defined to rob her of equality and to split her identity in value; by denying one side of who she is, her father implicitly rejects her altogether. Broyard by contrast remains uncertain (she never achieves what she calls the "Aha!" moment, an affirmation of an identity "deep in my bones"), but suffers little, rescuing herself from distressing bafflement by accepting that complex racial state as normative, perhaps even destined. Her father's secrecy initially forces her into doubt, but after sixteen years of dogged research, meeting her large multiracial family, and agonizing over her identity, she knows that she can never answer definitively the question "What am I?" (even with DNA testing, a discussion of which forms the Afterword to her text). Her own multicultural marriage intensifies an ineluctable complexity, and if her young son were to ask about his background, she would be ready: "Daddy is a Sephardic Jew with roots in Spain, Greece, and Turkey, and Mommy is Norwegian, French, black, and Choctaw Indian." With that realization she achieves a peace despite, or perhaps because of, the indeterminate answers. Her attitude transcends the problem that afflicted her father.

One identity she embraces accords with what her father had chosen: a writer. Here is where a story she inserts in her work takes on paradigmatic importance. Henry Louis Gates was about to profile her father as part of a series for *The New Yorker* that eventually became *Thirteen Ways of Looking at a Black Man*. Gates encouraged Bliss also to write about her father, but as he was about to publish his essay while she was just beginning her research, and because he was the more important author writing in a major venue, his version of Anatole Broyard would necessarily have prominence. For Bliss Broyard the key issue is who gets to control the story of her father and by extension of herself. Though Gates's description of her father is accurate—Broyard is "a virtuoso of ambiguity and equivocation" and "a connoisseur of the liminal" (110)—she has no desire to cede control of her father's narrative. In the introduction to his book, Gates quotes the cultural critic Stuart Hall in a statement referring to the identities of his African-American subjects but equally applicable to Bliss Broyard herself: "Identities are the names we give to the different ways we are positioned by, and position ourselves in, the narratives of the past" (xiv).

Gates never knew Anatole Broyard, while Bliss had known him for twenty-four years, but that fact alone hardly grants her sole right of comprehension and interpretation. The competition to define both father's and daughter's identities goes to the heart of her project. That competition, in which Gates fires the first shot, doubtless impels her into writing and confirms her conviction about her enterprise: to assert that the identities of both father and daughter, however strong the claim that they can be freely chosen, are nevertheless rooted in family and in history. Anatole Broyard had written in a *New York Times* column that he had escaped to Greenwich Village, "where no one had been born of a mother and father, where the people I met had sprung from their own brows. . . . [W]e outdistanced our history and our humanity." He needed to repudiate a past no longer useful to him and to embrace a myth that his self-fashioning was evidence of authenticity. But Bliss knows the deeper truth that one cannot fully escape the past, nor, in her estimation, should one.

In coming to write her story of the family, in narrating the secrets of the family past, Bliss Broyard accepts the necessity of her heritage, released to claim a rightful place in it. Gates makes a distinction between how Anatole Broyard viewed the world (as an opportunity for "self-creation") and how his children viewed it (as an imperative for a greater authenticity). Bliss too is capable of inventing herself, not to escape the past but to negotiate her legacy from that past. While I suspect that she has ambivalent feelings about her father's contention that even race can be "an elective affinity" as Gates has it, she does join with her father in affirming a right to choose.

Her choice connects her with a family, a community, and a history. Nancy Miller has argued that "Autobiography's story is about the web of entanglement in which we find ourselves, one that we sometimes choose" ("The Entangled Self," 543). Not only does Broyard's text demonstrate her need for the extended family in order for her to write her story, but her work is effectively one of collaboration, as by the same token her racial identity is itself "collaborative," a stew of multiple genes. If Washington-Williams chooses to expose the secret she had maintained for so many years, Broyard elects to entangle herself in a complex web of history, storytelling, and silences. She makes her research and her writing an integral aspect of the identity that, throughout the project, she is in the process of discovering. As a result she asserts that we may choose our race as much as race may choose us.

Here is where she is most respectful of her father's dilemma and choice. While one might conclude that Anatole Broyard's concealment made him anything but authentic, his daughter instinctively declares that even his rejection of his racial inheritance could be construed as a brave act of self-definition and a refusal to be definitively categorized, however different the reasons from her own. Her search for origins involving exposure of "the secret" should not be considered a betrayal so much as an attempt to join with her father in an act of understanding and love—not because his choice necessarily manifested generosity toward her but because that choice allowed her to explore the mysteries of identity and what it means to feel like an authentic subject. It is rare that uncovering a parental secret allows the child not only to understand what has been opaque but, more crucially perhaps, to disentangle the complex strands of her own distinctiveness.

Conclusion
Freedom or Exploitation?

I ended this study with a discussion of Bliss Broyard's work because she may stand for an aspiration all the writers of this book express, whether overtly or not: to achieve a degree of autonomy even though they claim to have been bridled by circumstances that have made freedom dubious or difficult. As I have argued, many of the men and women writing their fathers' lives undertake the searches for parental secrets less to complain they have been victims unjustly injured by those concealments than to show they have escaped the more harmful consequences of the deceptions and the evasions, in the process becoming self-fashioners if only in their ability to write their story. Of course if the freedom to tell the story led only to a tale of persecution and mistreatment, this could be a tautology, but Broyard's narrative is void of bitterness or castigation, and though she ultimately rejects an identity as a white woman she embraces the same kind of freedom her father elected, not out of protest against the race he chose or the idea of inheritance but, like him, to be as free as humanly possible to choose her own fate and write herself into a new identity. She therefore represents an ideal of self-transfiguration from a received model of selfhood. Her act of malleable regeneration recalls an apothegm of Michel Foucault: "One writes to become someone other than who one is" (182).

Rather than bringing this book to a definitive conclusion, I want to end by raising several questions, largely to affirm that the issues I've discussed are necessarily open-ended. One of the most important questions has to do with the relation of secrecy to private life. If we think that the right to privacy is part of what constitutes our personhood and that concealment is an almost sacred privilege, then we might insist that the secrets of others not be exposed under any circumstances. We might even ask if the anguished self-reflection in almost all the auto/biographical work I've addressed is sufficient to justify those writers delving into the secret lives of their fathers. If, however, we believe that secrets make intimacy impossible and family life constrained, we may have no problem in justifying their revelation, believing family members have the right to probe secret lives until they are brought to the light of day. Since we form our identity in part from others, to confront a father whose life is based on deception may ultimately be salutary for our self-construction.

A corollary question might ask if there is something important about one's *not* knowing the secret. Would a resistance to the knowing spare the child from having to confront dark truths and from increasing the distress he or she already feels? Could a decision not to investigate result from a generous desire to protect the father from the pain of exposure and raise hopes of increased closeness given that exposure might rupture whatever remains of the relation? On the other hand how could that ignorance not raise doubts about anything the father would say or do, aggravating unverified suspicions? This brings up another difficult question: How can we discern what a "satisfying" conclusion to such a quest really is? Satisfaction might be a matter of gaining full and complete knowledge of the secrets; of creating a comprehensive narrative accounting for what was believed or suspected but not fully known until the completion of the search; or of answering questions that allow the child to understand his or her identity in a way impossible before the accrued findings.

The *New York Times* book critic Michiko Kakutani, in a succinct statement about satisfaction in memoir applicable to the works I've considered, characterizes the motivating force of memoir writing and reading as "the belief that confession is therapeutic and therapy is redemptive and redemption somehow equals art" (quoted in Mendelsohn, "But Enough About Me," 70). Though Kakutani's characterization is doubtless meant to condemn what she takes to be the genre's foundational principles, it is true that the writers in this study do justify the exposure of secrecy on grounds of a therapeutic yield and consequent redemption defined as the acquisition of knowledge whose lack prevented a fruitful relation with the father. Only in the act of speaking out, the children seem to say, can they find necessary relief from the anguish resulting from the father's taciturnity. In the face of the revelations we readers function somewhat as priests or secular judges listening to the enforced confessions and pronouncing on the child's right to the narrative. As for art, while none of the writers makes the case for the project on the grounds of aesthetics alone, I have tried to show how these narratives tell complicated stories in complex, artful ways.

A critic who believes such texts are inescapably exploitive, self-serving, and mendacious once complained to me that in writing them those adult children reveal their inadequacies and "relational deficiencies," retaliating out of bitterness because they did not have the fathers they naively wished for, who would be forgiving, generous, and always available. Furthermore, he asserted, such children are unable to conceive states of mind other than their own. And yet we have seen many of these writers attempting to put themselves in the place of their fathers and to imagine what in those lives drove the older men to secrecy. More important, these children do not appear to write from a position of defensiveness nor punitive vengefulness so much as to show how the shaping power the secretive fathers consciously or inadvertently exercised over the offspring confused, regulated, and compromised the latter's self-understanding. The effects of paternal power could not easily be escaped, and whatever autonomy is expressed in these texts is achieved only with a struggle of conscience and will. Whether these accomplishments are fact or illusion, the writing of the complex relationships dramatizes the struggle between father and children, figures whose lives are inextricably entwined.

The same critic wonders whether the writers, should they have children of their own, will fear to be exposed in turn as inadequate failures and violators of *their* children's trust. This is a good question, if only because it would be interesting to know how the writers, especially those who show little forgiveness to their fathers, regard their project as they age. Auster, Gordon, Wolff, Washington-Williams, and Broyard all allege having made a conscious effort to treat their own children with an openness they missed in their fathers, so I suspect they would have no such obvious concern. Such parents recognize the importance that knowing one's origin, in all its difficult complexity, has for both self-understanding and a parent-child relation in which the two figures will become fully present to the other. Given this recognition, coming to be known by their children should hold no fear, only the promise of hard-earned accommodation.

BIBLIOGRAPHY

Aciman, André. *False Papers: Essays on Exile and Memory.* New York: Farrar, Straus, Giroux, 2000.

Ackerley, J. R. *My Father and Myself.* London: The Bodley Head, 1968.

Adams, Timothy Dow. *Light Writing and Life Writing: Photography in Autobiography.* Chapel Hill: University of North Carolina Press, 2000.

——. *Telling Lies in Modern American Autobiography.* Chapel Hill: University of North Carolina Press, 1990.

Appignanesi, Lisa. *Losing the Dead: A Family Memoir.* London: Vintage, 2000.

Auster, Paul. *The Art of Hunger.* New York: Penguin Books, 1992.

——. *The Invention of Solitude.* New York: Penguin Books, 1988.

Barbour, John D. "Judging and Not Judging Parents." In *The Ethics of Life Writing,* edited by John Paul Eakin, 73–98. Ithaca: Cornell University Press, 2004.

——. *The Value of Solitude.* Charlottesville: University of Virginia Press, 2004.

Bechdel, Alison. *Fun Home: A Family Tragicomic.* Boston: Houghton Mifflin, 2006.

Bersani, Leo, and Adam Phillips. *Intimacies.* Chicago: University of Chicago Press, 2008.

Besemeres, Mary. "The Family in Exile, Between Languages: Eva Hoffman's *Lost in Translation,* Lisa Appignanesi's *Losing the Dea*d, Anna Vlasopolos's *No Return Address.*" *a/b: Auto/Biography Studies* 19 (2004): 239–248.

Blaise, Clark. *I Had a Father: A Post-Modern Autobiography.* Reading, Mass.: Addison-Wesley, 1993.

——. "A Middle-Aged Orphan." *New York Times Magazine.* April 24, 1986.

Bok, Sissela. *Secrets: On the Ethics of Concealment and Revelation.* New York: Vintage Books, 1989.

Brooks, Peter. *Troubling Confessions: Speaking Guilt in Law and Literature.* Chicago: University of Chicago Press, 2000.

Broyard, Bliss. *One Drop: My Father's Hidden Life—A Story of Race and Family Secrets.* New York: Little, Brown, 2007.

Buckton, Oliver S. *Secret Selves: Confession and Same-Sex Desire in Victorian Autobiography.* Chapel Hill: University of North Carolina Press, 1998.

Cavarero, Adriana. *Relating Narratives: Storytelling and Selfhood.* Translated by Paul A. Kottman. London: Routledge, 2000.

Chandler, Marilyn R. "A Healing Art: Therapeutic Dimensions of Autobiography." *a/b: Auto/Biography Studies* 5 (1989): 4–14.

Chekhov, Anton. *The Russian Master and Other Stories.* Translated by Ronald Hingley. Oxford: Oxford University Press, 1999.

Chute, Hilary. "An Interview with Alison Bechdel." *Modern Fiction Studies* 52 (2006): 1004–1013.

Couser, G. Thomas. *Vulnerable Subjects: Ethics and Life Writing.* Ithaca: Cornell University Press, 2004.

Derrida, Jacques. *Archive Fever: A Freudian Impression.* Translated by Eric Prenowitz. Chicago: University of Chicago Press, 1996.

Dutton, Patricia. "Reconciliation and Life Writing." In *Encyclopedia of Life Writing: Autobiographical and Biographical Forms,* vol. 2, edited by Margaretta Jolly. London: Fitzroy Dearborn, 2001, 735–737.

Eagan, Susanna. *Mirror Talk: Genres of Crisis in Contemporary Autobiography.* Chapel Hill: University of North Carolina Press, 1999.

Eakin, Paul John, ed. *The Ethics of Life Writing.* Ithaca: Cornell University Press, 2004.

——. *How Our Lives Become Stories: Making Selves.* Ithaca: Cornell University Press, 1999.

——. *Living Autobiographically: How We Create Identity in Narrative.* Ithaca: Cornell University Press, 2008.

Fitzgerald, Penelope. *The Blue Flower.* London: HarperCollins, 1995.

Foucault, Michel. *Death and the Labyrinth: The Works of Raymond Roussel.* Translated by Charles Ruas. London: Athlone Press, 1986.

Freadman, Richard. "Decent and Indecent: Writing My Father's Life." In *The Ethics of Life Writing,* edited by John Paul Eakin, 121–146. Ithaca: Cornell University Press, 2004.

Freeman, Mark. *Rewriting the Self: History, Memory, Narrative.* New York: Routledge, 1993.

Fremont, Helen. *After Long Silence: A Memoir.* New York: Delta, 1999.

Gates, Henry Louis. *Thirteen Ways of Looking at a Black Man.* New York: Vintage, 1998.

Gilmore, Leigh. *The Limits of Autobiography: Trauma and Testimony.* Ithaca: Cornell University Press, 2001.

Gordon, Mary. *The Shadow Man: A Daughter's Search for Her Father.* New York: Random House, 1996.

Gray, Francine du Plessix. "I Write for Rage Against Reality." In *First Person Singular: Writers on Their Craft,* edited by Joyce Carol Oates, 246–250. Princeton: Princeton University Press, 1985.

Greer, Germaine. *Daddy, We Hardly Knew You.* New York: Alfred A. Knopf, 1990.

Hartman, Geoffrey. *Scars of the Spirit: The Struggle Against Inauthenticity.* New York: Palgrave, 2002.

Helmreich, W. B. *Against All Odds: Holocaust Survivors and the Successful Lives They Made in America.* New York: Simon and Schuster, 1992.

Henke, Suzette A. *Shattered Subjects: Trauma and Testimony in Women's Life-Writing.* New York: St. Martin's Press, 2000.

Hoffman, Eva. *After Such Knowledge: Memory, History, and the Legacy of the Holocaust.* New York: Public Affairs, 2004.

Kahn, Nathaniel, director. *My Architect: A Son's Journey.* A film by Nathaniel Kahn. Copyright © 2003 Louis Kahn Project, Inc. Copyright © 2004 New Yorker Films Artwork.

Kammen, Michael. *Digging up the Dead: A History of Notable American Reburials.* Chicago: University of Chicago Press, 2010.

Kimmelman, Michael. "The Last Act." *New York Review of Books,* October 25, 2007, 4–8.

Kingston, Maxine Hong. *The Woman Warrior: Memoirs of a Girlhood Among Ghosts.* New York: Vintage, 1975.

Kraus, Carolyn. "Proof of Life: Memoir, Truth, and Documentary Evidence." *Biography* 31 (2008): 245–268.

Kuhn, Annette: *Family Secrets: Acts of Memory and Imagination.* London: Verso, 2002.

Kurzem, Mark. *The Mascot: Unraveling the Mystery of My Jewish Father's Nazi Boyhood.* New York: Viking, 2007.

Lanchester, John. *Family Romance: A Love Story.* New York: G.P. Putnam's Sons, 2007.

Lane, Anthony. "The Disappearing Poet: Whatever Happened to Weldon Kees?" *New Yorker,* July 4, 2005, 74–80.

Lane, Jim. *The Autobiographical Documentary in America.* Madison: University of Wisconsin Press, 2002.

Langer, Lawrence L. *Holocaust Testimonies: The Ruins of Memory.* New Haven: Yale University Press, 1991.

Lejeune, Philippe. *On Autobiography.* Edited by Paul John Eakin. Translated by Katherine Leary. Minneapolis: University of Minnesota Press, 1989.

Lelyveld, Joseph. *Omaha Blues: A Memory Loop.* New York: Farrar, Straus and Giroux, 2005.

Levin, Meir. *Novarodok.* Northvale, N.J.: Jason Aronson, 1996.

Magids, D. M. "Personality Comparison Between Children of Hidden Holocaust Survivors and American Jewish Parents." *Journal of Psychology* 132 (1998): 245–255.

Malcolm, Janet. "The Silent Woman." *New Yorker,* August 23 and 30, 1993, 84–159.

——. *Two Lives: Gertrude and Alice.* New Haven: Yale University Press, 2007.

Margalit, Avishai. *The Ethics of Memory.* Cambridge, Mass.: Harvard University Press, 2002.

McCaffrey, Larry, and Gregory Sinda. "An Interview with Paul Auster." *Mississippi Review* 20 (1991): 49–62.

McCooey, David. *Artful Histories: Modern Australian Autobiography.* Cambridge: Cambridge University Press, 1996.

Mendelsohn, Daniel. "But Enough About Me." *New Yorker,* January 25, 2010, 68–74.

———. *The Lost: A Search for Six of Six Million.* New York: HarperCollins, 2006.

Middlebrook, Diane. "Misremembering Ted Hughes." In *The Ethics of Life Writing,* edited by John Paul Eakin, 40–50. Ithaca: Cornell University Press, 2004.

Miller, Nancy. *Bequest and Betrayal: Memoirs of a Parent's Death.* New York: Oxford University Press, 1996.

———. "The Entangled Self: Genre Bondage in the Age of Memoir." *PMLA* 122 (2007): 537–548.

Moi! Autoportraits du XXe Siècle. Milan: Skira, 2004.

O'Connor, Mike. *Crisis, Pursued by Disaster, Followed Closely by Catastrophe: A Memoir of Life on the Run.* New York: Random House, 2007.

Oliver, Anna Cypra. *Assembling My Father: A Daughter's Detective Story.* Boston: Houghton Mifflin, 2004.

Ozick, Cynthia. "*Omaha Blues:* In Research of Lost Time." *New York Times.* April 3, 2005.

Pederson, Martin C. "Interview with Nathaniel Kahn." *Metropolis Magazine,* June 2003.

Phillips, Adam. *Promises, Promises: Essays on Psychoanalysis and Literature.* New York: Basic Books, 2002.

Porter, Roger J. "Finding the Father: Autobiography as Bureau of Missing Persons." *a/b: Auto/Biography Studies* 19 (2004): 100–117.

———. "Love Is No Detective: Germaine Greer and the Enigma Code." *Life Writing* 3 (2006): 3–16.

———. *Self-Same Songs: Autobiographical Performances and Reflections.* Lincoln: University of Nebraska Press, 2002.

Prince, Robert M. *The Legacy of the Holocaust: Psychohistorical Themes in the Second Generation.* New York: Other Press, 1999.

Richardson, John H. *My Father the Spy: An Investigative Memoir.* New York: Harper-Collins, 2005.

Rips, Michael. *The Face of a Naked Lady: An Omaha Family Mystery.* Boston: Houghton Mifflin, 2005.

Roth, Philip. *Exit Ghost.* Boston: Houghton Mifflin, 2007.

———. *The Human Stain.* London: Jonathan Cape, 2000.

———. *I Married a Communist.* New York: Vintage, 1998.

———. *Patrimony: A True Story.* New York: Simon and Schuster, 1991.

Sarraute, Nathalie. *Childhood.* Translated by Barbara Wright. New York: George Braziller, 1984.

Skakun, Michael. *On Burning Ground: A Son's Memoir.* New York: St. Martin's Griffin, 2000.

Smith, Paul. *Discerning the Subject.* Minneapolis: University of Minnesota Press, 1988.

Spiegelman, Art. *Maus,* vols. 1 and 2. New York: Pantheon Books, 1986, 1991.

Steinman, Louise. *The Souvenir: A Daughter Discovers Her Father's War.* Berkeley: North Atlantic Books, 2001.

Tambling, Jeremy. *Confession: Sexuality, Confession, the Subject*. Manchester: Manchester University Press, 1990.

Thompson, Jon. *Fiction, Crime, and Empire: Clues to Modernity and Post-Modernity*. Champagne-Urbana: University of Illinois Press, 1993.

Washington-Williams, Essie Mae. *Dear Senator: A Memoir By the Daughter of Strom Thurmond*. New York: Regan Books, 2005.

Watson, Julia. "Autographic Disclosures and Genealogies of Desire in Alison Bechdel's *Fun Home*." *Biography* 31 (2008): 27–58.

Wilkomirski, Binjamin. *Fragments: Memories of a Wartime Childhood*. Translated by Carol Brown Janeway. New York: Schocken, 1996.

Wolff, Geoffrey, ed. *Best American Essays 1989*. New York: Ticknor and Fields, 1989.

——. *The Duke of Deception: Memories of My Father*. New York: Random House, 1979.

INDEX

Note: Italic pages numbers refer to figures.

Aciman, André, 47
Ackerley, J. R.: and father-child resemblance, 11, 138; and truth, 142, 145. See also *My Father and Myself* (J. R. Ackerley)
Ackerley, Roger, 140, 141
Adams, Timothy Dow, *Light Writing and Life Writing,* 105
After Long Silence (Helen Fremont): autobiography and biography melded in, 43, 48; and documentary evidence, 46, 47, 50, 53; and ethics of inquiry, 49; and falsified past, 45–46; and family relationships, 48–49, 53; identity in, 44, 48–49, 53; inauthenticity in parents' story, 45, 48, 53; and multiple identities, 50–51, 53; and narrative coherence, 52–53; and parental resistance, 18, 45, 47, 48, 49, 53; parent-child issues in, 12, 44; and parents' religious identity, 12, 18, 43, 44–48, 51, 52; and parents' secrecy, 51–52, 53; and parents' suffering, 12, 50; and power struggle, 49–50; revealing and concealing dialectic in, 47, 49; and silence, 45, 46, 47, 49, 50; and story of the story, 53
Albee, Edward, *The American Dream,* 163
Albright, Madeleine, 44
"American Masters" television series, 134
Appignanesi, Lisa, *Losing the Dead,* 52
Assembling My Father (Oliver): ambivalence about search, 124; and documentary evidence, 100, 120, 122–23, 124, 125, 126; and father-child resemblance, 120, 121; and father's absence, 119, 120, 122, 123–24, 125; fragmentary narration in, 126; and identity, 120, 121–22, 127; and imaginary dialogue, 125; and memory, 123, 126; and mother's erasure of father, 119, 120–21, 124, 126, 127;

reconstruction of father, 120, 122–27; and silence, 120; and uncertainty, 122
Auden, W. H., "In Memory of W. B. Yeats," 124
Auster, Daniel, 107, 108, 109
Auster, Paul: and detachment, 99; and detective work, 104–6; and openness toward own children, 188; and truth, 103, 104, 105, 106, 108. See also *The Invention of Solitude* (Auster)
Auster, Samuel, 102, 110
autobiographical narratives: and betrayal of secrets, 13; biographies within, 11, 14, 133; and cracking of parental codes, 3; and origins and performance of selfhood, 4, 11, 26; role of memory in, 10, 11; and secret lives of fathers, 1–2; as self-renewal, 118; and tracking of secrets, 2; and truth, 10, 11. *See also* life writing; memoirs of adult children

Bachelard, Gaston, *The Poetics of Space,* 125
Barbour, John D., "Judging and Not Judging Parents," 109–10, 160
Barthes, Roland, 124
Bechdel, Alison, 139. See also *Fun Home* (Bechdel)
Beckett, Samuel, 109
betrayal: and *After Long Silence,* 18; and *Assembling My Father,* 101, 121; and autobiographical narratives, 13; and *Crisis, Pursued by Disaster, Followed Closely by Catastrophe,* 79, 90; and *Daddy, We Hardly Knew You,* 72; and *Dear Senator,* 177; and *The Duke of Deception,* 149; and *The Mascot,* 24, 27; and memoirs of adult children, 4, 12, 16, 18; and *My Father and Myself,* 143; and *The Shadow Man,* 64